A Journey Of Riches

The Art Of Overcoming Challenges

Foreword

There is a malaise known as *the human condition*, an obstacle in life, if you will, that cannot be removed by a single human being until there is *recognition* of the obstacle, *clarity of mind*, and *purpose* defined as *action*. It is only after these steps are taken that change occurs in your life. Others call this change *transformation*, and well so because one can easily change a flat tire, yet one cannot transform the flat tire into its original, air-filled state to roll the car along.

The human being, thus, lives life, experiencing at a young age the beauty of the stars at night, the calm of mother's warm arms as she embraces us, the joy of learning to walk as much as the thrill of getting away with a lie. These experiences as we all know shape our life, and as we grow from child to teen to young adult we carry these experiences, often wanting to repeat them such as swimming in the Pacific Ocean with our best friend. However, the complete opposite happens sooner or later, meaning, there are experiences that we never again want to have, such as being beaten with a belt by your angry father. These negative experiences also shape our life, often leaving us feeling hurt, confused, angry, resentful and somewhat violated well into our adult life. These negative feelings then begin to dominate our life as we create a *story* about what happened to us and we stick to it as if it were written in stone! While reading this book I could not help but relive my own youthful struggles in life, my failed marriage, the profound lows of aloneness and such. But this not my platform, yet the urge to mention obstacles I faced come from reading these stories of the *down and out* who through a strenuous process overcame the obstacles on their way to the riches of success, their life dreams, achieving what they once thought was but a pipe dream.

This book proves that the force of will, coupled with a clear process and attentive, professional life coaching does and will transform your life. It is my personal experience that *believing* your life is going to turn out as you envision it, is the essence of this change, because belief demands time and patience, because belief is a driving force and these above essential elements are the gas in the human tank, as it were.

The process of changing one's unhappy and unfulfilling life also requires taking action and close attention to the vision, yet *trusting* the process is yet another necessary step in self-realization, or manifesting one's dreams. How can a person who does not trust others overcome this obstacle? By learning the process of recognizing the seed of the mistrust; in other words, *something happened in your life to have you say "I cannot trust people."* Well, then we live our life avoiding trust, not wanting to trust, doubting true love, and sheltering ourselves from intimacy such that we feel alone and unloved, yet the process allows you to understand this fully and to step into the world of trust such that you leave the past behind – where it belongs and create for yourself the new life that you sought for so long: fulfilling, joyous, successful and complete.

I believe that after reading these chronicles you will see yourself in the mirror, recognize who you are today and begin believing that your dreams are within reach indeed, waiting in the corner for you to snatch them up after mastering the process of personal development.

Dreams do come true. I know.

Daven Michaels
CEO of 123 Employee
New York Times Best Selling Author

Dedication

This book is dedicated to my Mum and second grade teacher Miss Day. While I was in third grade, I used to take my adventure stories to Miss Day with grammar and spelling mistakes. She was always accommodating, even if she couldn't read what I was writing. She called my Mum up to school and explained my situation to her. She went on to tell my Mum that I needed after school tutoring in the basics of English. She wasn't even my teacher, my third grade teacher had lost her passion for teaching and allowed us to do anything that we wanted. My Mum wanted me to repeat grade 3, Miss Day didn't think that was a good idea and said it would affect my self-esteem.

We lived on the Central Coast of New South Wales, Australia. I was nine years old and I couldn't read and write at a basic level. Only a few years earlier my mother had been through a nasty divorce and was working really hard to provide for her three children. Somehow my mother found time to take me to an English tutor and drive 30 minutes each way twice a week for a year. I remember feeling ashamed and when my friends ask me where I was going to after school, I told them a big porky pie that I was going to rep. soccer training. It wasn't long before I looked forward to reading in class. Instead of making a fool of myself and getting kicked out, I was now excited to read in front of others. I started with reading books in my spare time for fun. This experience is where my drive came from to share my stories and to help others to do the same.

Thanks to my Mum and my second grade teacher Miss Day, I have discovered the gift of sharing my experiences and hopefully, by doing so, I will inspire others to do the same. To look at your own past shame and to tell the story you just never know whom your story will inspire in the process.

Table of Contents

Chapter 1

From The Darkness Into The Light...

By John Spender

The time of the incident is still so real and vivid to me as if it only happened yesterday. I still remember lying on the lounge room floor watching one of my favourite TV shows at that time titled "Different Strokes". It was a Saturday afternoon and my Mum's boyfriend Phillip was sitting on the couch. I had a habit of wanting to go to the bathroom and leaving it to the last minute to rush off to the loo. On this particular occasion and unbeknownst to me, a nugget of poo had fallen on the floor before I could make it to the toilet.

Not long after, Phillip went to the bathroom. When I heard him shout, I was terrified. He stormed into the lounge room ranting and raving... is that your shit I just trot in? You filthy animal... he was furious. I was frozen to the floor unable to move, much like a rabbit caught in the headlights of an oncoming car. Phillip was a beast of a man, 6 foot 8 solidly built with a thick handlebar moustache that created a mean demeanour even when he wasn't angry. My mother came in from the other side of the lounge room from the kitchen.

I thought, "great my mum is going to step in and protect me". My mother asked Phillip what was going on, Phillip yelled "I just trot in this disgusting animals shit, what are we going to do about it?" I was still frozen with fear and I was unable to say anything. My Mum screamed 'rub his face in it like a dog'... that will teach him and he won't do it again. I couldn't believe what I had just heard and with that Phillip grabbed me by the ankles and dragged me into the hallway, over to the doorway to the bathroom before the carpet met the tile floor. He then drove me head first into my own faeces over and over again, before dropping me to the floor.

They both began to berate me saying I was dirty and that I wouldn't want to do it again and they yelled at me to go to my room. Totally humiliated, I felt confused, ashamed and angry. Didn't they know that I was only seven and that it was an accident? I couldn't stop crying. My Mum came in soon after still angry, she took me into the bathroom and told me to wash the poo out of my hair. Back in my room, I cried and cried into my pillow still in absolute disbelief at what had just taken place. I felt completely betrayed, angry and confused.

After the incident life just went on. It's maybe a surprise to you, that my childhood was mostly exciting, playful and a happy time of my life. Apart from a few isolated incidents involving my mother and her partner, my Mum was an amazing woman, hardworking, determined, kind and warm hearted. She actually divorced her ex-husband because his abuse towards me was becoming too much to handle. Although they were dramatic experiences, I can recall many more moments where she was kind and loving. She has always been there for me if I ever needed her love and support. Over time I had completely forgotten about the incident.

I remember our first family holiday together flying to the Gold Coast. Months prior my brother, sister, mother and I use to get up at 4:30am in the morning to deliver the local newspaper, the Central Coast Express. Although it was cold in the mornings, as we did this through autumn and winter, it was easier working together as a family and sharing a common exciting goal. We did this for about six months to make sure we had enough money to have a good time. It was an amazing two weeks with many memorable moments, we even shared a limousine ride to the Denning's restaurant in Jupiter's casino for dinner. It was a real buzz and a family moment that we all enjoyed.

We really had so many magical moments growing up as a family, especially on my grandparent's farm.

***

It was my darkness that brought more into the light of what I needed to do in this life. I had built a brick wall around that wounded part of myself never to be looked at again. I avoided taking a look for a very long time, unaware that I needed to look at it, part of me inside began to rot and it became clear to me that I needed to explore this part of myself. I needed to love my unloved parts.

Pacing through my apartment feeling incredibly nervous, I knew this was going to be a difficult phone call to make. There was no other way around the situation. I had been avoiding this conversation for a long time. I was about to make the toughest phone call that I was ever going to make and it was a culmination of 25 years of pretending that this incident never occurred. I felt so torn about shining the light of the truth and knowing that I was about to tear my mother's heart out with what I was about to share. I steadied myself, gained my composure and called my Mum knowing that it may not end well.

I love my Mum so much and she sacrificed many years of her life to raising me, my brother and sister. Taking us away from my Dad who was quick-tempered at the smallest of things. Also, little heavy handed at the time towards my brother and me, even my mother on one occasion. It's hard for me to put into words how much she has done for the family and continues to do, to this day. She really has been everything to me and her love is completely unconditional.

Now I have her breaking down in tears on the phone as she sobs that she can't remember the incident and it is a complete blackout. I was confused and annoyed at that time. I couldn't understand how that could be so. How could she forget such an emotionally significant event in my life?

I felt that I needed to have some closure and understanding about what took place that afternoon. All I could hear in my mind was "why are you doing this to me?". I responded by explaining to my Mum in the best way that I could, that we can't sweep the situation under the carpet anymore and we need to bring it into the light so we both can be healed. She agreed.

I felt like I needed to gain a deeper understanding of her childhood. I had only found out a few years earlier from her brother that their father had committed suicide when she was only 14. I asked her why she kept it a secret. She explained that my grandfather had played the role of her father figure for so long. By the time we three children were born, she didn't feel it was necessary to inform us. I asked her about her real father and it was difficult for her to remember. I could tell that it must have been a painful experience for her. This was also the very first time that she had spoken about her feelings, about what happened long ago. What an emotional phone call. We ended the call by agreeing that I would help her recall the event and paid for her to see a clinical hypnotherapist.

Unfortunately, even after regular phone calls, my Mum felt afraid to dig any further and trying to recall the events of that afternoon. The pain of that experience was too great for her and I didn't want to push the situation further. I felt let down. All I received as a way of an apology was "I'm really sorry I can't remember". I felt like I couldn't get any closure. I could sense her resentment towards me for having raised the issue. I was disappointed and I thought that she could have at least tried.

I underestimated the deep fear that my mother was feeling, and she hadn't been doing the therapy sessions releasing the pain of that experience like I had been doing. This painful and heavy experience had affected us both in a deep way, leaving wounds that may never completely heal. We hardly spoke to each other and I never went around for Christmas for a couple of years. When we did speak, I would call her Suzanne. At the time, I felt like she didn't love me enough to admit what happened, I felt completely unloved. My friends at the time drank and took recreational drugs to forget about their problems so I felt like I couldn't talk to them. I also had deep trust issues and I found it really difficult to open up to anyone. I spent a lot of my time alone feeling unworthy and unlovable. During Christmas, when the pain was too much for me to handle, I would get completely drunk and wasted on drugs.

After spending Christmas with my friends in Italy snowboarding, drinking, smoking pot and generally running amok, my mother called me in an emotional state expressing that it was too much for her to bear, that she was sorry and that she would like me to call her Mum again. She told me that after her hip replacement she had spoken to my brother and sister about what happened and even though she watered the incident down, I was relieved and accepted her apology. After all the work I have done on myself over the years, many tears shed and a lot of trapped pain released, I really am proud to have my mother in my life and to call her Mum.

The Catalyst

A year before the emotional phone call with my mum, my second landscape gardening business was doing quite well. I had set up a good lifestyle where I would travel to a different country each year with my girlfriend. While the lifestyle was good, the relationship wasn't the healthiest or most wholesome, looking back in reflection.

There were many moments of joy and abundance. We were both drinkers, mostly beer and red wine. We would smoke joints and occasionally take recreational drugs. We planned a dream trip to Southern Africa for six weeks after being together for over two years. This was our fourth overseas trip together, leaving at the beginning of July 2007. We had also discussed starting a family and that we would try while we were traveling through Africa. She was eight years older than me and she was approaching 40. We had booked a three-week tour starting in Cape Town, South Africa and we would travel through the Western Cape up to Namibia, across to Botswana and concluding the tour in Zimbabwe.

First off, we had a week in Cape Town exploring the surrounding areas. On the second afternoon, we were in a park overlooking the majestic table mountain sharing a long neck of beer feeling in awe and in complete gratitude. Around 15 black men were walking through the park towards us and they just looked like they had finished work and were walking home, laughing and joking with each other. I noticed that my girlfriend had become scared and she suggested that we leave before they walked past us along the path in front of the park bench where we were sitting. I assured her that everything would be okay and nothing bad was going to happen to us. Before I knew it, she took off like a flash and ran to the main road.

I kind of laughed as I saw her take off and the group of men walked past, completely ignored me and went on their way. I felt safe, enjoying the surrounding beauty and I began to reflect "hey, if those men were violent, she completely left me to face them on my own". Inside I felt somewhat abandoned, let down and shocked that she would just run off like that. Neither of us was very good at expressing our thoughts or feelings, let alone being able to express ourselves from a place of vulnerability.

Our discussions were confrontations, each of us expressing from our wounds and never really seeking to understand the other person's perspective or point of view. Our emotions would eventually simmer and everything would be okay again. We mostly had a really enjoyable time exploring Cape Town and the surrounding beaches.

We were both excited about the safari and on the second night after a long day in the truck, we set up camp on the banks of a river in the western cape of South Africa. After dinner, most of the group sat around the campfire drinking red wine and singing songs. I drank way too much and I couldn't really remember making it back to our tent. I woke up early the next morning to find that my shirt was ripped. My girlfriend was already awake and she said to me that I attacked her last night for no reason.

I asked her what happened to my shirt? She calmly said she was screaming while I was punching her arms and legs, luckily one of the guys from the group came and pulled me off her, I then fell asleep in a drunken slumber. I immediately apologized and I was confused as to why I would do such a thing. She showed me her bruises and it didn't look good, I felt so ashamed. I needed to go to the bathroom and take a shower and while I was drying myself, I heard two of the girls from our camp asking each other if they had heard all the screaming from the night before.

They both agreed that it sounded like a woman was being attacked. My heart sunk even further and the feelings of shame were almost overwhelming. My girlfriend was still resting in the tent when I came back. We were going to go Kayaking together along the river that morning, but understandably she no longer wanted to go and she insisted that I go so she could have some space.

In my mind that was shameful, inexcusable behaviour, I couldn't believe that I would do something like that. As I walked over to the meeting place for the kayaking trip, it was clear that everyone in the group knew what had transpired the night before. I said sorry to Rob my new friend in the group, the one that had pulled me off my girlfriend and I thanked him for helping her. He accepted my apology and told me not to worry about it. Everyone else in the group was looking very uncomfortable and I felt terrible, I just wanted to hide underneath a rock.

We all had to double up with the kayaking and I thought here we go, no one in their right mind would want to choose me as their paddling partner. You can imagine my surprise when one of the girls instantly chose me, I couldn't believe it. I'm sure it surprised the group as well. You mean she didn't think I was a monster? Paddling down the river was soothing, therapeutic and a tranquil experience. I ask my paddling buddy why she chose me to share the kayak with her. She simply smiled and said I looked like the strongest paddler in the group and she laughed.

That's, at least, one person who didn't think I was a terrible person and she was willing to sit in a kayak with me for an hour and a half. On the bus back to the camp, I was feeling so shameful trying to remember what had happened, but I was so drunk that it was all just a blur. The oldest guy in the group began talking to me. He was a baggage handler for Qantas from Brisbane and he came on the safari with his wife.

Our conversation was just idle chit chat, but I sensed a feeling of empathy from him as if he had done something similar and making conversation was his way of saying that everything is going to be alright. I did feel a little better and I was ready to face the enviable words from the tour leader 'John you will need to find your own way back to Cape Town'. In the Aboriginal culture, they call that the pointing of the bone and the person is banished from the tribe never to return. Completely ostracised from the group, they wander off into the bush and curl up and wait for death. It may seem like an exaggeration, but that's how I felt at the time. Like I just wanted to curl up and die.

After breakfast, the tour leader took me aside from the group. She began explaining in a surprisingly pleasant manner that she had spoken to my partner and that her response was that she didn't want me removed from the trip. The tour guide kindly smiled at me and said that she had been through a similar situation with an ex-boyfriend. She added that she was willing to sit down with me anytime if I ever needed to chat about things. I was completely floored with amazement. Not only had my girlfriend or maybe ex-girlfriend, I still wasn't sure about that yet, either way, she had let me stay on the safari and the tour leader had basically offered to be my counsellor.

I was still feeling incredibly shameful for what I had done and I still needed to speak with my best friend for the last two and a half years. I knew the first thing that I needed to do was curb my drinking. I didn't really know how to do that either, I felt so overwhelmed with guilt and shame.

I didn't know that one of the best ways to release shame and guilt is to talk about the cause of the undesirable emotions, expressing from a place of vulnerability, feeling the emotion and it is then released. It sounds easy enough, but back then neither one of us knew how to express our thoughts and feelings without becoming overwhelmed with emotion.

We did briefly talk about the situation and she decided that she didn't want to kick me off the trip and that she still wanted to be with me. I wasn't sure if I still wanted to be with her. I was feeling totally overwhelmed with heavy emotions mostly shame, guilt and unworthiness. I didn't know how to express what I really felt about the situation or how it may be related to my past experiences.

For the rest of the trip, I hardly drank and we really had a great time together. The safari through Africa was an amazing experience and one that I'll never forget. I got on well with everyone in the group. I was surprised people in the group were friendly towards me. We had some good laughs together and I felt that people in the group genuinely liked me and were happy to be my friend.

During the rest of the trip however, I mostly felt that I didn't want to be with my partner. Partly because of what I had done and partly because deep down I knew she wasn't the woman for me to move forward with on my journey of self-discovery.

We live in a world of the duality of twoness, hot and cold, black and white, negative and positive. Just as a wheel goes round we experience different spectrums of this duality. One of the ways I have learnt to not be at the effect of this duality is to find the centre of the wheel. If you are too negative about a situation you need to find the positive to equilibrate the experience and vice versa.

The positive of that experience with my now ex-girlfriend was that I knew I had to work on myself and that there was a lot of work to do, I just didn't know where to start. On reflection I would say drink less, quit the recreational drugs and to ask for support. At the time though, being in that situation, it was much easier said than done. I found that the very thing that I needed to give up was the very thing that I was using to help me deal with the pain I felt inside. It felt like without those substances I just wouldn't be able to cope with day-to-day life. I didn't feel confident, worthy and strong enough to face my life. As for asking for help, that was very hard to do because I found it difficult to trust anyone to support me with my pain and vulnerability.

Looking within

We arrived back to the apartment that we shared in Sydney at Bondi Beach, getting on much better, although the passion in our love life had died and the feelings that she wasn't the right partner for me continue to grow.

She smoked cigarettes, drank and smoked pot regularly. I didn't want that kind of thing in my life anymore, but it felt like there was no escaping it, as my friends all did the same thing.

My Dad and his wife came over from Adelaide and stayed with us for a weekend a couple of months after our trip to Africa. They wanted to know all about our adventure and we really did have some great stories to share. Seeing lions eating a zebra, bungee jumping next to the waterfall in Victoria Falls, spending time in the Okavango Delta in Botswana when a herd of elephants walked straight past our campsite, such magical moments.

My Dad's wife asked if it was safe in Africa, I explained that you needed to be careful but it was safe. My partner disagreed, saying that she didn't feel safe and I felt a deep sense of resentment towards her and I blurted out the experience of her running off and leaving me in the park when a group of workers were walking past. It was an embarrassing moment and it highlighted to everyone in the room that there was a little bit of tension between us.

I didn't know how to forgive myself for what I had done to her and I felt that I didn't really love her enough to want to spend the rest of my life with her either. She was getting older and I wanted to give her the opportunity to find someone else and settle down and start a family. It took me about three months to break off the relationship even then she instigated the conversation saying that she felt that I was not that into her anymore.

I confessed to her what I was feeling and that I felt we should part ways as friends. She agreed the passion between us was no longer there. She started crying and asking that I hold her hand over the weekend. I knew I needed to be firm and to make the separation as clean as possible. It wasn't easy, but I felt in my heart of hearts that it was necessary. She moved into a share house just around the corner and wanted to see me, hinting that we should get back together. At the same time, she was telling my family and our mutual friends that I was a monster and really dangerous to be with, so she had no other choice but to leave the relationship. I didn't blame her, she was obviously hurt and I really had done the wrong thing.

Simultaneously, she would make excuses to come over and make a move on me hoping it would bring us back together. Eventually, she moved to Byron Bay, explaining to me that it was too difficult for her to live in the same suburb. I think when you are only in a relationship because it's convenient, comfortable and you don't want to be alone, something has to change. It was pretty clear that we both needed help and support. I just didn't see us growing together as a couple. I didn't have the awareness or understanding at the time to really know what I wanted, I just knew that something wasn't right within me but I didn't know how to confront the pain.

My relationship with my ex-partner ultimately forced me to look within and seek answers to my life. I felt like I was in so much pain and self-medicating with recreational drugs and alcohol. I found a Reiki healer who was also psychic. She really helped me to explore my heart space and my wounds from the past. At first, it felt like the deeper I went into my heart space the more painful it became. After around 10 sessions while also consistently going to group meditations and meditating by myself, I began to feel much better within my own skin.

Although I felt like I had undergone an open-heart surgery, I felt completely uncomfortable socially when I wasn't drinking or taking recreational drugs. Mostly I would drink to feel confident in social situations. All my friends at the time were into partying. It sounds weird, but they were the people that I felt safe to be around.

The John of God meditation group that I was going to was the only real safe haven that I had. Emotionally, I felt like a little child again and completely vulnerable. I had transitioned from being a caterpillar to a butterfly, but one with no wings. I eventually stopped doing the group meditation and I would sporadically meditate on my own.

Taking Responsibility...

The beer was flowing. A friend and I had been into the cocaine enjoying the Australia day celebrations. While part of me was enjoying the day and night of partying, deep down inside I was dying. I was in the bathroom ready to do another line and I looked in the mirror and thought what the f^*k am I doing. I certainly wasn't happy and fulfilled, that's for sure. I hated cocaine, but here I was snorting it anyway.

It was January 2010 and it was the last time I touched cocaine, enjoying almost 6 years of sobriety now. It wasn't so much of an addiction for me, and as I have mentioned before, I just didn't know how to deal with the pain of my childhood. This was after discovering personal development back in the year 2000. I had read various self-help books, attended paid seminars, seen councillors and Reiki Masters. They all helped me to understand where a lot of my behaviours were coming from.

I just found it really hard to face some aspects of my life. I didn't really want to open up old wounds. I first tried marijuana and alcohol when I was 11 years of age. I had been intermittently taking drugs ever since. Most of the time, it was to escape life and I enjoyed the feeling of being high or drunk. I felt that nobody really understood what I was going through. I thought that my pain and experiences made me special from everyone else.

Unless you had been through some kind of intense emotional abuse, you wouldn't understand what I was going through, that was my thinking at the time. This was a difficult story to let go of and one that wasn't serving me at all. I realised we are all equal emotionally, we all experience heavy and light emotions just at different levels of intensity. I was sick and tired of not being completely fulfilled in my life. I was going to do whatever it took to face my life, to take responsibility for my pain and flush my own toilet so to speak. No turning back this time.

I joined a $40k 12-month coaching program called Coach the Coach, which was an excellent launching pad for starting my own life coaching practice. The course consisted of 6 fortnightly calls to begin with, 3-

weekend boot camps, NLP training at practitioner and master practitioner level, speaker training, RG146 (basic finance training) and coaching at live events around the country after you pass your basic NLP qualification. The courses were held on the Gold Coast and it was refreshing to get out of Sydney. I met many amazing people and did some mind boggling things, which really expanded my perception of myself.

As <u>Ralph Waldo Emerson</u> said "The mind, once stretched by a new idea, never returns to its original dimensions. In the first NLP training we did 90 hours in 5 intense days of learning process after process. On the second last day, we started at 8am and finished at 6am the following morning.

The last 4hrs seemed like a complete waste of time to me. Practicing hypnosis techniques on each other. The theory behind this was to bypass the conscious mind and program the hypnosis deep into the subconscious mind. It actually worked and I now can do hypnotic language patterns without much practice.

What really struck me with NLP was how fast you can learn a new skill or enhance an old one. I actually didn't learn how to read and write at a basic level until I was 10 years of age. And although I learnt how to read and write at a satisfactory level, I still found it difficult to spell. I found out in High school that I was dyslectic and one of the traits is getting all the letters in the wrong order. In NLP, I learnt a spelling strategy that uses the memory. Soon after that, I was providing NLP spelling lessons in my lounge room. This was such a powerful and empowering experience! Imagine earning an income from an area that you totally suck, and delivering results.

I was completely changed in a 3-month period. I mean dramatically changed. I started meeting people who would tell me their challenges. I would do a quick NLP process on them and they would be amazed and come on board as my client. The momentum I had built was awesome and I kept moving out of my comfort zone into bigger challenges. On the recommendation of my first mentor, I started looking for a charity to work for.

I had done some charity work before for another organisation in early 2000, but I found that it was a complete waste of time. My mentor recommended that I feed the homeless, but the organisation that he recommended was no longer running. The founder was caught gambling.

Something as simple as volunteering for a charity became a real challenge to find an organisation that was trustworthy and ran programs to help the homeless. After many phone calls and online research, I had an interview at Mission Australia in Surrey Hills **Sydney.**

In the interview, I found out that they didn't run feed the homeless programs. The premise of the centre was to enable people to get back on their feet living some sort of normal life again. It was all about empowering and supporting the people. The centre was broken into sections. They had temporary accommodation upstairs for people that were in crisis situations and needed somewhere to stay. Downstairs they ran university pilot programs, art and photography classes. They had a job centre with computers and support staff, free dental, counselling and each resident had a case officer supporting them.

I was amazed by the facilities, the level of support they had to offer the residents was incredible. When the lady asked me if I would like to teach there, I was amazed. I heard the yes word escape from my mouth before I even realised what I was saying. I had been a landscape gardener for 14 years and I had never done any form of public speaking before in my life, I had done some sales presentations and I quoted all my jobs. I knew I could find the confidence but those were all one on one interactions and this was going to be a class of around 15 people.

My mentor used to always say, 'Start with confidence and the competence will come'. We agreed that I would teach and share about personal development topics for a five-week trial period. I needed to prepare for a two-hour class and when I heard her say that, I did a Scooby-Doo face, like what, two hours? Again, I heard the words come out of my mouth 'that will be fine', I really wanted to catch those ones, two hours wow! I walked out of that interview and I had no idea what I was going to talk about.

I ended up watching a DVD on how to present to a group, it was Tony Robbins presenting formula and it was someone else teaching it. I came up with topics like facing your fears, developing an attitude of gratitude, letting go of bad habits and many more. I had written out my own blueprint for my first presentation and I hadn't even started my NLP master practitioner training yet. On the drive to my first class, I thought I was going to die.

I could hardly breathe and I was thinking that there is no way I can do this, I'm going to have to cancel. When I arrived, I found a parking space right out the front of the centre. Time was on my side and I had 25minutes before the class started. I began doing my breathing exercises, where you breathe in for 4 seconds, hold for 4 seconds, breathe out for 4 seconds and hold again for 4 seconds. I did this for 10minutes or so and I felt much better. I also did a swish pattern where you imagine in a still frame image "this is not going well" and then replace it with "things are going really well". You do this back and forth for a minute or so. Next you imagine the negative frame exploding into a million pieces and now you only have the positive still frame of things going really well.

I then expanded that imagination making it clearer and brighter, saying I'm a powerful presenter and my presentations have a positive powerful impact on my class. I kept saying this over and over. You can also anchor this into your physiology by squeezing your right hand into a fist while the emotional state is just about to peak. I was then able to fire off the empowered state while in the class simply by squeezing my right hand into a fist. I was now pumped and ready for my fist class.

The class went so much better than expected. I remembered everyone's name, I gently looked him or her in the eyes and treated them with respect. These were people that society had forgotten about and I don't think that anyone had treated them so kindly for a while if ever. I went on to teach at the centre for 3 months and I also did a lot of one on one coaching sessions with many of them as well. They thought I was teaching them life skills, but it was them who were teaching me about the power of helping others.

Of the many success stories during this period, one stands out in particular. When Tyrone came to my first class, he was clearly on something, I later found out that he was on heavy doses of anti-depressants. His eyes were glazy and bulging out of their sockets, he wasn't really present. When it came to his turn in the group share, he could hardly say his name.

We went through a number of exercises together and everyone was laughing uncontrollably at the end including Tyrone. It was like he was completely back to normal again. He became my biggest advocate bringing many others along to the group. We also did half a dozen coaching sessions together and he shared his dream of reconnecting with his children again, his hopes of working and living a normal life and owning a Harley Davidson Motorcycle. I was able to help him collapse heavy emotions of fear, guilt and shame. Within three months he found a job, left the centre and began speaking with his children again.

It was so gratifying for me to see him succeed and I knew then that coaching would become part of my life. At the end of that year, I sold my business and I started speaking and coaching full time. I have now travelled to over 50 different countries and territories around the world, exploring exotic places and helping many people along the way. I now live in Bali Indonesia, running my coaching sessions online and can run them from anywhere in the world, I also put this book together to give people insights into the various challenges that people face in their lives.

I think it's easier to change our perspective about our current situation through reading about other people's viewpoints and experience. Whatever path you are going down, it is never too late to turn around. To change the way you see your current reality, to think different thoughts, to make a new decision and take new actions.

This wasn't an easy chapter to write, but I'm better than I used to be and I have moved from my darkness into my light. I think too many people hang onto shameful experiences to their own detriment. Having worked with thousands of people around the world, I haven't met a single person who doesn't have a shameful experience or dark secret to share. Everyone has done something that they are not proud of and the more we hang onto those experiences, the darker they become. Ultimately what you run away from runs you.

Chapter 2

Embracing Change

By Angi Kim

It felt pathetic to be hiding in the middle of a cushion fort I'd built on the floor like a child again, hoping it would provide some kind of protection and comfort while I bawled my eyes out in huge body wrenching sobs.

I did not want to be heard. Sydney didn't feel like home anymore. I hadn't actually called anywhere home since my marriage had ended almost two years earlier, and I was still struggling to adjust to being alone after growing apart from my best friend of over eleven years. Without a relationship, a house, a job, or close friends nearby, there was nothing good for me here. I was ready to pack my bags and leave again.

A few weeks earlier, I'd arrived back in Australia after an incredible year of travel. Backpacker style, I'd lived in my tent, couch surfed, hiked, dived, island-hopped, taken thousands of photos and met wonderful people from all over the world. I'd felt alive and free.

With my laptop in tow, I was lucky to pick up bits of freelance design work on the road. But for the most part, I'd just roughed it, lived on savings and was content to make things up as I went. I'd given myself one year to be carefree and spontaneous, but that time was now up.

Travelling had been the dream escape for me. I was inspired by stories from my uncle and aunt who, back in the day, spent four years exploring the globe in their trusty four-wheel-drive. I was now temporarily staying in their "treehouse" on the outskirts of Sydney. Away on another adventure, they would be back soon.

While staying at their place, I felt terribly alone, overwhelmed and sad. I felt so sorry for myself, thinking of all the bad things that had happened in my life. I cried and cried until I was angry for being so wretched, which just made things even worse! I hated my own company and I was at breaking point.

It had been a few years since I'd taken anti-depressants or spoken to a counsellor, but I could feel myself slipping back into the depression that had held me for so long and I knew something had to be done. With just two weeks to sort out my living situation and find some kind of life direction again, a wave of helplessness washed over me. At that moment, I was totally incapable of making any decisions about anything. More tears…

The spider

Earlier that year I met John, a tall, smiling, fellow Australian sitting in our outdoor yoga area in Bali. Surrounded by rice fields, the open bamboo room with its high slanted ceilings reaching to a centre point was the perfect spot to focus, unwind and meditate. Or it would have been if a rather large black spider wasn't dangling from its web, right above where we lay on our mats. I hated spiders with a passion and actually had nightmares about them.

Chatting to John after class, I mentioned the spider was bothering me. As I'd secretly hoped he did what most men in the same situation would do and offered to help. I was pre-prepared with a chair and a broom, ready for imminent spider removal, but John suggested leaving the spider in peace and doing an NLP process instead. This was not what I had in mind at all! Seriously, couldn't we (as in John) just get rid of the spider first and then maybe try a process later…?

Having only recently learnt about NLP I was very sceptical. I thought it was something pick-up artists used to trick girls into bed, not something that could help in this situation, and the very idea that my lifetime phobia of spiders could be cured in just a few minutes was laughable. John was confident it would make a difference though, and there seemed no harm in trying.

So not knowing what to expect, I closed my eyes for the 'fast phobia scramble' process. Using his voice as a guide, John asked me to remember back to the time when I was first scared of spiders. It took a little while to locate because I had so many scary memories of them, however, one instance stood out soon enough.

On a family road trip when I was really young, I was sitting in the backseat of the car behind my mum, my sister next to me and my dad was driving. A big hairy spider crawled out from behind my mum's head, making its way around the front passenger headrest and stopping just inches in front of my face. It was huge! I started to scream and so did mum and my sister. Avoiding a crash, Dad hurriedly pulled over and we all tumbled out in a hysterical pile. Checking the car thoroughly, the spider was nowhere to be found. Convinced it was just hiding and would make a reappearance at any moment I refused to get back in, I was terrified and had felt that way about spiders ever since.

As I relived this memory in my mind, I retold the story to John in great detail and with much emotional horror, physically shuddering at the thought of the spider. John asked me to repeat the story by running it backwards in my mind, forwards in black and white, backwards again, forwards telling it out loud and so on. After many repeats, I was laughing and the story had been reduced to a 'Once I was in the car with my family and there was a spider. We all jumped out.' So despite my disbelief, a mere ten minutes after we started the process, John had me standing up on the chair, face to face with the spider I'd previously been wishing death upon. I stood there calmly watching her weave away, and finally said 'You're really quite beautiful, aren't you?'

The process had somehow reprogrammed my fearful response to spiders, and neutralized them so I was no longer afraid. For months afterward I waited for the effect to 'wear off' and find I was frightened again. That time never came. Telling the story to friends back home, I don't think anyone really believed me, but the process was that simple and it actually worked!

So while I was hiding from the world in my pile of cushions, John sent me a message and we started chatting again. I knew he did life coaching and that he could probably help me because he already had. Once I got over my initial financial objections, general trust issues and concerns that our conversations would be over Skype and not in person, the decision to get support through coaching over the next 12 months proved to be one of the best I have ever made.

The sad story

In our first coaching session I started to rehash my life story, the sad version full of reasons to feel bad and sorry for myself that was constantly playing in the back of my mind. Rejected at birth, I was adopted from an orphanage in Taiwan when I was just two months old. My birth mother didn't want me and we knew nothing about my father, not even a name. My adoptive parents brought me back to Australia and all was great until my teenage years when we started to fight and eventually they had kicked me out. I didn't talk to them for a long time, and although we were in contact again, the relationship was extremely strained. I became anxious for weeks before attending family gatherings.

A severe clinical depression set in and I was on and off medication, seeing doctors and psychologists to varying degrees of success for years. It became a huge effort to put on a happy face and pretend everything was okay, and I developed a social fear that people didn't like me. I remember lying in bed one morning wondering if I would ever feel 'normal' again. It wasn't that I even wished to be happy. I was just so tired of waking up and automatically feeling bad.

My partner at the time had been amazing throughout all of this. We'd met when I was 18 and he was my best friend and rock, I am still grateful for his love and support and was absolutely devastated that our relationship ended years later when it turned out we wanted different things from life. Alone, unloved, abandoned, and unworthy, I had really messed things up. Nothing I wanted seemed to matter, and with no home, no job, and no support I felt like a failure. It was humiliating to admit.

Having heard a lot of this before from previous conversations, John said, 'Okay, so these are all the things you don't want, what are the things you do want?' I wanted to use my skills and creativity to inspire and encourage others — to become a photographer and get paid to do what I enjoyed. I wanted a loving supportive relationship with my parents and to be accepted as I was. I needed to be more decisive and in control of my emotions instead of so up and down all the time...

John suggested we do a values alignment exercise. For this exercise, I had to identify what my ideal values were and then list how I'd spent my time in the last week and then a month. The theory was that the most similar these three lists were, the more aligned my life was and the happier and more fulfilled I'd be. My list included having good relationships with my family and friends, health and fitness, getting out of nature, travel, adventure and new experiences, fun, spontaneity, creativity and getting paid for it, financial independence, and the freedom to make my own decisions. It was a good checkpoint as the lists showed that while I was fulfilling some of these values in everyday life, other areas were much less aligned, causing discontent, hurt, anger and frustration.

I couldn't imagine having a good relationship with my family when we were barely speaking, or how I would satisfy my desire for adventure now I was back in Sydney. I could easily get graphic design work, but my heart wasn't in it then. I wanted to take photos, and while I had taught myself a lot through trial and error, I was very far off a professional standard.

It was time to brainstorm. I had to come up with 50 possible ways of how what I wanted could become a reality. It seemed like a lot I thought, but John said it was an exercise in lateral thinking, to allow yourself to be open to new realms of possibility, no matter how far-fetched it may seem at the time. I also wrote out positive affirmations about my creative work and family relationship on a small card so I could carry it around with me. These affirmations were to counteract the negative beliefs in these areas that I had held onto for so long, and I started to repeat them over and over instead of the sad life story that was usually there.

Taking action

It was late January and I had missed out on my chance to study photography that year, as it seemed like course enrolments had already closed. I could always keep travelling with my camera and learn through experimentation, but I felt this would take longer and be less effective. I also had a working holiday visa for the UK that would expire soon. Perhaps I could live over there for a year and study when I got back? Or maybe I could study photography in the UK? But then, I would be paying international student rates and I still would have missed enrolments and need to wait. Alternatively, I could just get a job in Sydney to tide me over while I was being so indecisive…

Checking my email later that day, I was intrigued when an advertisement for a photography course popped up on screen for a private design school in The Rocks, a beautiful location right on Sydney Harbour. It was a yearlong full-time course starting in a few weeks, and applications were still open! I looked into it more… the curriculum sounded good and the teachers were all photographers currently working in the industry. To get accepted into the course, I needed to fill in some application forms and send in a few photographs I'd taken to show my current skill and prove interest. Excited, I got all the bits together and applied. Online application sent! I could expect to hear back within a few days, the onscreen message told me. So I was surprised when less than an hour later I received a phone call saying my application had been accepted and whether I would like to come in and visit the campus?

Things started to happen very quickly and fall into place on their own accord. A good friend of my friend had a room to rent at Cremorne Point. I visited the apartment and met my new housemate who seemed really happy and friendly and wanted to show me around the area. We walked a short way down to the ferry terminal, where the ferry would take me straight to the city and drop me right near the design school campus. With beautiful ocean views overlooking the Sydney Opera House and Harbour Bridge, I couldn't think of a better way to commute! The timing worked out too. I was able to move in the weekend before classes started, and a day before my aunt and uncle got back from their trip as well. It was perfect!

Another surprise was just how supportive my friends and family were as soon as I shared the news I would be studying photography. My parents helped me buy a scooter, which made it a lot easier to get to jobs with my laptop and camera gear. One friend gifted me a camera bag she had hardly used, and another gave me a tripod for my birthday. My aunt had some great lenses I could borrow and I was also put in contact with someone who was able to get a huge discount on the rest of the equipment I needed.

Just when I thought things couldn't get better, I found out a photographer I'd met during my travels would be staying up the road from me for a few months. He was a willing mentor and happy to help with assignments. Feeling totally in awe of how everything had unfolded so smoothly and unexpectedly in those two weeks, I know that I couldn't have planned it better if I tried.

Shifting focus

The course workload was full on, but I was thoroughly enjoying learning and seeing the improvement in my images. I started to notice correlations between photography and what John was saying in our coaching sessions. Previously, I'd just been pointing the camera and trying to make pretty pictures. The idea that you can tell a story with an image and have the power to change that story simply by what you focus on and how you frame it to include or not include elements was fascinating.

So with that sad story I had been running in my head for years, I consciously decided to shift the focus, reframe and tell it from a different perspective. I sat down one afternoon and rewrote my childhood from another point of view. I wrote, 'My birth mother cared about me having a good life so much that she was willing to give me up for adoption to a loving family who could look after me' and so forth.

Just by looking at things with an attitude of love instead of anger and negativity, I felt more positive and better about the past. Some of the resentment I had held towards the people and events in my life started to melt away, and with this new understanding and compassion, I finally started to forgive. From then on, and with John's constant encouragement, I began to look for the good or as he called it 'the gift' in every situation.

Courage to fail

The biggest thing that was holding me back now was self-confidence. I was worried my photography work wasn't good enough. I was worried I wasn't good enough. I felt quite intimidated by the talent I saw around me and was extremely shy about showing my work.

As a graphic artist, I was used to sharing my designs, but this was different. With the luxury of an almost open brief, I was free to create — and I put so much of myself into this creative process that it left me feeling exposed and vulnerable. I allowed doubts to creep in about my ability and how hard it was to 'make it'. I wanted to protect myself from judgment and potential criticism. Job opportunities were presenting themselves, yet I was hesitant to take them for fear of failure.

'But what is the worse that could happen?' John asked. 'I don't know... People won't like it. My work will get criticized. It will confirm that what I'm creating isn't good enough, which means I'm not good enough... and then I'll feel bad' I shrugged. 'But what good could happen?' he continued. 'People might love my work and commission me to create more. I could win things if I entered competitions and begin to build up my portfolio and profile. I'll get constructive feedback to help me improve' I answered.

I made a goal to start posting work online every week and enter competitions. Soon, I received an honourable mention, it was a small win in a small competition, but it was just the boost of encouragement I needed to persist and keep going. Next, a couple of my images were marked as editors' favourites by a magazine I practically idolized, and then I was ecstatic and jumping around the house with excitement when they chose one of my photos, from amongst thousands of entries, to be published.

Feeling inspired and loving the city views across the harbour, I was out shooting and experimenting almost every night. Two of my cityscape images were selected for a Sydney theme exhibition in the Rocks. It was the first time I had exhibited photographs and I was amazed and overjoyed when both prints sold on opening night!

I started to accept paid photography jobs. I had overcome the fear of failure by accepting that I may fail but was determined to do better each time no matter what. I would take opportunities as they came and learn from the experience. After all, everyone has to start somewhere! By having the courage to allow my work to be seen, I gained more confidence. I acknowledged that not everyone will like what I create and that it doesn't necessarily make me or my work bad, other people may love it! Those little doubts about not being good enough are still there, but when they come up, I can thank them for trying to protect me, and keep on creating.

Finding gratitude

At the end of the term I was utterly exhausted and in our next coaching session, John found himself consoling a blubbering mess. I had a total meltdown and wanted to quit. It was too hard to study full time and work enough to support myself. I'd let my freelance design work slip so I could keep up with assignments, and I wasn't earning enough to cover my weekly rent and expenses. There was no way I could continue like this…

Plus, bad things kept happening. Some of my camera gear was stolen, and I crashed the scooter. I wasn't hurt badly, but I was much shaken. My housemate had been acting strangely as well. The happy facade he had put on when we first met was wearing off and my gut instinct told me things weren't quite right. However, being so caught up with everything else, I simply ignored it.

The best way to stop feeling sorry for myself, John said, was to go out and do something nice for someone else. So I did. I donated some money to charity and I made a conscious effort to do something kind for someone each day — even if it was as small as buying a coffee or giving a compliment.

It was time to change my focus again. Instead of looking at all the bad things that had happened, I needed to be grateful for all the good I already had and be open to accepting it. In the meantime, John had me re-evaluate my finances and work out a budget so I knew exactly how much money I needed each week. We agreed that I should drop back to part-time study and find a steady income. The course would take longer to complete but I wouldn't have to worry about money this way.

I received a job offer from a very talented photographer who wanted an assistant. Excited, my head was saying, "take the job"! You won't get another opportunity like this! But instinctually my heart was telling me to wait, and that something more suitable for my current situation would come along. His specialization was not an area of photography I wanted to go into, and the pay wasn't nearly enough to cover my expenses. Even so, I agonized over the decision for days before finally turning the job down.

A week later and just before it was time to go back to class again, an old client called, she said they needed a designer a few days a week and could I please start immediately? The pay was over double the last offer, and there was even the opportunity to use my photography skills. With a steady income and lighter study load, I felt like I could finally breathe. I was indeed grateful for how things had worked out so providentially yet again.

Angel

Days spent in front of the computer were disappearing rapidly and I hadn't ventured out of the city for months. I didn't feel like I could afford a holiday, and logically it seemed like I'd have to wait until I finished studying and saved up again.

My home situation had gone downhill from slightly uncomfortable to the point where I was actively avoiding spending time there. Having been fired from his job, my housemate was now in our apartment 24/7 and didn't seem interested in looking for more work. He started smoking inside which made it hard to breathe and gave me allergies, and played music in the living area that was so loud I could still hear it locked away in my own room with both the hall and bedroom doors shut. With my quiet sanctuary and personal space gone, I started to feel like I was going crazy and found it impossible to be productive.

I was still getting photography competition notifications but I hadn't been taking the time to enter them anymore. One got my attention, though, it sounded amazing. The prize was a two week $20,000 'trip of a lifetime' to go down the east coast of Australia with three friends, taking photos and blogging about adventure activities for a travel company. I had a really good feeling about it and sent my talented photographer friend Angel a message to enter as well.

In the meantime, I continued to practice gratitude and use my affirmations. I told myself I had a peaceful home and that my life was full of new experiences and adventure. I rearranged my schedule so I could work late at night when my housemate was asleep.

'It was time to move' — a thought that was confirmed one morning when a notice at the ferry terminal announced it would be renovated and closed for 6 months. The design school was also relocating to the other side of the city, meaning my daily commute would be much more complicated and involve connecting three different buses.

I agreed to housesit for a friend, as the person they had lined up originally cancelled at the last minute, and the arrangement would be mutually beneficial for us all. I'd get a quiet space to myself for five weeks, the pets could remain in their beautiful big home, and it wouldn't cost the family a whole lot of extra cash for a kennel.

However, just as I was about to move in, Angel called and was so excited she literally squealed down the phone in delight. I was talking to a finalist in the travel photography competition! Even though I'd had an uncanny feeling when I first saw it advertised, I'd almost forgotten about it by that stage and hadn't entered anything myself.

Before choosing a winner, each finalist had to put together a team proposal of which friends they'd take and why. I was genuinely surprised when Angel asked if I wanted to come. Although we got along and shared the adventurous creative streak, we hadn't known each other for very long, so her wanting to share this experience with me was an unexpected honour.

The only catch was I had to confirm I could go the next day, and if we won, it clashed with my housesitting commitment. What to do? This really was a fantastic opportunity but I didn't want to let my friend down. I said I'd go, and amazingly things fell into place perfectly yet again. I got time off work, and could manage with the study. A friend who was a very experienced house sitter happened to be back in Sydney and was free exactly at the same time the prize trip started. I had been so nervous when I called the family to explain about the competition and ask if I could share housesitting with a complete stranger to them. But they were more than understanding and happy as long as the animals were taken care of. So, I was off!

The trip was incredible. Four girls, six cities, we travelled 3000kms in 14 days. It was VIP treatment all the way, and our schedule was packed with at least three activities each day. To name but a few, we went bungee jumping, scuba diving, white water rafting, spinning on jet boats, hot air ballooning, rode rollercoasters, feed dolphins, swam with seals, learnt how to surf, swung through treetops, climbed towers and hugged more koalas than I can count.

From a photographic point of view, it was a crash course in having to deliver images on time to brief. Each night we went back to the hotel to edit our photos and write the blog for social media, often not getting to bed until 3am and waking up at 6am. It was one of the most intense yet fun and rewarding things I have done. We also got a lot of practice being on the other side of the camera too, as numerous TV and newspaper teams came to interview us and we learnt to pose on demand.

By the end of the trip, I had had more adventure than I'd even dared to imagine or thought physically possible in a two-week timeframe, and it hadn't cost me a thing. I was able to use some of the photos for assignments in my course. I'd become good friends with the other girls. And as a bonus, I got some quality time with my friend while we housesat together for the last week after I got back.

My friend encouraged me to look for a new place to live, and I found a lovely home near a rock climbing gym and close to the city and new design school location. Quiet home sanctuary and holiday dreams answered. I didn't have to know how things would happen or plan every detail. I just needed to trust that things would work out and be ready to take the opportunities when they came.

'The gift'

My housemate did not take the news that I was moving out well. For the last month I was met with a sullen silence and he wouldn't even acknowledge me if we were in the same room together. People suggested I should stop paying rent for the last few weeks just in case I didn't get my bond money back, but I wanted to do the right thing by him and thought he would do the same for me. I was wrong.

After I moved out, not only did he refuse to return my bond, he also claimed that I owed him more money for damage to the house. He wouldn't answer the phone or respond to my requests for more details, and instead, emailed me a tirade of abuse.

I called the real estate agent directly and found out that he had abandoned the property a week after I left. He must have been living off the rent money I gave him as he hadn't paid rent on the apartment for months and owed the landlord thousands of dollars.

It was hard for me to understand how anyone could behave so badly and treat me this way, especially a good friend of a friend! I was very upset about losing my bond money and was shocked by the sheer hatred in his messages so when John asked me what the gift in this situation was, I was pissed off and didn't want to hear it. There was no gift. The man was a jerk and had ripped everyone off even though I had done the right thing. I wasn't interested in finding the positives here. There weren't any. I just wanted to be angry.

After I'd calmed down and thought about the situation more, I realized that there was indeed a lesson I needed to learn here. I should have trusted my gut instinct earlier. I hadn't felt comfortable with my housemate soon after I moved in but had ignored the feeling. I had also done this in business deals and other relationships to similar effect.

The gift was in helping me to learn to trust myself more, and to not take things personally. My old housemate had his own drama going on and needed to believe I was a bad person to justify his actions. The abuse had nothing to do with me and was certainly not a reflection on my character. Sometimes it's just a matter of letting go and getting on with life. There would be no reasoning with this man.

The silver lining was that he hadn't bothered to put my name on the rental agreement. This meant I wasn't blacklisted from the property market for abandoning the place, and I couldn't be held liable for the rent still owing and costs to empty and repair everything. That was a relief. Again I focused in on the good, and although it was hard, I aimed to see things through eyes of compassion, forgiveness and letting go.

Months later, I found out that my old housemate had just snapped and was sentenced for assaulting a bus driver in the face with a rock. I am so grateful he is not part of my life anymore and I was able to get out of that situation before something worse happened.

Once more, friends helped me move and the new house immediately felt peaceful. I set up a lifestyle I was really happy with, and for the first time in years, I felt content and at home.

The ropes

It was January again, and my steady stream of income ended with the end of the year. Ideally, this work would have lasted until I completed the course in a few months' time, so I was a little frustrated. I took the opportunity to visit my parents in Tasmania though. Our relationship had improved so much that I could hardly believe it. This was the first time I had really looked forward to spending time with them, and I finally understood what it was like to have the loving, supportive family I had dreamt of for years.

Living so close to the gym, I'd been doing a lot of indoor climbing, and I was keen to get some outdoors experience while I was in Tasmania as well. A friend put me in touch with a climbing guide she knew, and we ended up having some great adventures. He was in town for the holidays and joked that we were the only climbers in that part of Tasmania, which was great for me because having no one more experienced to climb with he was quite willing to take me out and literally teach me the ropes.

So in the safe hands of my personal guide, we spent the next few weeks doing mini road trips where we camped, hiked, kayaked and of course climbed. I was learning new skills, getting outdoors, taking photos and really loving it.

On one of my favourite days, we climbed 400 metres up the side of a mountain. I was shown how to place and remove safety gear in the rock as we progressed, and the view kept getting more and more beautiful. It was such an incredible feeling to be up so high, immersed in nature just hanging off the rock face!

The sun was already disappearing by the time we reached the top and we still needed to get back down. I hadn't done much abseiling before and it was a rush descending into the darkness not being able to see the bottom. We reached the ground by midnight and started on the relatively short hike back to the car, but the trail markers weren't visible in the dark and we were soon lost and wandering around.

My guide looked stressed and finally admitted that he'd been waiting for me to spit the dummy, and refuse to go any further. But how could I be upset? I'd had an amazing day climbing, the weather was good, and we weren't in any real danger because we knew there was a main road nearby... In a weeks' time, I would be back home doing something comparatively boring indoors wishing I out here, lost in the dark!

When we finally stumbled across the car hours later, we lay outside and just looked up at the stars for a while. What a day. I had fully enjoyed every moment.

For my last weekend in Tasmania, I was invited to travel south and visit a bird conservation project. An online publication needed photos of scientists in the field, and I spent the day documenting their work. My climbing harness came in handy as I was able to join the research team climbing tall trees in search of nests, and I learnt more knots and additional rope skills. The article was published and the photos were picked up by other publications as well which generated some bonus holiday income for me! Life was good.

Alignment

When I got back to Sydney, I just wanted to be outdoors and take photographs. I themed my course portfolio around climbing and adventure and I spent the following months scaling cliffs and hanging off ropes with my camera. It was such a joy to be able to combine these passions!

An opportunity came up to assist one of the photography lecturers from the design school. Grateful for the work, it was also a little humbling at first. I was still doing my own shoots, however, there is so much to learn from more experienced photographers in the commercial realm and I needed to be willing to start at the bottom again. On set where I used to be a senior creative / art director, I was now getting coffees and occasionally acting as an HLS (Human Light Stand). My new-found rope and knot tying skills are useful, as I've spent a lot of the time balancing on ladders, rigging up lighting and electrical cords before pulling them all down safely to create the next scene.

When I finished studying, I received great industry feedback on my final portfolio and was asked to show my work at the end of year exhibition for the design school.

At the moment, work is creative and varies between photography, assisting and design. My income is increasing and it's wonderful to be getting paid to do what I love as I build up my portfolio and business.

My weekends are spent climbing or enjoying other outdoor activities— it's a great way for me to stay fit and healthy, experience new things and have fun spontaneous adventures. I am much more in control of my emotions, my choices, and am able to see the world in a positive new light. I really relish time alone and enjoy my own company. Add to all this, the great relationship I now have with my family, some loving supportive friends, and my values lists are starting to look pretty well aligned!

I'm not sure what's next, however, I trust good things will happen and have learnt to embrace change, to flow with life instead of fighting it.

Chapter 3

My Mother, My Heart

By Ais Sarah

Six Months

Six months is not a long time when you think about it. It isn't enough time to squeeze the rest of your life into and not enough time to say goodbye. That's all the time I would have left with my mother. She was my inspiration, my hope and my life. The doctor was saying that I had, we had, to accept all that we thought we would be doing together in the future, would have to be let go.

I remember that day like it was yesterday. Yesterday I woke up optimistic about life, anxious to get back to school and finish my master's degree. Yesterday my mother was healthy, happy, and looking forward to sharing my life with me. Yesterday I took my mother to the doctor and his words changed our lives forever.

When I think about that amount of time now, it feels like a lifetime of possibilities. I felt life was being stolen from my soul, tearing my mother right out of my arms. But yesterday is gone. So are the six months of days that followed. That morning, I woke up and it was just another ordinary day but nothing would ever be the same.

Yesterday

I woke up one morning to the blaring of my alarm clock. Today was going to be a wonderful day. I had been waiting for a special message from God and thought that it would come on this day. That kind of excitement, that can only come from life, didn't help me crawl out of bed. Sleep still clung to me with its warm embrace.

I had noticed in recent weeks that my mother had been a little slower in her routine. Getting ready in the morning, moving around the house, and doing her normal everyday things. I didn't think much about it, people slow down, as they get older. I got dressed and then we finally made our way through the busy streets of Singapore to the bus that would bring us to the clinic ten minutes away. Mother had wanted to go to the clinic for a check-up.

Life always seemed to move so fast in my hometown. The world was cursing and rushing on their way to work, running late, as usual. School children decked out in their uniforms laughing and giggling, oblivious to the trials and tribulations of adult life that would haunt them in a few years. Housewives hurried to the market to pick up poultry, vegetables, and fresh fish for a wonderful family meal at the end of the day when everyone had returned home.

I was still shaking the sleep from my mind as we rode the short bus trip to the clinic. My mind was a blur of all the things I had to do in order to get ready for my return to Perth where I would be continuing my master's degree. It was both exciting and stressful at the same time. Two opposing forces that didn't seem to fit together but so often do without any remorse. I missed my mom when I was away but I knew what I wanted to do with my life. I had always wanted to run a business but had a goal of completing my master's degree first.

That morning everything seemed to line up for us, as though God had taken a moment to reach down and make our day easier, almost carefree. When we reached the bus stop, the bus arrived at the same time. Then the bus proceeded to make it through every one of the traffic lights. Not once hitting a red light, which is almost unheard of. I took note of this, still feeling that today was going to be a truly extraordinary day. After all, who would think something terrible could happen when everything else was working out so well? It was like a red carpet being rolled out before us with a special invitation.

When we got off the bus and started walking to the clinic, we still encountered no delays. I felt a presence of something around us. It was as though we were being watched carefully. It was comforting. An entire city belonged to us at that moment.

We walked into the government run clinic and noticed the crowd of people. The young and old intermingled, weary faces keeping their eyes cast down on the floor, or flipping through magazines. An occasional cough broke the silence and eyes drifted toward the culprit, suspicious of the ailment. My mother checked in and we hovered in the corner of the room. My mother leaned against the wall and I wasn't sure which one was holding the other up. I spotted a young man hunkered in a corner, resting on a chair. I was about to ask if he would mind giving up his seat when my mother's name was called. We both looked to each other, a little stunned. In this clinic, waiting two hours was average. Nobody ever got in that fast, especially with so many others waiting.

If we had arrived first, before all these other people, then I could have understood that we could get to see the doctor within ten minutes of arrival. My mind was telling me that something was wrong but a stronger part of me was pushing that idea deep down. I think some of the puzzle pieces were beginning to come together, one at a time but I didn't want to see it. Yet there we were, having arrived well after eight in the morning, being ushered into the doctor's office. I could feel envious and angry eyes stabbing at our backs as we disappeared from the waiting room. I couldn't blame them.

The doctor who came into to see us was not the usual morose, serious, grim doctor we usually dealt with. This one was a bubbly Malay doctor who bounded in through the door, cheerful as though everyone he would see this day would be cured of his or her ailments with the wave of his hand. I wondered if his exuberance would last through the whole day. The signs started coming fast now but I couldn't catch them. I couldn't put any of them together. I had this growing sense that something wasn't right. "What can I do for you today?" the doctor said in a tone that matched his apparent mood.

My mother told the doctor that she had been uncomfortable lately because of excessive bleeding during the past month. I listened intently as I hadn't heard this level of detail about the situation yet. She first realized that something might be wrong during her cousin's wedding. At some point during the ceremony, my mother noticed bloodstains on her dress. My mother was strong emotionally and she knew something wasn't right.

I was away on a vacation to the United States at the time so she waited for me to return to go for a check-up. When she finished recounting her tale to the doctor, his demeanour hadn't changed, but there was a more serious look in his eyes that I noticed right away. I think my mother noticed as well. She had tensed up a bit more.

The doctor wanted to run some blood tests and also asked my mother to lie down on the examination table. The doctor's face ran cold when he examined her cervix. My mother couldn't see the change but I did. She looked to me and the worry in her eyes jabbed at my heart. I wanted to tell her not to worry, that everything would be alright, but it wasn't all right.

The day suddenly seemed to make sense to me, but I was a long way from imagining the news that would come to us later that evening. For the time being, I knew my mother wasn't well, but she was young, not even 54 yet, and that meant whatever this was could be dealt with and cured.

The doctor's face had grown grim. I guess it was moments like this that changed their day. My mother finally saw that expression and hers grew just about as dark. Now we both knew something was wrong.

I wanted to crawl back home, back into the warm comfort of my bed and sleep this day away. Bad news can't come if you don't hear it, right? I had to be strong for my mother. Whatever it was, we were going to get through it together. Somehow, I knew at least that much.

We were ushered from one room to the next for tests, and I never left her side. After what seemed like hours of moving through different rooms, having blood drawn and tests done. We arrived back in the doctor's room. A nurse came in behind us and handed the doctor a report.

His face turned ashen, "You must go to the hospital, immediately. You have half the normal amount of blood. You shouldn't even be walking around. I can't believe you haven't fainted. You need to get to the hospital now!"

I had always believed doctors were calm and cool under just about any situation, but this one apparently hadn't learned that skill. Something was seriously wrong and they had to run more tests to be sure what it was. I don't think he wanted to deal with the burden of telling my mother the truth and instead wanted to pass it off to another doctor. The doctor said that he would call for an ambulance, but my mother was a stubborn sort. She said a taxi would be more than adequate.

My mother and I walked silently out of the clinic, past the angry and befuddled eyes that had been waiting long before we arrived and who were still waiting. We made our way out onto the street into the middle of a crowded and chaotic world. A cab waited for us outside.

I eased my mother into the back of the cab, recalling the words the doctor had said, 'I can't believe you haven't fainted.' I was afraid to let go.

The moment we stepped into the hospital I thought there would be hours of waiting.

I looked briefly to the heavens and handed a letter from the previous doctor to the nurse. Mother was moved next in line to see a doctor. We were escorted to another examination room. A female doctor entered and after my mother recounted what she had told the clinic doctor, the examination began all over. As the doctor checked my mother, her demeanour never wavered. In her world, she probably dealt with the worst-case scenarios every day.

The doctor finished and my mother struggled to sit up and we turned to the doctor, hope and fear spilling from both of us in waves. The doctor calmly looked to my mother and said the words I still hear in my sleep today, "I am sorry to tell you this, but it looks like you may have third or fourth stage cervical cancer. We'll need to do further testing to confirm".

Time stood still. The word was as potent and powerful as anyone had ever described it. Cancer. I didn't know much about different types or stages, but third or fourth stage sounded ominous and terrible. My mother didn't react, it was almost like she expected it. My jaw remained fixed to the floor as I struggled to process the information. I didn't want it to be confirmed because then it would be real and when it's real, there's always an end. My mother was to be admitted for a few days so that they could run more tests.

As my mother spent the next few hours being checked in, getting into a hospital gown, I had to make the dreaded calls to family. They cried and worried about what would happen in the coming months. During the next few days, my mother went through a battery of tests and I couldn't go in with her. I never was able to get a handle on my emotions during those few days, but my mother was so calm, relaxed, even comforting. She was the one who was sick, who was dying, and she was comforting the rest of us.

Then one afternoon, the doctor came in with the results. Stage four cervical cancer.

My heart sank and then everything came crashing down when she said, "You have less than six months left to live." The room fell silent. Inside I was screaming, "Six months?" Six months was nothing. It wasn't enough time. I needed more! Regrets that I didn't even know I had started funnelling into me in waves. All the things I wanted to do with her and never did, the trips we talked about taking someday, my graduation that we would share.

My mother lay calmly on the bed. She seemed to accept it as though the doctor had merely told her she couldn't have children anymore at her age. I wanted to be strong for my mother, but she was the one who was giving out strength like candy.

The doctor excused herself from the room and we sat alone, looking at one another, neither one of us knew what to say. We sat in silence, listening to the sounds of the hospital move around us. Nurses came in regularly to check on my mother and each time they tried to usher me out. My mother needed her rest. In her eyes, I could see her wanting to say that she'd have plenty of rest soon enough. I cried each time, desperate to stay with her.

They let me stay for a while but at ten o'clock, the evening nurse came in and told me I had to leave, that it was hospital policy. I could come back tomorrow. I walked to the door and the nurse had to guide me the rest of the way out. Every moment was precious now. Every moment had always been precious but there hadn't been a time limit before. Prior to today, my mother would live forever; there would be plenty of time for everything we wanted to do.

Today everything had changed. I found my way home that night though I'm not entirely sure how. I walked in, closed the door behind me, and a dozen sets of eyes, from aunts and uncles, all stared at me. I caught them and then ran into my room and slammed the door shut behind me.

I collapsed on the floor and spent the next several hours crying. I never felt as alone as I did at that moment. The world was suddenly far too big and frightening. I wanted to crawl under my blankets and keep the world, with all of its pain, away. From that first tear that streamed down my face, it just wouldn't stop. I wondered at some point whether I would run out of tears.

Then, suddenly, just as it had started, it stopped. I simply sat up as though I was slapped and told myself that I couldn't feel sorry for myself anymore. It was my mother that was dying and I had to be strong for her. I had to be strong for everyone, so I wiped my face and marched out into the living room to deal with the family that had gathered. I knew that I had to deal with this one step at a time, one day at a time, as the tired old cliché goes.

***

I called Momma K who lives in Michigan for some advice as she had dealt with a similar situation. She told me to write a letter to my mother. In it, I should say everything positive that I wanted to say to her. She told me that my mother would read it over and over in the coming months, so I should be sure to not leave anything out. I spent all morning composing this letter. Thinking about everything I loved about her, our memories, the way she had inspired me, and that I would be there every step of the way for her.

I apologized for anything and everything that I said out of anger, resentment, spite, or simple defiance while growing up. I wasn't a perfect child, she knew that and I let her know I knew it too and I let her know that I was sorry for all the times I hurt her.

I delivered it to her at the hospital with a bouquet of purple balloons and purple flowers, her favourite colour, to brighten her room. I let her read the letter. I watched her take in every word and though tears welled in her eyes at times, she never let them out. She was fighting to be strong for me. All I wanted was for her to let go and know that I was there to catch and support her.

She finished the letter, folded it neatly with a smile, and thanked me for it, "Don't worry about me," she said softly. Mothers always put their children before themselves. It's simply their nature to not want anyone to worry about them.

***

The next week went by like a flash. Each day brought us a little closer together and we began to laugh a bit more. Family and friends came by, delivering flowers, cards, candies, and words of encouragement.

My mother hated all of the attention. She hated anyone worrying about her, but she couldn't escape it. She soon found herself enclosed in a sea of symbols of love and hope. Sometimes we go through life thinking we know just how much we are loved, but never realizing the full scale of that affection. My mother knew, at that moment, all about the love she had spread because it had returned in full force.

When the doctors finally told my mother that she would start chemotherapy and radiation treatments, it sounded hopeful. I took it upon myself to research everything I could.

I had almost forgotten about school in Perth and managed to transfer to a local centre for 'distance learning'. This allowed me to stay close to my mother and do what I could for her.

I learned that during chemotherapy, the immune system is greatly compromised. This meant that our home had to be extremely clean. My family agreed to help clean from top to bottom before my mother came home from her first chemotherapy session. I had an idea to change my mother's bedroom so that it would be easier for her to deal with the complications of the treatments. We put up purple wallpaper, inspirational cards, and fresh purple flowers everywhere.

At the end of the long week, the house was sparkling clean and her bedroom was completely different. Just before my mother was set to come home, we hung banners and prepared a surprise party for her. I arrived at the hospital to pick her up. Mother was so excited to finally be coming home after weeks in the hospital, we all were. "What would you like for dinner?" I asked. My mother didn't hesitate, "Thosai."

It was her favourite meal from little India and I agreed without question. We headed to little India and picked up her meal to bring home. My mother was weary but so happy to finally be out of the hospital. I sat beside her, holding her hand the entire ride home. We walked through the front door and my mother's face lit up with a glow I hadn't seen in a long time. Tears finally broke free and she thanked everyone for their kindness.

Strength

From my research on chemotherapy and radiation treatments, I knew it wasn't going to be easy. We travelled back and forth to the hospital several times during the next few days as the doctors ran more tests and prepared us for what was to come. My mother had been preparing herself for this procedure, gaining strength of spirit, mind, and body.

She knew enough about the side effects apparently. I suppose the doctors had told her enough about them. I spoke with other cancer patients and their families. They all seemed to hold the same hope that the treatment would work for them. I sat with my mother as the nurse inserted the long needle into my mother's hand. We watched comedies on my laptop and counted the minutes until the drug entered her body and began its work. I kept expecting her to double over in pain or begin to vomit. She did none of that. Her face was like stone. "How are you feeling?" I would say several times. She would simply smile and nod. Okay.

My mother surprised me as she had a lot in recent weeks. She had proven resilient, stronger, or more prepared for the effects of the chemotherapy than most people. Each treatment she received left her stoic. She showed no signs of the normal side effects.

She took it as well as I could have imagined anyone dealing with it. I think what got her through was her strong will. My mother wasn't a stubborn woman, or so I believed. I think she simply had a stronger belief in herself to overcome things and deal with them on her own. The doctors seemed impressed with her resilience to the side effects, and even when they started radiotherapy, she showed few outward side effects. She lost her hair, of course, from the chemo, but I don't think any amount of willpower could prevent that. And so it went for weeks on end. She would receive needles in her frail hand, waiting for the chemo to course through her body and more radiation.

Hope

When someone you love is dying, you tend to open yourself up to more possibilities. Anything that could help the cure was something I wanted to do. My mother's chemotherapy and radiation treatment were moving along well enough, considering, but we were willing to try whatever we could to help. Chinese medicine has long had a history of success in millions of people's lives. Natural, homeopathic treatments began to fill our home as the weeks rolled on.

I brewed traditional herbs for hours, it was cleansing to the spirit to focus on something other than the inevitable. You can't focus on what's going to happen if you're doing everything you can to prevent it. All you can do is keep fighting and plodding along. My mother drank whatever I gave her for the next three months.

Everywhere we looked during those days was miserable and full of suffering, people dying all around us. It can be difficult to feel upbeat and positive surrounded by all of that every day. We made a point to laugh often and loudly whenever we could. Laughter itself is said to be one of the best forms of treatment for just about anything. That old adage states, "Laughter is the best medicine." My mother's face always had more colour and her eyes had more life whenever she laughed. She was looking better every day.

One Sunday afternoon I had to get online for my classes, so I headed down to a local McDonald's, I sat down and set about working. After some time, I noticed a young man place a sticker on his bottle of water. I could read the word, calm on it and asked him what it was for.

"Dr. Emoto found that water molecules react to words around it. They vibrate in a certain manner and you can actually taste the difference."

I wasn't sure what to make of it but I thought about all that love we had placed around my mother's room before she came home from the hospital. All those words, those memories, that feeling had to have the same effect, didn't it? When I returned home later that afternoon, my mother was up and about, smiling, laughing and feeling great. I spent the evening posting positive words on all the bottles of water in the house. We didn't talk about it; we didn't have to. I could tell my mother was feeling the same way.

We spent the next few days experiencing a range of emotions, from hope to fear, happiness to despair, and then back again. My mother and I simply didn't know what to expect anymore. We wanted to believe. We wanted to hope. After all, she was doing so much better that it hardly seemed real. When we returned to the hospital for a routine check-up, the road seemed to open up before us once again. I felt a familiar pressure build at the back of my mind, as the pieces of another puzzle began to fall into place.

I turned to my mother and said, "How about we skip the appointment and just go into town." Why?" she asked. "You've been doing so well, I just figured there's no need to go today, right?" She saw right through me. I should have known she would. "It'll be fine. I feel great. Don't worry!" and with that, she guided me along toward the hospital.

We waited for more than an hour in the doctor's office. A nurse came in and called me out into a room, I swallowed hard, not wanting my mother to notice. I had asked the doctor to inform me of any bad news in private first and mother had agreed. Our doctor stood in the hall with a look I refused to acknowledge. I couldn't look at her face. "I think it's time you prepare," she said "Prepare?" I answered, choked up.

A long pause lingered between us, "Yes. Your mother's cancer has spread. It's consumed over ninety percent of her liver in less than a month. There's nothing more we can do. We're going to stop the chemo and radiation treatments." My mouth searched for words but came up with nothing. There was nothing left to do except wait. "We can make her as comfortable as possible," the doctor said again.

My head shook and then the tears rolled once more. I thought about my mother dying slowly in a hospital bed in pain, surrounded by family. I thought of my mother waiting inside the room for me and realized that I needed to be strong. I wanted to keep this from her; I wanted her to hold on to that wonderful feeling, and that hope that she had found recently. I couldn't tell her yet.

"What's wrong?" my mother asked. "Nothing, doctors just wanted to ask a few questions about how you're feeling." She didn't say anything. I thought she would. Maybe she read it in my face. If she did, she didn't react. I decided that I was going to break the news to her the next day. Tomorrow was going to be the most painful day of my life.

One Last Trip

I couldn't sleep that night. I kept trying to figure out how I was going to tell my beloved mother that the doctors had given up hope. I prayed all afternoon for the strength and courage to be able to tell my mother it was over. My mother could tell something was wrong.

She cornered me in the afternoon but by that time I had already worked up the courage to tell her. When I broke the news to her that we needed to prepare, my heart shattered into pieces. My mother listened and said nothing, she was calm, just as she had been the first day we found out. It was as though she already knew. I wept by her side uncontrollably and she comforted me, stroking my hair and asking me to stop crying. I wiped my eyes finally after some time and looked into hers, "You already knew?" She nodded slowly, somberly. "How?"

"I could feel it," she said. "My body has been telling me for some time. It could have been the treatment but it wasn't. I knew."

I asked her what I could do, if there was anything I could do to help, if there was anything she needed. "No dear, God will take care of me. He has other plans for me. I'm ready."

We spent the next few hours nibbling on fruits and watching television. Then, out of the blue, my mother turned to me and said, "I would like to do one thing before I go. "Okay," I said, "anything." "I'd like to go to Kuala Lumpur."

We headed out to Kuala Lumpur and spent a few days visiting. When we returned home, we found out about Kampung Senang. Kampung Senang was a non-profit holistic healing place that helped cancer patients. My mother looked at me and we both thought the same thing, we weren't ready to give up the fight just yet.

Kampung Senang is a holistic centre that helps cancer patients where the positive good will emanating from it seemed to be infectious. The staff were warm and friendly and we even got to meet the founder, Mr. James Low. We had a lot of questions and he gave us a mountain of literature and videos to take home.

I was sceptical about this from the start as we had little money. The setback with the chemo and radiation treatments made us both a little wary of getting our hopes up. Mr. Low assured us that due to our financial situation, we were eligible for free organic fruit. Mr Low introduced us to a book by Betty Khoo called, "Cancer Cured Naturally" as well as Dr. Ishak who practiced holistic medicine in Malacca. When we returned home, my mother was so excited about some of the exercises she learned at Kampung Senang that she started right away.

***

Within a few days, my mother and I made the six hour bus ride to Dr. Ishak's clinic and were greeted by an impressive clinic. We quickly learned that the philosophy behind Dr. Ishak's treatment is treating the root cause of the problem and positive thinking. By holding positive thoughts, and rejecting the negatives, one can greatly reduce their risk of disease and illness. Within days, my mother was feeling better than ever.

Even with cancer ravaging her body, she was active, energized, and believing in life. With my mother feeling so well, we signed up for one of Dr. Ishak's wellness detoxifying camps. We called it our 'holiday retreat' and I couldn't wait. When we arrived, the serenity of the place surrounded us. An Indian doctor, Dr. Priya, greeted us. We were briefed on programs that had been designed for us.

My mother was to be on a strict, all organic juice fast for one week. Dr Priya explained that we would be woken up at 6:30 in the morning to start drinking our first juice. Then at seven, our first yoga session and after I would return home for my mother to do her morning colon cleanse. We were then given a juice every hour and a half and were instructed to drink a glass of purified water in between. This diet kept us full. My mother was given a massage in the afternoon and by evening, she was to do another colon cleanse. She was also given time to rest in between, which she needed.

The days were fairly routine. A mixture of massage, yoga, water, and colon cleanses. Then my mother was instructed to write a letter to release her emotions. It could be about anything, but it should be about things she wanted to let go of her past. She wrote for an hour and then we burned it together.

We both did two enemas daily, one in the morning and the other in the evening. And somehow, what I had initially thought of as juice fasting was so different from what it actually was. I never felt hungry during the entire week. On the last day of our juice fast, a delicious aroma of hot soup entered the house and our mouth started craving the taste. I will never forget how fortunate we were to come across Betty Khoo's book.

The News

My mother had planned on doing chelation therapy one Saturday morning with Dr. Ishak until he realized that her blood count was too low when we arrived. Then things started to go downhill. Mother started feeling sudden pains in her stomach and she wanted to go back to the hospital in Singapore. Her colour was fading and I knew something terrible was happening. We arrived at the hospital in Singapore and mother went through another round of tests and after three days, the doctor finally wanted to speak with me.

"I'm afraid your mother is getting ready to leave," the doctor said. "But she was doing so much better. We went to the new clinic, she was responding." I argued. "She was becoming comfortable. She wasn't getting better. We see this all the time. I'm sorry."

My mother would soon be gone. I had to prepare myself for this. So I sat with her in her hospital room. The nurses tried to make her room as comfortable as possible. They didn't ask me to leave after ten o'clock. My mother began pointing to things in the room and asking me what they were. She would describe them but there was nothing there. I wondered what she was seeing, if it could be ghosts.

Then she began speaking to me as though we were out shopping. The doctors said this was normal. Her mind was no longer able to sort and organize imagination, memory, and the real world. I ended up sleeping on a chair in the hospital room. At the crack of dawn, the doctor was at my mother's side and he urged me over. He told me that my mother might depart over the next hour.

It was coming to an end and I couldn't fight the tears. The past six months or so wasn't enough. I wanted more. My mother called to me and I turned to her. Her voice was weak and frail and I leaned close to listen. A smell lingered around her and I will never forget it. It was the odour of death and though I had never experienced it before, I knew it without a doubt. My mother whispered, "Don't cry, it will all be all right soon."

I hurried to call all of our relatives to let them know. When I returned to my mother, she was hallucinating again. It must have been a party because she was talking about people I had never met, asking for a drink, laughing lightly. In the afternoon, my mother was in so much pain that the doctors finally gave her some morphine. She rested for a while and by evening, her colour had returned and she seemed so much better again.

One Last Evening

I stood by my aunt as we all cuddled near mother. She was definitely more comfortable after the morphine. We watched mother give us a small smile and I felt very grateful that the doctors had been wrong. I looked around the room I saw how much love mother had shared with us all and how much sacrifice she had gone through for me. I stood reflecting on her life when I suddenly heard mother muttering a prayer. I burst into tears immediately.

My beloved mother was passing away, leaving us at this very moment. Everyone crowded around mother, holding her hands and muttering prayers with her. We watched as mother struggled with her last breaths. My body suddenly seemed to detach itself from the moment and I took few steps back as I watched the reality unfolding in front of me. I could see my mother reaching for me, trying to hold me so I hurried over to her side. I held her hand and leaned close and whispered, "Go Mom, we love you very much," I said it twice, tears streaming from my eyes and mother breathed her last breath.

The days that followed were a blur. I recall snippets of what had happened, but not the entire days. For the funeral, my mother was dressed in white and looked like a healthy, glowing bride. The day befits my mood, being grey, overcast and full of sorrow. Just as the service ended, though, the clouds began to break and a rainbow spread across the sky.

My mother never blamed anybody for her illness. She accepted her fate from the beginning. I don't know what she was thinking during those weeks leading up to us going to the clinic, but I wonder if some part of us knows when something is seriously wrong. It was as though she knew it was coming. My mother had stage 4 cervical cancer that spread to her liver. It was the liver cancer that ultimately took her. She was radiant and vibrant and for so many of the final weeks, it actually seemed as though she was getting better. I believe that the combination of our faith in God, laughing often and trying the natural holistic cures helped a great deal.

I am glad that she had a strong will and determination to beat the disease because it made her last week's better than they could have been. She accepted her fate and put her trust in God. I will always cherish the years we had together.

After she passed away, all I wanted to do was to withdraw from the world, to hide from family and friends and I told my best friend this. Then she asked, "Are you going to pull away from me, and your grandmother, too?" My best friend and my grandmother were the two closest people I had in my life and I was not going to pull away from them.

Yes, I hurt and missed my mother terribly. I cried often and for hours, but as the days wore on, the pain eased a bit more. I had to appreciate that I had time to say goodbye to my mother. Six months didn't seem like much at all at the time but so many never get the chance to say goodbye to their loved ones when they finally pass on to the next life. I was granted that blessing and I needed to appreciate it. I was only twenty-two at the time.

I had my entire life, so hiding from it wouldn't do my mother or myself any honour or grace. I decided to move on. I went back to school after two weeks and worked on my master's degree. Many of my family and friends were surprised that I did it so quickly afterward. Getting through some of the classes was difficult. My mind kept wandering back to the sadness and heartache, but I learned to deal with it. Whatever the future holds for me, I'll be okay with it. I know my mother is with me. I can feel her smiling down on me with every bright sunny day.

And I always remember to smile back.

Chapter 4

The Epiphany

By John Newman

The only way that I could have described it was as an "epiphany".

For the previous fifteen years, I had been working in the Western Australian mining industry. I was first employed as a truck operator, driving the two hundred ton dump trucks and over time I worked my way up to operating the other heavy machinery, bulldozers, loaders and face shovels. The trouble was that after working in the industry for over a decade, I was sick of it. Yes, I was earning good money, but I was bored.

There were the long hours, shift work and the work was very repetitive. I was either pushing dirt around or digging it. Then there was the time away from my family. Just about every significant event that I wanted to attend, I was always working. I just felt trapped. Here I was, middle-aged, I had been through broken relationships, I was paying child support and I was drinking too much. I looked at my financial situation.

Sure I had a house, a car and some savings. I also had some credit card debt and I wondered where all my money had gone. I was nowhere near where I thought I "should" have been with my finances. I quickly realized that I would have to keep working this job that I was slowly starting to hate for the next twenty years or maybe even longer. I couldn't work out where the last ten years or so had gone. It was like I was asleep at the wheel. At least not literally! I knew there had to be a better way.

I decided to do something about it. Some of the people I worked with had an investment property, so I started reading some property investing magazines. In one of these magazines somebody had recommended a book written by an Author named Robert Kiyosaki called "Rich Dad Poor Dad". So on my next break from work I bought myself a copy. Now this book really opened up my eyes to the way I had been thinking about money and investing and reading it has totally changed the rest of my life. You see one day while I was at work, the machine that I was operating was on standby. I was sitting on my machine and I was reading my new book when I heard this noise behind me. I looked around to see what it was.

At first I couldn't see where it was coming from, but then this bulldozer started to appear from the edge of the pit. I looked a little closer and I saw one of my workmates Ross in the cab. Now this guy was a lovely bloke. He was about sixty years of age and has been working in the mining industry for at least thirty-five years. I kept watching him as he was pushing this huge rock with his dozer and he was struggling to move it. He was positioned at this weird angle. He tried to push the rock but the dozer was rattling and jerking around.

I could see him being thrown around in the cabin. It was then that it hit me. What I mentioned before that I could only describe as an epiphany. I asked myself, was this going to be me in another twenty years. Well not if I could do anything about it. Right then I decided that enough was enough. I could no longer go on the way that I had been. I knew that I had to educate myself on investing, change the way I was managing my money and take control of my own financial future. I didn't want to work myself into an early grave or have to rely on the Government to take care of me in my old age.

I realized that I had just been living in my comfort zone, doing what was easy and just hoping that things would work out. I finally knew that if I wanted things to change that I would have to make it happen myself. Thinking back to my childhood, I realized that I had always taken the easy option. I grew up in the island state of Tasmania in Australia and I loved it. I lived in a small country town and I was always out riding my bike, playing cricket, footy or golf with the other kids. There was just my Mum and myself growing up.

She worked as a cleaner at the local Hospital, but I never felt that I was poor or I was missing out on anything. Mum had a lot of help from her parents, my Nan and Pop, and I was a little bit spoilt, after all as I was the first born Grandson. At school, I just coasted along at half pace. My marks were okay, but just about every report from Grade one until Grade 10 stated that "if John would just apply himself more" or "he has done well at subjects that capture his interest but he is capable of so much more". Even with my sport as I got older I started to lose interest and I just wanted to "have fun" with my friends. Year eleven and twelve was really just a party for me and I had no idea what I wanted to do when I "grew up".

At age nineteen I got a job at a bottle shop, which I quite enjoyed, but I wanted to travel. So when I got a phone call from a mate suggesting we head over to Kalgoorlie in Western Australia, I jumped at the chance. We packed up my mate's Toyota Corona, boarded the Spirit of Tasmania and headed off across the Nullabour Plain on an adventure to the Kalgoorlie Goldfields. We had some fun for a few years. Once I started working in the mines and started a family, the time just flew by. One day I seemed to wake up from a deep sleep and I began to wonder where the time had gone. I felt that I had a good life. I had a dream job in many people's eyes earning good money, but I had to ask myself why I was so miserable? My financial situation was one thing. As I said before I felt that I should have had a lot more money than I did. I also realized that I was living in my comfort zone. My whole life was predictable, safe and comfortable. I knew something had to change.

Luckily for me it did. First I married the love of my life Natalie and shortly after my eldest daughter moved in with us on a permanent basis.

I had "the epiphany" and I had a new goal for my life… to achieve financial freedom. I had an interest in property investment but my first challenge was that I wasn't sure where to start or what to do, but I decided to take Rich Dad Poor Dad's advice and start educating myself. I began reading property investment books, magazines and going to seminars. All the advice seemed to be to get a mentor so I started to look into a couple of companies.

At this stage, I was pretty gung-ho about everything and I was desperate to "get in the game". Eventually, I chose a company that had a ten thousand dollar mentorship program. Shortly afterwards I had bought two investment properties through their buyers agency.

At the same time, my wife and I were building our dream home and I rented out my three-bedroom cottage as another investment. Now suddenly being in debt for well over a million dollars didn't bother me in the slightest. The problem was that we had a huge non-tax deductible debt on our main home and cash flow was becoming a huge issue.

It also didn't help that our new accountant (recommended by my property mentor) talked us into buying one of the properties in a trust and our finance broker, (another recommendation) didn't set the loan up correctly and at tax time it became one huge mess. I tried to hold on to all these properties for as long as I could but I was getting into further credit card debt just trying to service the loans. I wasn't exactly living on baked beans, but it was becoming harder and harder to fulfil my financial obligations.

My wife was saying that we should sell a couple of the properties and start again but I did not want to admit that I had stuffed up and I wanted to buy more not sell. I then started to look at ways to increase cash flow.

I spent hours on my laptop researching information and strategies, and then I read an advertisement… "Free seminar: How to control millions of dollars' worth of property… without using any of your own money". You must be thinking that surely the alarm bells were ringing? Not with my current mindset! Next thing you knew I was sitting at this seminar listening to the speaker telling stories of controlling millions of dollars' worth of property using none of your own money. Learning about options, property developments and even an offer to use his money to fund deals.

The way that it would work was that I would find the deal, he would fund the money and split the profits. Sounds fair, right? All that was needed was six thousand dollars to learn all of his secrets. Of course, my wife didn't want me to do it. I was convinced that this was the answer. Next thing you know I was handing over my credit card details. So then I threw myself into this new project. I watched his DVD's, read his manuals and a couple of months later attended his three-day seminar on the Gold Coast in Queensland. Even my wife enjoyed the seminar and was on board.

The only problem was that the deals that this guy would fund had to be a lot bigger than he originally had said at the free seminar. That was alright I said to myself, I could do this. So I started looking for deals on the Internet, sending out hundreds of letters to owners, negotiating with them on the telephone and trying to make the numbers work. But they never did. I tried and I tried, but I just could not find anything with enough profit in it that my new mentor would provide the finance. I did not want to give up but I just could not make this work. I needed another strategy.

Eventually, I sold two of my properties, paid down the loan on our house and paid off the credit cards. I had to ask myself the question. Did these property guys scam me? Maybe, maybe not. I certainly got some bad advice. I choose to believe that they were trying to do the right thing and help people. I certainly learned heaps of information in these programs and I have learned so many valuable lessons.

I now know exactly what NOT to do with property investing and what to do differently next time, and I am still a big believer in growth assets such as property being part of my wealth strategy. A lot of this was my own fault because I did not have a proper money management system in place to start with. I bit off way more than I could chew and just hoped it would work out rather than having a proper strategy. I'm responsible for my life, my decisions and financial situation. I now realized that I would need to concentrate on cash flow or some sort of an income accelerator to help fund further properties.

I was determined to make sure that I didn't get myself into that sort of financial mess again. I decided I needed both a cash flow and a growth strategy. Once again though I wasn't sure where to start but I knew I had to keep educating myself.

I had also started to become interested in the mindset side of wealth accumulation and personal development. So much so that I decided to throw myself in and devour as much information as possible. I read that success is achieved 80% in the mind and only 20% is a strategy.

I thought I might as well work on the 80% and the rest will eventually take care of itself. Once again I threw myself into my education, reading books, searching the Internet and going to seminars. Anything that had to do with the mindset for success, I threw myself into it. I started doing affirmations, taping and plastering my goals all over my bathroom mirror and all around the house. Don't worry, my Wife thought I was going crazy. I believed I could turn my results around, although I must admit I still had a lot of doubts.

Eventually, I went to a seminar which was all about your mindset and how it relates to money. I started to discover a few of my old self-limiting beliefs around money and how they had been holding me back. The best part about this seminar though was that the presenter was offering a free online course. He and his wife had created the program about building the foundations of financial freedom. I thought to myself why not it's free. Like a lot of the seminars I had been to I believed that if I can learn even one thing that can help me it is well worth my time.

About a month later I started to do this online course, which went for 5 weeks. To say that this course was to me a complete game-changer was a total understatement. The founders of this course really concentrated on the mindset for achieving financial freedom. They also led by example as they had created true financial freedom themselves before they began teaching others to do the same. They became my mentors, coaches, role models and a true inspiration going forward.

Throughout the course, they inspired within me a true belief in myself that I could actually achieve my goals. One thing they said to me really stuck in my mind: "The goal is not the money or to get rich, the goal is to BECOME the person capable of becoming rich that matters".

After I finished this course I now had a new goal and strategy. I decided that I would start an online business. Once again I started to educate myself on the ways to make money online, how to build websites and starting an online business. At this stage, I had a general theme that I wanted to build my business around.

I also thought I needed a product to sell while I built my business up. I really had no clue how to build a website and all the technicalities involved. All I knew was that I would need some training. To be honest, I am not very tech savvy. I still remember going to a store to buy my first laptop a few years earlier and telling them that I knew nothing about computers… And boy, didn't they run with that! This thing was so slow… it literally took me hours to check my email and bank balance. My wife helped me pick out a new laptop a couple of years later, what used to take me a couple of hours took about five minutes and I said to her "well what do I do now". Anyway, even though I have come a long way since then I still had no idea how I would do all of this technical stuff.

I kept researching and discovered that there was so much information on the Internet about how to make money online. I was also wary. There were so many opportunities and promises of riches and I knew that many were obvious scams. After my experiences in property investing, I made sure that I researched everything thoroughly. At the end of the day though I could sit on my hands forever or I could trust my own judgment and take some action. I made a decision and started working with an affiliate marketing group and I created my website which I called "My Road to Financial Freedom". The general theme of my site is to help other people with the money management, mindset and strategies for success and financial freedom that I have learned along my own road to financial freedom.

For the next twelve months, I threw myself into my new business, blogging, marketing, building up an email list and building up my brands online presence on Facebook, Twitter and other social media sites. I also kept up my training, learning new skills and strategies. I started to make some money, little bits and pieces at first, gradually I started gaining a belief that I could actually make my business a success. The most satisfying thing was when I started to get some feedback from people that had read my blogs or had started following me on social media.

To hear that something you have created or written has actually helped someone, somehow is an amazing feeling. A great analogy I once heard was that it was a little bit like climbing a mountain. As you get to the next ledge you can't climb any further until you help pull up the people behind you. Then you climb to the next ledge and once again you help up the people behind you until you reach the top of the mountain. I truly want to help others with all that I have learned and as I keep learning more I keep helping people more. I now believe that it is my mission to educate, lead and inspire people. Helping them to achieve and experience their dreams and goals with confidence and courage. I provide world-class education, motivation and inspiration on money management and creating financial freedom.

I just remember the pain and feelings of emptiness that not having control of your life and finances felt like. If I can help anyone get out of that place I'm fulfilling my mission. On Reflection the main things that have helped me make my business a success:

Firstly, it is your mindset that is the key. When I first started out I heard that success is achieved 80% in the mind and 20% strategy. I certainly agree with that statement. First you have to deal with your old programming and negativity from the past, plus numerous doubts and fears. A fear of not being good enough is quite common amongst first timers into investing. A fear of failing is another.

A chronic fear of what other people will think was a big one for me as well as overcoming my natural shyness. Even the fear of success is a major one for people. Dealing with people that say you are crazy or obsessed or say you have to face reality. This comes from the people closest to you most of the time. It is so easy to give up or not try something, or procrastinate or make excuses and play the blame game. Sometimes you know what you need to do but you just can't get yourself to do it.

That is why working on your mindset and getting your mind to work for you instead of against you is vital to success. Doubts and fears still come up from time to time. The old procrastination monster will occasionally rear its ugly head, but by constantly working on my mindset and taking consistent action keeps the monsters at bay. And that is another key learning: taking action!

If you want success, you have to take consistent action and work at it. I make it a habit of taking daily steps towards my goal no matter how small. By taking continuous action, although it starts off slowly, eventually, as you build up momentum, things start to snowball. You need to be determined and committed to your success and really focus on what you want to achieve. It is definitely true that as you start taking the action you will start to receive heaps of opportunities for other projects and people try to bring you into their own agendas. That is why it is so important to remain laser focused on what you really want to achieve and keep taking action towards its attainment. I think it was Richard Branson that said: "opportunities are like buses, there is another one coming along every five minutes". Also don't be afraid of making mistakes or failing. You never really fail anyway unless you actually give up and quit! I use the phrase of measure, monitor and adjust. Just see what works, what doesn't and keep adjusting accordingly. As long as you keep taking that consistent action and don't give up you will eventually start seeing results.

A major element that I have learned is the habit of self-education. A great quote that resonates with me is from Jim Rohn who said: "Formal education will make you a living, self-education will make you a fortune". Remembering back to before I started my journey of personal growth, I felt bored, miserable and directionless. I have to believe that was the case because I wasn't growing. I was just drifting along in my comfort zone. I believe that to keep learning and growing is an essential human need for happiness and fulfilment.

I now absolutely love learning all about business, money management and personal development. Constantly learning new things makes me feel truly alive. It is also vital to success. After all, if you already knew how to become rich you would already have done it. Luckily like most things it is also a very learnable skill. Other people have already achieved what you want to achieve. That is why it is so important to be able to find great mentors and coaches to learn from and model their methods for success. Finding like-minded people you can mastermind and bounce ideas off is important as well.

As I said before, sometimes your friends and family won't understand your journey. So being able to find a group of people heading in the same direction as you are vital. The main thing to remember is a success and financial freedom is a learnable skill. The information is out there and other people have achieved what you want to achieve. You just have to find it, learn it, act on it and never give up. So what does the future hold for me? In many ways, I still feel like a toddler just learning to walk in the game of financial freedom. I still need to learn to run, ride a bike, drive a car, and maybe even fly a plane!

The sky really is the limit! I'm starting to create my own products and I have several plans in the pipeline. I have created and started selling an eBook and I am half way through creating an online course. I have some plans for several niche websites and have some ideas for a membership and coaching site.

One of my mentors once said to me that the purpose of the goal is not the obtainment of the goal, it is striving to achieve the goal that makes you a better person.

The secret order is be, do, and have. Be the person that you want to be. Do the actions necessary. And then you will have everything that you can dream of. I once read a book from some successful guru and he said: "if I can do it, you can do it". I didn't really believe it at the time, but now I say it to you. If I can do it, you can do it too. I truly wish you all the success that you can dream of. Dream it, believe it, and then achieve it!

Chapter 5

Dared By Love

By Jane Thorpe

I've spent most of my life reacting to the world. Reacting to the "external" world, you know life's circumstances like relationships, or different people and the events presented to me. I'm not quite sure at what point I took my focus of appreciation and everything in my world happening for me. Everything appeared to be happening to me.

I guess it was a series of events; like being at the beach and a set of waves knocking me to and fro in the water. All the time forgetting to dive under these very waves to find the stillness and peace that sits beneath. Instead, I let myself get knocked under gasping for air, struggling and fighting, becoming more apprehensive and afraid with each wave. It has felt like a great portion of my life has been one set of waves after another. And this is how I began to discover there is a stillness and peace that sits beneath.

And what of all these sets of waves? They are events that have sewn together my life. What is the purpose of them all thus far? And before I recount one of these sets of waves or events, allow me to confess my own resistance to getting to this very moment.

Recently I came to the realization that after many years of striving ambitiously and working to pay the bills, all under the guise of getting ahead or getting somewhere, I was finally confronted with the idea that writing on and off with long gaps of years and years in between was not going to cut it. Hadn't I been aware of a gift and that gift was writing and what's more, one day it was going to be a huge success, widely accepted and make me lots of money? Hmm, that's just it. After attempt and attempt, something always stopped me.

There's a name for it and it's called procrastination, or writers block. Well, let's just say I've known more of the procrastination than the writing…It's taken a very long time to see the real "why" in sitting down to write. In fact, it had nothing to do with being a huge success, widely accepted and making lots of money. It's been a series of challenges that lead me to see the real reason to sit habitually allowing space for the words to flow to the page.

Here, as I am sitting open-hearted and vulnerable, I find myself finally surrendering to receive love into my life even more now. You see this is the 11th hour for this very chapter that will be open to the external world and its scrutiny and judgment and the resistance has been huge just to be here. The amount of anxiety in the middle of my stomach that has been screaming loudly as soon as I put my fingers on the keyboard has been like bringing two magnets together that repel each other.

The anxiety was causing me to feel nauseous. So after deciding to ask myself what am I afraid of, two things became clear. The first, that perhaps I didn't know what to say and the second, which stemmed from the first "what if it was rejected". There! Right there! This time I was able to see that all of this was more reacting to the idea of the external world again. Hadn't everything I had experienced brought me to the point of no return? Albeit in many increments so that I would start to know my internal world, maybe just maybe the whole journey was all about giving me more opportunities to observe myself, to know my True self rather than judge myself?

What if none of my experiences were a mistake? From all the awareness I knew of, I had many challenges where I was given the gift of being able to see that it wasn't me writing. It wasn't me having to make everything happen in my life. If I could just "be" and let the Love take over. In other words, let God, let the Universe, Surrender, get out of my own way, get out of my head and allow my Heart to guide me. Those waves or rather, challenges…Probably the biggest challenge of all has been running from the pain instead of embracing it. I've spent time after time running from pain.

Luckily sometimes the pain has simply gotten so intense that I have thrown my hands up like a criminal finally cornered by the law and for this metaphor, I'll call the law "Truth". The Truth usually appeared not when I was winning externally. In my experience, it was revealed only after my darkest moment of which I have had several. All of these darker moments were not really that dark at all once the light was shone on them. It was the thoughts I was unconsciously entertained by (aka the ego) that had me believe I was hopeless or not worthy enough.

Take the Depression I went through back in early 2001-2002. The thoughts in my head had me convinced that sadness was bad. You have no right to feel sad. You should have your life together. You are hopeless, shameful, not good enough, a fraud. The self-doubt was overwhelming.

Here's the thing. At this very time, my life was looking good. I was newly married to the man of my dreams. I was living in a great apartment, owned a retail business and was at a place in my life that I liked a great deal. Everything was falling into place. I had reached goals that I thought were unreachable and my life was coming together like a magical fairy-tale. I was even pregnant with my first daughter. Why then was I feeling so low in energy and not wanting to get up and go? The desire that was usually there to go after whatever I wanted simply wasn't there anymore. My spark seemed dim. In fact, I imagine it would be like being locked in a coffin alive although I wasn't feeling alive at all.

Over time, I started to withdraw from social engagements. I didn't answer the phone as much. I lied to my friends that I couldn't catch up because I was too busy. This was strange behaviour for me, not the norm at all. I'm usually outgoing and a talkative. I found myself sleeping in or not getting up at all. Sleep was my vice along with loads of ice cream and basically any junk food that I could eat - secretly of course.

The guilt and the shame I felt were overwhelming. "If they could see me now" was the constant thought running through my head. I found myself crying most of the time, fighting with my husband and most detrimentally had entered into this negative self-talk beating myself up continually. At this point, the "you can do it" approach that had always worked for me in the past was not working. I was feeling like a failure.

My husband insisted I see a doctor and before I knew it I had filled out a questionnaire confirming my depressed state. This was partly a relief that I had an illness yet equally despairing was coming to terms with the so-called "Mental illness", which I was prescribed pills for anti-depression. At the time I was unaware that taking the pills - which undoubtedly got me out of the initial wrath and helped to produce more serotonin to the brain, was still a Band-Aid to my reacting to circumstances.

Several months went by and in September 2001 I gave birth to a beautiful baby girl. All was well for a while. I seemed to be feeling better. Perhaps it was the miracle of life or maybe it was the hormones from breastfeeding. Whichever, it was short-lived because eight weeks later, coincidentally when I stopped breastfeeding, I fell into the darkest depression I never thought imaginable. From here on, negative thoughts spiralled with momentum. Suddenly the identity I had been familiar with was gone. I no longer recognised myself. Hopelessness, lost and confused would only begin to describe the way I was feeling. The false reality my belief system had led me to this point in my life had disappeared. Therefore, everything I knew was wrong. A mistake. Blurred! Physically I couldn't talk.

With the incessant chatter in my head, it was no wonder. The passion I had for anything I had once enjoyed had evaporated. I was trapped. It seemed like there was no way out. Depression then changed to frustration, which was even worse. Every day was another life sentence. I appeared to be making progress yet the negative voices in my head wouldn't stop and were building up to the point I decided I must be going insane. I was alone and very separate and no one seemed to understand. I knew I was nowhere near my real self. The pills allowed me to attend the "daily grind" yet my spirit was still missing in action. This was slowly torturing me. My new self-medication of alcohol and cocaine that somehow I knew deep down was not the answer. It was all I was capable of attempting at the time, given my new world was still not the one I was familiar with.

There was no sign of it changing either. I just couldn't fix it this time. Throughout this period I was really beginning to hate myself as a disappointment in not sorting myself out had set in. Uncertain of anything, I really hit Rock Bottom when I couldn't get out of bed at night to attend to my four-month-old daughter. Despite the pills and the attempt to be counselled, I felt dead inside. After a night out - getting as comfortably numb that I could be whilst still trying to hide this - it occurred to me I had one option that might work for me. That option was Suicide. Sheer frustration was my motivator. Where was the light at the end of the tunnel? It was definitely darkest before the dawn.

Once my husband was asleep, I cut a piece of rope from the balcony blind awning and took a chair into the shower recess in the bathroom, where - after deciding it would hold my weight - attempted to make a noose. I slipped it over my head and stepped off the chair. It hurt like hell. I very quickly stepped back on the chair. Realizing this option involved pain I hadn't anticipated, I retreated to my bed feeling useless, shameful and hopeless. All I recognised was a failure. I was pathetic and weak. What a feeble attempt. I couldn't even do that! It took me a few days to finally confess to my husband what I had done. The courage or the sheer desperation or the fact that I had no alternative but to ask for help was my saving Grace.

With encouragement, I came forward and told a psychologist I was seeing. I accepted that the best option was the hospital for a few weeks and it was finally okay to admit defeat, surrender to my fears and hopefully overcome this desperation. Possibly come out the other side even…? I checked into my new abode. Home for the next three weeks would be a mental health clinic. At first, I was reluctant. If one more person called me "Darling" and told me I would be okay, I might explode. I was completely disconnected. After a week of foetal positions and lots of crying, I was able to make a step toward wellness. Monday morning was my first cognitive behaviour class. I realised one thing, everything I had been doing was not helping me. Therefore trying something new was suddenly not a bad idea. There had been so much thinking going on and no action that I was happy to ignore the thinking at this stage. Ironically, the "just do it " approach made me realize I had nothing to lose and possibly something to gain.

Once the decision was made, everything changed. Songs on the radio seemed to reflect the way I felt. I still recall the lyric on the radio at the time went "Can't you see? Life's easy when you consider things from another point of view". OMG, it was one of the first times I had noticed life reflecting how I felt. Throughout this time, I started exercising and eating well even though I was being fed medication like a guinea pig. I looked forward to the way I felt when I got out in nature for my daily walk. Every couple of days, however, I had to try a new pill. One type of medication would speed me up, keep me awake half the night or another would make me anxious.

Unfortunately, my epiphany about my clear path to recovery didn't last long. The Professor of the Clinic - and I hold no blame here- had now concluded I must be Bi-Polar. Another label. I was improving far too quickly for their liking. The simple fact was that I was ready for the change required to move forward. I had done my suffering for months on end at home. I had to stand up to the Professionals and trust what I believed and what I felt.

They had all their textbooks and testimonials to prove that I should be prescribed Lithium. I knew in my heart I was on the road to recovery and another pill was not the answer to what they thought my problem or labelled condition was. Hey!! I had attempted -albeit half-heartedly thank heavens - to do myself in. Did they think I was there for a joke? I wanted to get better and get on with my life. I was asked to take pills - Lithium- and maybe after a year assess the situation. I said NO. If I went downhill again I would know they were right and I was wrong.

The only way that I would know I was right was to follow what my heart said and the ever so brightening glimmer of a spark that had been getting brighter. I would not take the pills. Didn't they realize the impact the cognitive behaviour classes had on me? Could I replace bad thoughts for good ones? Perhaps I could find me again? I left the hospital after a total of three weeks. I kept up the day classes for a while to ensure my environment didn't regress my steps. It was like playing a game of snakes and ladders. I had climbed a ladder and slid down a snake that took me many steps back, only to find the next ladder took me way beyond where I had been before. I had so much more awareness even if it was only about my thinking at this point. It was enough to make me embrace life again.

For two long years after I was nervous the depression would return. Anytime I felt tired, I felt guilty and thought "Oh No, here we go again". This angered me as I felt I was looking over my shoulder always scared that any day the demon would return. I then asked myself "Why me?" Even though I was no longer depressed. I was living in fear and still wasn't free of the thought that it might return. I felt robbed of the future. Wasn't I happy before all this had taken place? Now I was scared of the future in case it happened again.

I was carefree before. Why did this need to happen? Bit by bit I began to live in the present again and became clear that the thoughts were not actually real unless I entertained them and believed them to be true. Perhaps I didn't need to pay attention to as much of the thinking that went on in my head? Perhaps the thinking was simply on repeat and I could choose new thoughts. And if I was tired I could simply rest and that was ok.

I began to realize I had ignored the way I felt and the resistance to simply being aware of how I felt was what was creating so much thinking, which created more emotions which created more thinking and so on. A while later, it occurred to me that I was back. No depression and no fears of it shadowing me either. Aha. I was living in the NOW. I was out of the coffin and I was feeling Alive. Embracing the pain was more about observing it and the thoughts attached to it. It was more of a portal to know myself a little more. Maybe there was more to me than who I thought I was and sure, I didn't know myself as well as I thought I did at all. It seemed I had been taking myself for granted and life was showing me how to reveal my true potential.

I realized that making sure I do things I love were a big part of feeling good. Simply attending the daily grind was not fun. Especially not fun given I had always been trying to get somewhere or work something out with my head. Allowing more time for me be it looking after myself through a healthier diet and making time for some kind of movement in my life that I enjoyed was fundamental in keeping my mind clearer.

Exercise also helped to increase my energy levels rather than opting for lower vibrational choices like drugs or alcohol. I discovered that instead of always looking for something more I could be more grateful for where I was. I could appreciate my experiences rather than run from them. Each and every one of them was giving me something or at the very least revealing something to me. I also became gentler with myself and have more compassion for others. Life wasn't about fixing or changing whatever I thought was wrong. That was simply my judgment and it was all those judgments that had made me my own prisoner in the first place. It was also apparent that the more attention I gave these self-doubting thoughts the more they created emotions and more thinking to include this belief system of helplessness.

I could start to love and accept myself by focusing more on what I loved and start to refrain from focusing on all the fearful thoughts. I could choose to be my own worst enemy or my greatest hero and it all was stemming from the relationship with myself. Life is a journey and knowing all the things I was becoming aware of, took some time to integrate. There were steps forward and steps back and bit-by-bit I became aware that life was not really how it appeared. Even people were not whom they appeared to be. I started to notice more and more. I also noticed that I was still reliant on the external environment giving me happiness.

The only trouble with this was that if it changed, it then affected my mood and emotions. If my husband was stressed at work I sometimes took his stress. Life was full of ups and it was also full of downs. We had our second daughter - UP. We bought a new house - UP. My husband Chris's stress of being a CEO in a publicly listed company raising funds or the threat of being bought out - DOWN. Now there was this new awareness of how topsy-turvy everything was depending on what I thought brought me happiness or stress. I started to write sporadically. Putting my thoughts and the way I perceived my world down on a page felt somewhat empowering. As much as this was getting most of it out I was starting to find myself arguing with Chris. My typical thoughts were if only thoughts, if only he wasn't this way or if only he was that way inclined everything would be just fine.

It hadn't occurred to me for one moment that just like the house or the circumstances being external, that the very man himself was external. I started focusing on all the negative things. These were all the reasons why I was feeling empty or bored. He was always away overseas. I was always doing things by myself with the children.

I even redecorated our home. After not gaining the interaction and approval from my husband I began to paint a picture in my mind of him not caring. Little by little we were arguing more and not getting on. This was when something magical occurred for me. Although at the time I couldn't see any magic until months later.

After the entire nit-picking between us, Chris had suggested that I must be Bi-Polar after all and insisted I see a Psychiatrist. I said I still didn't believe it, however, I would go along and talk and perhaps I would learn something more. After a meeting with Chris and myself and the Psychiatrist whom I recall at the time was looking at both of us to see which one of us was there to see her. After her suggestion that we are all a little Bi-Polar from time to time and that she could see no immediate signs of being manic it was suggested that if I was to take anything, that I take the mildest medication available. As I don't like swallowing tablets - Thank Heavens - I asked for syrup instead. I left her office with this syrup all the while knowing I really wasn't Bi-Polar. I must have had a little doubt though as I called my girlfriend when I got home and she said "Are you serious?" There's nothing wrong with you. You are more switched on than most people I know.

With this confirmation, I hatched a plan. And this is where the magic started…My plan was to slowly get rid of the syrup. Every day for the next six months I proceeded to tip a little of the syrup down the drain. Not once did it ever touch my lips. If I really believed that there was nothing wrong with me then I would placebo affect my husband. I never heard another word about it for months and months until one day whilst on holiday, Chris said, "I have not seen the level on the medicine bottle go down. Have you been taking it?" "No, I have never taken it."

It was then that I realized that Chris was playing a role for me. And I could believe the external world or I could believe myself. This time, no one could convince me as I was focusing on myself instead. Chris had been showing up to reflect my doubts and I could run with them or not. So the external world only had an influence on me if I allowed it. I had stopped blaming my relationships and my circumstances for my happiness and started to see that I was responsible for my own happiness. Oh, the silver linings were everywhere if I looked a little deeper. Life was definitely not at all what it appeared. In actual fact, I could thank Chris for playing this role for me.

Without him, I wasn't able to see this. It took these very people and circumstances to reflect my fears or triumphs. After a few more years of observation and the support of more conscious intentions and actions, I started to see that everyone was reflecting or playing a role for me. Instead of fixing the outside I started to attend to the inside. I had been living my life outside in rather than inside out.

The outside was a reflection of how I was feeling internal. If I focused on the lack I got the experience of lack. If I focused on being enough and having enough then life reflected back abundance. If I trusted then life showed up effortlessly. If I worried and doubted then, sure enough, I had the experience of insecurity and fear. The relationship that was of paramount importance was the one I had with myself. All other relationships reflected this. If I went back on my word to myself, someone I knew others went back on his or her word to me. If I took time for myself I noticed the calendar cleared and the phone was quiet enough to be able to embrace the space for myself.

Little by little I noticed my choices came more from love than fear. I was responding less and less to the external. Whether it be reacting to someone in my life or to my own thoughts. Instead of reacting, I would catch out the moment I had let my actions direct me by giving the moment space. Not doing anything with it and simply leaving it alone.

Noticing instead my own self. The reactions usually came from wanting to be accepted or approved and not being rejected. How was I not accepting myself or approving of myself? How was I rejecting myself? Everything became a microscope for me to see whether I was acting from love or where my patterns of sabotage from a well-rehearsed ego being in control.

Recently I did a 55km walk for charity. My intention was to do something new and to challenge my fitness. It turned out to be an incredible learning curve of self-observation. I got so much more out of it than I expected. I thought I was simply getting fitter and checking something off a bucket list. It wasn't until the training had finished and the 55Km walk completely that I discovered so much more about this outdoor challenge. And what those discoveries were really surprised me. Most of the training myself and the other three women in our team did was every third week we went to a different coastal walk in Sydney ranging from 11km to 33km.

There were the obvious learning's like having the correct lightweight backpack and water supply. The right socks, shoes and copious amounts of Band-Aids for blisters. That staying together as we walked made for more conversation and kept us entertained. It was the observations of the thoughts in my mind that blew me away. And from these very thoughts I could see how much we live our lives listening to the orders these thoughts bark at us, putting off all the things we love in case of failure or not being good enough or not being liked etc....

It was on the very last training session from Coogee beach to Vaucluse and back, which was a mere 18km compared to the 33km session we had done 2 weeks previously, that really opened my eyes. The walk started off well. The now, three members who include me - we were down a team member who hadn't been well that day - set off at a fair pace. It was a scorching hot day and I had all my necessities, water - check, sunscreen - check, Band Aids - check, snack- check, hat- check, mind - almost check. Today I was about to discover the tricks of the mind. By the time we arrived at Bondi Beach the other two women were charging ahead leaving me just out of earshot of the conversation. Okay, no problem. I'll just admire the view and carry on walking. That worked for about another kilometre.

As we started up the hill towards Vaucluse the thoughts kicked in. "You're falling behind, you're not as fit as these two. You don't fit in anyway. They are both married and you are divorced. You don't have a husband. You have nothing to add to the conversation anyway. I wasn't expecting to walk this far today. I thought we were only walking 12 km.

Perhaps I should ask them to turn around now. Oh boy, it was a running commentary. I brought myself back to the present moment again however that was short lived as today my blisters were hurting a bit and my legs a little sore. The thoughts continued. A moment later one of my team members suggested we turn around as she had to be home to do something and we all agreed it was a great idea. Phew. That was getting difficult. My thoughts subsided for a while as we walked downhill. The other women still a good eighty meters in front of me.

By the time we were approaching Coogee again the thoughts were back in full assault. "What were you thinking entering this 55km walk? You can't keep up with your team. Why don't you just stop here and now anyway? Best to save your sore feet and blisters for the actual day. It won't matter if you stop now.

SHUT UP I thought yelled at them. No! As much as I wasn't enjoying it at this stage and it hadn't been a fun walk like the others I wasn't giving up either. I would just talk to my team and tell them my awful experience. I don't know how many times I brought myself back to focus on my breath simply to disengage with the enemy in my head. I did talk to the team and much to my amazement they had had their own meddling thoughts going on. They had walked so fast to try and get it over with as quickly as possible.

Oh right. I was so busy being entertained by these thoughts I hadn't even considered they were having their own demons. What was most prominent to me, however, was how much and how quickly the thoughts (aka the ego) would come in to sabotage and distract me as soon as I was out of my familiar comfort zone. And how if I simply chose not to engage in them they eventually hushed. The Big day arrived and thankfully because of my last training experience I was already prepared for my mind's brutal attacks.

That was until I got to Coogee Beach at 5:45am that morning and looked around the beach at the other 2000 women and men. Are you kidding? The majority of these people look like athletes. Look at the muscles and the sinew. These people look like they do marathons as a regular form of exercise. I was a 47-year-old mum with a reasonably fit body and a desire to try something new. I definitely didn't have the appearance of a well-seasoned Queen of the Outdoors Fitness Junky.

Looks, of course, can be deceiving. Perhaps it was the energy of the day itself or the sheer reminder of the last experience I had from falling behind my teammates, probably both and I was off to a thrilling start. With every step, I lunged forward increasing my pace to keep the lead of my teammates. "Hey, what did you have for breakfast this morning? 'they joked. For me, falling behind was not an option today. No way. We traversed the stunningly beautiful coast from beach to beach, bay to bay stopping here and there for the toilet or to reapply a Band-Aid and by the time we reached the other side of the Bridge - we were walking to Balmoral Beach- I was well into a comfortable stride and not one single sabotaging thought.

It appeared the training and "practice" had supported me in many ways. All was well with the team until the 45km mark. With 10km left to go and the next 9km being the most difficult, I suddenly winced in pain. My two very large blisters on both my feet that were wrapped in about their seventh or eighth Band Aid by this stage let out the most incredible stinging pain I have ever encountered. This was my worst nightmare come true. Apparently more people stop long treks due to either heat exhaustion or blisters.

Earlier one of my teammates had stopped, riveted to the ground limping and doubling over and with further application of new Band Aids, some neurofen and a great attitude had come through it. It was my turn. I stopped and hobbled to sit down. The thoughts were going crazy now. You can't walk another 10km like this. You will fall behind again. You can't concentrate anymore. You are limping. You are slowing down. It will be midnight at this rate by the time you get there. Everyone is passing you, maybe someone can come and pick you up by car, and so on and so on.

I took the advice of my teammate to have some neurofen too. The next two kilometres were not easy although there was a definite pleasure in the choice of ignoring those thoughts and proceeding. I went from all my attention on limping and the excruciating stinging- which I had to remind myself was simply raw skin and that my leg hadn't fallen off - to suddenly somehow noticing that the pain transformed into a new sensation of numbness and no longer was I limping. I could feel pain, however it wasn't too bad and definitely was not taking all my attention any longer. My focus returned to the breath-taking beauty of my surroundings. Sydney on a twenty-eight-degree day on a coastal walk was no less than stunning. A beautiful yet gentle breeze in the air on a glorious summer day and I was feeling Alive and somewhat invincible. Well well. Pain transforms and disappears if you keep going through it. Embrace the pain.

The last 8 kilometres were even more satisfying because I had triumphed my circumstances rather than giving in to them. This was a new high. I had seen first-hand how I could overcome the limits of the thoughts in my mind and certain physical barriers that were not as bad as first perceived. Before I knew it we were arriving at Balmoral by 5:00pm. We did it! I did it. And as I stood watching the Sunset sipping a Winners glass of Champagne I noted that some of those super fit women right back at the start were still finishing way after we had crossed the line. In fact other than the crazy people who ran the entire 55km we actually did really well time wise and finished before most of the other entrants?

Appearances were not just deceiving. The thoughts in particular about those appearances and circumstances were definitely deceiving. I certainly didn't expect to see what comes from the constant practice of something. It reveals so much about yourself and going beyond your own self-imposed limitations. Getting out of my comfort zone was more rewarding than I had anticipated. That's the benefit of a new awareness that's been embraced from Love and not from fear. It opens up more and more space to go beyond what you already know. It became apparent to me I must write habitually simply for the space it inspired me to create for myself and all those jewels that come from not giving in to those thoughts that seem like they know everything.

In fact, that was a very clear message to me to give space to the thoughts more and more. If I don't engage in my thoughts their power diminishes. And then what? Perhaps I can keep creating more rather than reacting…Hmm? Where to from here? In service of my dreams and not my conditions… All in my life, as in your own life, is a necessary experience in order to fulfil a mission. All of it is dated by love. The dropping of ego and returning to live as a creator and not a reactor was a valuable lesson for me to learn. Go on! Love dares you.

Chapter 6

Overcoming Challenges

By Cecilia Yeung

Rock Bottom – 2009-2010

2009 was one of the worst years in my life. I had just turned 40 and did not expect that within a few short months of celebrating this milestone with close friends in joy and exhilaration that I would hit rock bottom with no job, no relationship, no home, no direction, no money and completely alone to face my bleak future. The worst part was that my new found circumstance took me completely by surprise and I had to keep my malaise a secret from my family and friends. In short, I had just moved to Australia after a life of 16 years in Hong Kong. It had not been an easy decision because by doing so, I gave up my business, my apartment, my network and my friends to start a new life with my significant other.

I was reluctant for a long time to make this drastic move but after months of his persistent persuasion, I finally decided to take the plunge. Within six months of this move and after a seemingly routine fight, I was told rather unemotionally and bluntly that the relationship wasn't working out. Was I to leave because he said it was over? What on earth am I supposed to do now? I had uprooted my entire life to commit to this relationship and our future. I was too shocked to believe what had happened. I was ashamed to share this with anyone and was just plainly and blindly confused by it all.

I spent time with my family in Canada and travelled to complete some work assignments in Hong Kong and Asia during this ambivalent period. Surely he wasn't serious about breaking up? Maybe he just needed some space and we would continue on with our lives together that we had been planning for several years after he realized how foolish he was being. The last time I was in the home we were sharing, I left with a large suitcase for a one-month trip to Asia and Canada. I was confident that we would work this out even though I was also overwhelmed with fear and sadness. "He is just going through a phase," I told myself as I flew out on that flight. It would be three years before we met again.

I Just Have To Share My Homeless Story - 2015

I was recently at a 3-day personal development seminar and on the last day, the organizers arranged a number of guest speakers with 90-minute slots to share their proprietary success tools. They, of course, were selling their products and were doing their best to convince the audience that their program is the absolute easiest and quickest route to wealth, success and happiness. What struck me was that out of the six speakers, four of them had a "homeless" story. I had to chuckle a little because I realize that the secret to success is not what we've been fed over the years by countless self-help books, gurus and motivational speakers.

You know what I'm talking about. The success formula: work hard, seize every opportunity, take risks, build relationships, have a vision, be hungry, be relentless, be persistent, take massive action…and so on. The real secret to success is to end up on the street! So if you want to be wealthy, successful and happy, you should try to become homeless? Now I am just here joking and this is in no way being disrespectful to the millions of people around the world who in fact, have no homes and struggle for survival every single day of their lives. You see, I also have a homeless story though I was not living out of a cardboard box like one of the speakers at that seminar but I was hopeless and struggling and it was indeed, the lowest point in my life.

And also because being homeless is one of the most feared or one of our most basic human needs not being met. Abraham Maslow taught us that food and shelter are a human being's most fundamental need for survival and if this is absent, we kick into our most primal drives to meet these needs. According to his hierarchy of needs, the next level is safety and security after shelter, as in family, a job or social stability followed by love, connection and a sense of belonging. Well, for a long time, I was without a home. True, it was not total devastation I faced and some may say it was glamorous homelessness by choice. With hardly any financial means, I still managed to fly business class, travelled across Asia for work and across to Canada to visit my family.

I stayed in five-star hotels (when organized by the client) and the luxurious homes of my friends. No, I was not destitute to the level where I was starving or living on the streets. I had very little means, dangerously low self-esteem and lost complete faith in life and myself. I was only focused on getting through each day. I ponder back on that period of my life and on how I got through each day. I believe it is firstly an innate survival instinct that protects us and keeps us alive. Our brains go into total and laser focus on how to nourish our bodies, how to get through the day and plan for the next day. I also believe this was developed at an early age when I learned how to take care of myself and be independent, without the support or security of nurturing adults. My childhood was very solitary and without a lot of interaction with my parents. This, I believe, is the reason I am completely self-reliant, fiercely independent and where my core values originated from.

So Everything Is Going To Be Ok?

My parents did not impose any religious views on their household nor did they talk to me about such matters. When they did communicate with me, it was usually perfunctory instructions such as ordering me to finish my dinner or telling me it's time to go to bed. I can hardly recall a conversation about my homework, my studies, my interests or my well-being. That can't be right you say and as I write this, I am incredulous at just how little input my parents had in my development as a human being.

I discovered the library at age seven. To me, it was a mammoth haven of information and answers. It was an incredible entertainment and a fantasy for a young child who was starving for guidance and direction. I learned at an early age that whatever questions I had, I simply had to look for it in a book. I did not ask teachers, the librarian or other adults in my life. In fact, I do not really recall asking questions, it just wasn't something that occurred to me. I think it was because I usually felt pretty insignificant as a child and asking an adult questions may seem to be bothersome.

I simply searched for the answers myself. It is amazing how this conditioning set me on a path of development and completely defines me to this day. In how I solve problems, make decisions, seek answers, make discernments and draw conclusions about life. It has been a strength and driving force but it can also be a setback. During my worst times and challenging moments in life, my default drive is to turn inward and figure it out on my own. It's not stubbornness or arrogance. It is simply a survival instinct kicking in when I have to figure out how to get out of a mess. I was a "latch-key kid", termed for my generation, the children of baby boomer working parents, growing up in the 70s in Vancouver, Canada.

My younger brother and I learned to take care of ourselves early on. Both our immigrant parents worked and struggled to fit into a very new and daunting world that was drastically different from where they came. The term denotes wearing a house key around one's neck and visually communicating that there were no parents at home when you finish school and definitely no one to pick you up. I took care of my own breakfast and went home to cook lunch for my brother and I. After school, I would clean the house, do my homework and basically, managed all my needs without bothering my parents. It's amazing how adaptable children are. I was never asked about my difficult transition to a whole new life. I was adjusting to a new and daunting environment as well! I was simply given directions on how to get to school, where the food in the kitchen was and the basics on taking care of each other after school.

I was given chores and one important responsibility was collecting our mail from the main lobby of our apartment building every day. Then placing it on the dining room table for my mother to review when she got home. This responsibility I took very seriously because my brother was too young to handle it. I would take the mailbox key from its place every day after school to check the mail and one afternoon to my horror, the key was missing! I could not find it anywhere and sheer panic set in as I contemplated how my mother would react when she discovered that I had lost the key.

I was fraught with terror and fear. I searched and searched and could not find it anywhere. I had to figure a way out of this. I retraced my steps from yesterday's collection and searched the apartment hallway, scoured every corner of our tiny apartment but to no avail. I remained in panic and suffered through an agonizing evening of anxiety. My mother did not notice that there was no mail on the table that day. There were days they didn't get any mail and I was temporarily relieved that I bought a little more time the next day to search for it. I went to bed full of dread and doom so I did the only thing that I could think of in my young and childish mind. I prayed.

My parents had never taken me to church nor discussed religion or any form of ideas relating to faith with me. I came across the Lord's Prayer in school and in the mind of that terrified seven-year-old, I needed help so I asked God to help me find the key. I said the Lord's Prayer over and over again until I fell asleep. The next day while I was getting ready for school, I noticed out of the corner of my eye, the mailbox key on the carpet near the door. I was ecstatic! I was relieved beyond words. It was a miracle! It was one of the greatest sensations in the world to have such a heavy and dreadful burden lifted.

No, on that day I did not find the light or path to God or became religious but something did change in me. My seven-year-old brain made a connection that things work out if you have enough faith and believe in yourself. This has guided and assured me during my worst times and there were many. I recall a moment after I left Australia and I was sitting on my bed at the Ramada Hotel in Hong Kong. I was in town for a few days for work, which was going to provide some much-needed income. I was counting the money I had left to live for the next few days and calculating when the next incoming dollars would be. When I was not working or preparing for work I was constantly plotting on how to organize my next meal, my budget for each day and how long I can last with the dwindling amount of money I had.

Even though the situation was dire and I was morose with hopelessness, there remained a firm belief that I was going to be okay. Why wouldn't it be okay? After all, there were benevolent spirits and angels looking out for me. Otherwise, why would I be upgraded to a suite at the Ramada with a nice little living room and a beautiful sea view? Glamorous homelessness right? How I wished I opened up and reached out to friends during this time. It's not like I didn't have any. Honestly, I just couldn't face anyone. Especially when I wasn't even sure myself what my relationship status was and I didn't want to lie to my friends. The shame and humiliation I wore so gallantly did not allow me to have any conversations about it with others. It was a cross I had to bear, an epic challenge that was up to me and me alone to overcome. I was a gladiator and I was going to get through this!

Years later when I finally opened up to what I was going through my friends were aghast. Shocked and disappointed that I did not trust enough in their friendship to let in their help. Of course, the ones that truly know me well understand that this is my way of dealing with calamity. I know that relying on others and getting support is an important part of overcoming challenges. That is just not part of my DNA and not how I face problems. I am getting a bit better at asking for help these days. Whenever there is a serious challenge, I know I will kick in my proven and well-used success formula. My faith got me through it. The faith that was drilled into me got me through moment to moment when I cried out with anger at why this was happening to me.

Then the signs would appear that things would be okay. A payment I wasn't expecting to come in yet would magically appear in my account. I would get upgraded to business class for a flight to Singapore. Or the hotel reception would say to me with a smile, "Miss Yeung, we have upgraded your room to a harbour view suite for your three nights' stay." Or I would wake up in the morning, look out at the blue sky and for a split second, the woes of my homelessness and tattered relationship momentarily forgotten.

I would feel the grace of divinity coursing through my body. A grace and knowing that I am beyond this existence and that I will be okay. Developing a strong belief in yourself and a deep knowing that it is going to work out and resonance to the divine that exists in and around you. It has pulled me through many dark moments. When times are tough, recall the inner strength you have and the times that you were trapped but found a way out. Life has a magnificent and beautiful way of guiding us and providing support, in the most unseen or unexpected forms.

People of depth, with compassion and humility,did not achieve these traits by having a smooth ride. The strong, wise and empathetic light beings out there in this world developed their depth in their soul through countless etchings of painful struggle and turmoil. The story of miners trapped for 69 days underground in Chile in 2010 sent waves of horror for those who can only imagine their ordeal and their inhumane struggle for survival. I read about this with deep compassion and admiration. Their strength and courage to get through each day, moment to moment with only faith on their side that they will survive. I will never know exactly what they went through.

I can take their story as a metaphor for times of struggle in darkness when light and escape seem impossible and out of reach. Whatever I have been through will never be close to the magnitude of physical and emotional suffering these men went through. I can certainly glean lessons from knowing that hope can keep you alive. In those moments of utter defeat and buried hopelessness, what can you do to maintain your sanity and get out alive? Whatever your darkness may be, whether it is for one, 69 or 169 days, know that there is a way out. Keep your faith alive.

Resourcefulness Will Get You Everywhere - 1987

My parents did not fulfil the immigrant dream as in work hard, save money and provide a better future for the next generation. They suffered marital problems and were constantly fighting and struggling to keep our family together while going through financial challenges.

They tried their best and through all the turmoil, we were somehow blessed with two additions to the family, my sister and baby brother. Because of their continued dysfunctional parenting of being absent and providing a lack of care, I became the caretaker of my younger siblings from a young age. When I was 19 and they were still quite young at age, nine and seven, my father finally left us for good. My mother, shortly after that traumatic event, decided that she needed to "get away". She did not share her plans with me other than to tell me that she would be gone for a while and left some money for us to live on. I stepped up and without any consideration of how pathetic our situation was, I just took over.

I was going to a community college at the time and had three part time jobs. Like I said, I had always been independent and had been taking care of myself financially for a number of years by this time. This was the first time I was fully responsible for the household, all the childcare and even though I took care of the kids, now I was 100% accountable for the welfare of these two little beings. All the money that my mother left us went to groceries.

I wasn't clear on when she would be returning so I didn't budget very well. When the money ran out, I had to be resourceful on how to feed the family while working my part-time jobs and going to school during the day. My sister and baby brother were great and were very resilient kids, we did not know any better so being left on our own to fend for ourselves was our normal. They were responsible for getting themselves to and from school every day and I tried to be around as much as possible.

Nights that I was working, my brother who was 17 at the time, took up duty to make sure they brushed their teeth and went to bed on time. Breakfast was cereal and toast and I had been packing their lunches since they were in kindergarten so that was not too difficult. It was the planning of evening meals and what to feed them every night that baffled me. I didn't know how to cook except for heating up processed food, which we had plenty of in the house. My mother was great at stocking up lots of canned food as this was my main food staple since childhood. She was and still is, an obsessive hoarder. Keeping supplies of every household item in the basement as well as a freezer full of mystery food that she keeps buying on sale. When the funds were running low, I decided to tap into the freezer for our dinners.

I defrosted a package of mystery meat every day. The obvious packages like chicken, sausages or hamburger patties were quickly eaten up. But as time went on and there was no sign of any parent returning, I had to keep digging into that freezer for questionable saran-wrapped chunks of ice that may have been there for years. I learned to flavour the mystery meat with highly processed and flavoured pasta, such as Hamburger Helper and the kids seemed to love every meal. I just wanted to make sure they had a hot meal every night and I prepared every meal with love. There were disasters or meals that did not turn out well at all. The kids, however, didn't seem to notice and loved our evenings together, eating at the table as a family and enjoyed every disgusting meal I prepared for them. At one point, there was no more money and I wasn't expecting a pay check until the following week. What was I to do in the coming days to feed the kids? In my resourcefulness and in the spirit of making it fun and light, I designed a game for them to look for coins and old lottery tickets around the house.

The instructions were to look under the sofa, in coat pockets and in drawers and the contest was to see who could find the most coins. We played this game several times and to our delight during the first round, we found five old lottery tickets that had winnings of about $50! We promptly cashed in the tickets and then headed straight to Safeway to get groceries and much deserved treats for the kids. We laughed, danced in the aisles and went home to enjoy a scrumptious meal that night.

Thankfully, we got through this period without any traumas, starvation, neglect or physical harm. In fact, the kids recall this as a very happy time, full of fun and laughter. It was only years later when I told them the real story behind the search for lottery tickets that they cried about how strong I was for them. I didn't see it that way at all. I was just being resourceful!

How to Become Un-Homeless – 2010

Tapping into my well-used prowess in resourcefulness, I created a regime that not only helped me get through a tough financial situation but also positions laser sharp focus on getting out of my demise. All I knew was that this homelessness and insanely illogical circumstance did not define me and I was not going to stay there for long. JK Rowling once quoted, "Rock bottom became a solid foundation on which I rebuilt my life."

This became my mantra and inspiration. Getting a job, I decided, was not the answer because I would only be doing it for money. I knew that my heart would not be in it. I combed through my network to see whom I may contact for part time consulting. Sure enough, just as I started planning it, a magical email came through from a client while I was in Canada for Christmas. Asking if I could meet with him in the New Year to discuss some freelance marketing consulting (yes, faith works in wonderful ways!). By this time, end of 2009, my family was aware of my situation and was forming a coalition to persuade me to finally move back home.

As much as I was tempted, I did not wish to leave Hong Kong with absolutely nothing to show for it except my failure. I had to work this out. When I finally decide to leave, it would be on my terms not because I was completely broke. I do have to thank my family for giving me the emotional and financial support during this time. They all knew I had no money so they sent me a ticket to spend Christmas at home, which I had only missed once in all the years I lived away. It was a bittersweet Christmas for me as there was a black cloud of uncertainty hanging over me. I was also in the relaxing comfort of family. When I returned to

Hong Kong, I found myself a tiny studio. I started working on several projects that provided a steady income. I kept up with my consulting and training that I had reactivated with clients and also managed to secure some new projects. I was on a total mission, a mission to get back on my feet financially.

This became one of the most disciplined, austere and structured periods of my life and I set the standard very high. I had no choice but to create a structure that kept me focused, healthy and productive. I am a lot more relaxed today and I certainly do not recommend this level of extreme discipline for everyone. All I know is that in less than a year, I doubled my income, got out of my dire financial straits, rebuilt my life, and regained my health. I started my day with a meditation, and then spent an hour on incantations, affirmations and emotional tapping, followed by a healthy breakfast and my thoughts were completely focused on income generating productivity every day.

When I wasn't working in a client's office or from home, I went to yoga, listened to my personal development CDs, did my visualization exercises and spent long periods of time on my own. I wrote in my gratitude journal every night. I declined all social invitations as they did not contribute to my income productivity and was perfectly content to spending my free time reading, preparing healthy food or exercising. Did I mention that I was on a vegan raw diet as well during this time? I guess when I set out a tough regime, I went all the way! For someone who enjoys a glass of wine every day, it was the first time in my adult life that alcohol was completely cut out. I even stopped drinking coffee and my energy, focus and mental sharpness increased each day.

It's funny that when the body starts cleansing and detoxing, the mind will follow suit. I made a conscious choice to stop watching TV and reading newspapers to remove negative images and mindless conditioning from my life and it was entirely effortless. The gossip magazines that I once enjoyed reading were, and are still now, distasteful to me. Music also played a big role during that period of time. I bought a rebounder (a mini trampoline that is labelled as one of the best forms of exercise for cardio and detoxification) and bounced every morning to a couple of happy tunes while singing along.

The purpose was to set off the positive mental conditioning to the physical level and to surge the uplifting energy through my cells. It certainly worked because each day gradually became better and brighter!

Two (or Three) Minds Are Always Better Than One - 1984

Napoleon Hill, in his timeless classic, "Think and Grow Rich" shared that "No two minds ever come together without thereby creating a third, invisible intangible force, which may be likened to a third mind." I have been fortunate in my life to meet soul mates and dear friends that I will count on until the day I die.

One of these friends is my true blue and lifelong best friend I met when I was 12 years old. Friends come and go and a few stay for a lifetime. My best friend and I dealt with the agonies of puberty and woes of being a teenager with each other through thick and thin. Because we both came from dysfunctional families and we lacked role models to nurture our minds and provide us with direction, we had to guide each other through this trying and emotionally painful period of growing up. No longer a child that had to obey orders but not yet an adult with the freedom and decision-making power.

We thought we knew everything and assumed to know what was best for us. I honestly do not know how I could survived the tumultuous period of my teenage years without her counsel, unconditional love, support and alignment. She was my anchor, my soul sister and someone I would trust with my life. During the summer of 1984, Vancouver Transit went on strike. All the public buses operating in the city were kept idle and the bus was our only form of transportation aside from walking.

At ages 15 and 16 respectively, we were facing an entire summer of staying at home unless we walked or got rides from our parents. Because the latter solution was not available, we had to figure out a way to get to the beach or social gatherings with our friends. We put our heads together and came up with a plan on how we would get around, and more importantly, to our favourite Kitsilano Beach. The famous and most popular beach in the city about 4 km's away from me and 6 km's from my best friend.

Without the bus, our only other option was to walk or hitchhike. We were greatly concerned about our safety and came up with a system of walking to meet each other at a halfway distance between our homes, we than hitched hiked together as close to the beach as we could get, walking the rest of the way. Our number one ground rule was that we would never hitchhike alone. We were safer together and we developed a screening process. Women with children were totally okay, as with the elderly. We were also okay with couples, regardless of age but we checked them out first. We were very wary of lone men and viewed them with scrutiny and scepticism. We made sure we sat close to the door within close reach of the handle and only hitchhiked during the day, and never at night. We devised all these rules on our own through debate, detailed planning and preparation. I even recall sitting down together to make a list of these rules and guidelines.

When the beach day was over, we would hitchhike together to one of our homes and after dinner, wait to be picked up in the evening by a parent. I am cringing as I write this because this was so dangerous! Anyone reading this, especially teenagers: do not ever hitchhike and get into a stranger's car! Vancouver today has an efficient public rail system and to my knowledge, there has never been another bus strike ever since.

The strike lasted all summer and we got through it safely and with a lot of fun and sun I might add because of our resourcefulness and relatively mature heads. We even had the bronze tans to show for it!

Soul Brothers and My Ultimate Mastermind - 2011

Towards the end of 2010, I attended a high impact personal development program focused on mastering stage skills and becoming a high-profile public speaker. The life transformation did not come from the content of the program, which was amazing, but through a couple of significant people I met there. This program, which I could not afford to attend, was held in Phuket, Thailand. Through the graces and the benevolent beings that always look out for me, the CEO of the organizing company knew I wanted to attend but could not pay the US$10K fee and offered me to come along as a helper. This meant that I would not be participating, but help out behind the scenes and of course, be able to sit in to learn from the speakers.

A friend offered a spare bed in her room at the high-end resort, it was held for five nights. I had just enough air miles to book my flight so off I went! I was totally in my element, learning from the world's masters on presenting to audiences of thousands and I was also part of the organizing team, spending personal time with the teachers and other helpers. I connected with many friends, old and new, who were either attending the program or volunteering their services. I am very lucky to be a part of a regional personal development network of many professionals, teachers, presenters, entrepreneurs and overall, just genuine and lovely people. I connected very well with one participant, a vibrant, larger than life and deeply emotional and soulful Australian living in Kuala Lumpur, whom I had recently met in Sydney where I was working at another event.

As the program was nearing its end, and we realized that we would soon be parting ways, I thought of a possible way for us to stay in touch but we needed a third person to make this alliance complete.

Another participant that we both enjoyed the company of is an American artist living in Singapore. We love him because of his gigantic heart, mind-staggering talent (that was totally under-utilized and not made commercially viable for him) and just his overall, innocent and graceful presence that infects you with waves of warmth and goodness.

I brought up the idea of forming a Mastermind Group after the program to stay connected and they quickly agreed as we all wanted the growth to continue. We also knew that it is very easy to slip back into our old habits and it would help greatly if we had people around to hold us accountable. We agreed that when we returned to our respective countries and hectic lives, we would communicate on a regular basis. Checking in on each other's progress, challenge each other, to lend support and encouragement.

At that time, we all had our personal challenges and business and personal dreams that were unfulfilled. One thing we knew for sure, we were all resourceful, talented and extremely passionate individuals whose tipping point was just around the corner. We had all the ingredients, knowledge, grit and desire to be successful but something (and it was unique for each of us) was holding us back. We decided on a weekly one-hour Skype call and our format was we would each take 10 minutes to give an overview of our week. We would devote the remaining half hour on a rotation to one of the three, to discuss, explore, challenge, encourage or just listen to any topic or the current issue of that person's choice.

We quickly became each other's closest confidantes. Sharing intimate details of our personal lives with utmost trust and gaining valuable guidance and support as we each maneuvered our way through our obstacle-ridden paths. We became so close and connected that it felt like we were soul mates. Our partners did not seem to mind the intimate yet totally platonic relationship. In fact, they were very much a part of the conversation. We met up in person for several retreats throughout 2011-2014, spending quality time together, sharing our dreams, ideas and our progress.

This alliance obviously has had an effect on us because, after a year of our conference calls, we all exceeded our goals in just about every area of our lives. When we reflect back on when we first started, to see how far we have come and how much we have grown. We all grin from ear to ear as well as share a moment of disbelief because every one of us has outrageously exceeded our own expectations. Now that is a sensation one should feel often! I am so indebted to this Mastermind Alliance and to my true soul brothers (as well as their wives) for their love, unconditional support and loyalty the last five years. Today, we continue to communicate on a regular basis and meet in person whenever we can. They are my family away from home.

I'm still learning today to call on my friends and family for help when I need it. It may not be a big issue for the next person but it's something that will continue to be my life lesson. My faith, resourcefulness, independence and ability to solve problems will only get me so far on my own but with others, we can truly create miracles. And it is indeed, a magnificent life when shared with others.

Chapter 7

Limitless - There are no limits in life except the ones we place on ourselves.

By Helen Ingrid Appleton

What if I were to ask you this one question. I really want you to think about this. Don't just read it, please ask yourself this question. Did I do everything I could with everything that I was given?

That not only includes the good things you attracted into your life for that is easy, but also the so-called bad. This really is a great question to ask yourself and one that I continually ask others and myself almost every day. However, as I first stated I really encourage you to think about this question. It's so easy to just skim over the words and not take them in.

I personally believe it is one of the most important questions you could essentially ask yourself. I first heard this question being asked at a seminar I attended many years ago by one of my leading mentors, Dr John Demartini. And it has stuck in my head ever since because it is so profound. In fact, Dr John Demartini has had an incredibly strong impact on the way I now look at life. His teachings have helped me enormously in all aspects of my day-to-day existence. The more I learn, the more I realise I have to learn, and it's a continually evolving journey that is infinite.

Let's now go back to that question. I will ask it again. Did I do everything I could with everything I was given? If you were really true to yourself, the answer in most cases to this question would be NO. Ask yourself why? Reflect back on your life and take a good hard look at it. How many opportunities have you passed up along the way? Countless opportunities I would imagine. I know from my own experience that this is the case with most people and it was with me too. And that is okay? You can't change your past but you can make the choice to do the most with your life from today onwards.

The best way to do that is to learn more. Acquire skills and techniques in order to do this and to ask better quality questions about your life. Chances are, like the rest of us, you didn't make the most of what you were given. We get one life, which sadly most of us take for granted until we reach old age. Then we start to really get scared because we finally realise the value of time and how precious it is. Why? Because time is now limited. My advice here is to use your limited time to create limitless opportunities for yourself and others. For we all have the ability to do this and time really is our most precious asset, so please use it wisely.

One of the greatest discoveries we can honour and realise in our lifetime, I believe, is the unlimited and untapped source of power we potentially have within us. Why potential? Because if this power isn't used we cannot create the life we desire and we end up wasting our lives.

We actually have limitless potential, and opportunities surround us all the time. We are simply not honouring them. Or most of the time not even realising that they even exist. Why is it that some people achieve more than others? Why is it that they have more money, more success, more friends, do more, have more, be more etc.?

We all have the same amount of hours in the day. In fact, if time is our most precious asset, then why are we not valuing it more? It is limited and it is vital that we spend it carefully, for this is one thing we never get back. I will explain a good way to make the most of your time later and prioritise your day to get optimum results out of it. I want to share a little bit about myself first, part of my journey and how I have managed to overcome some of my own personal challenges along the way.

From a very young age, I was always driven by an intense desire to know more about myself and study human behaviour. Watching people interact with each other always fascinated me. I was always asking questions and I drove my parents mad, particularly my mum, by my constant rebellious nature. I always did things differently, in fact, I was a problem child in some ways. Why? Because I didn't conform to the norm.

In fact, I still don't, so I guess I grew into a problem adult. I was a strong individual. Outspoken and believed that I deserved and had the right to question the society's standards. It's so called rules and regulations and then decide that if I didn't agree with them then why should I conform? I'm not saying that I broke laws and acted stupidly, well most of the time anyway. I simply decided for myself that I was the master of my life, not other people. I didn't want society to dictate to me who I was supposed to be. I always stood out and was in fact ostracised for being different.

I was a geeky looking kid, wore glasses since I was two years old, had buck teeth, was extremely thin and was always extremely strong willed. I was constantly being called four-eyes because of my coke-bottle looking glasses. I absolutely hated wearing them. I decided at the age of thirteen I had had enough of being teased because of my eyes. I stopped wearing my glasses and haven't worn them since. At the age of nine I was wearing clothes that would fit a three-year-old as I was really skinny, I hated that too. So I felt extremely unattractive.

There was also just an energy about me that was different as well, and people seemed to pick up on this. This created an extreme amount of pain for me, as I knew I was different and I found fitting in very hard. Making friends was at times even harder. My friends were always just a little bit different too. Ironically though people looked up to me and I tended to get on better with adults. I was great academically and loved learning.

In fact, I actually loved school. I excelled in all areas and represented my school in state sports carnivals, debating teams, dancing and musicals. I was a member of the school representative council and was elected to be school captain, and the list goes on. In fact, the world was my oyster. Whatever I touched seemed to turn to gold. This seemed to be quite a feat since I moved around a lot as a child. I went to six different primary schools.

I did correspondence school at times because we lived in a remote region in the country for a number of years, and attended three different high schools. In spite of my achievements I actually believed I was stupid and ugly. Mainly because others put me down so much and deep down I lacked belief in myself. As a result of this feeling of inadequacy intellectually, my yearning for knowledge was enhance. I am not writing these childhood achievements down to big note myself, for as you can see I really felt the opposite.

Later in life things took a downward turn for me and I began to really question whether I was good at anything at all. In fact,my self-worth plummeted to such a low level that at times I questioned what on earth I was doing and why I was such a failure. I am merely sharing these experiences with you to let you know that no matter how tough life may get and how low you may feel at times, there is always a way through.

My parents divorced when I was seven. My mum, twin sister and brother just packed up and left my dad, wearing nothing but the clothes on our backs and taking nothing with us. All possessions had been left behind. The breakup of my family absolutely crushed me. I remember when we left. I didn't really understand why my family broke up at the time but had to deal with it nonetheless. I remember the day it happened that life would never be the same again. At that moment, at the age of seven, I grew up instantly and there was no turning back. I was now an adult in a child's body. It broke my heart. We then moved to a very remote region in the country, as unfamiliar as anything I had experienced before. We managed, as kids do, to adapt fairly easily, but this certainly had its challenges. We lived in a decrepit run down house (which we eventually turned into a lovely home) without electricity and running water. I had to walk 5 miles to the bus and back each day to go to school along with my brother and twin sister. I can tell you now that living without electricity and running water was extremely challenging.

And walking five miles to the bus and back each day, travelling over two hours or more simply to get to school was really hard. We left when it was dark and got home when it was dark. Rain, hail or shine. I did my homework by Tilly lamp or candles. My brother and sister and I were lucky enough to watch TV for an hour or so each evening. In order to do this, we had to run a cable from the car battery to the TV in order to make it work. Well look on the bright side, at least we had a car.... and a TV.

I had chores to do since we lived on a farm and most of my days were packed full with all of these experiences. I ran wild as a child as did my brother and twin sister since we lived on 150 acres of land. We had free reign and I absolutely loved this. This also came with its own set of challenges. We had to deal with the constant challenging forces of nature, flash flooding which was incredibly dangerous and severe droughts.

Our livestock would die because of the lack of water and deadly snakes and there were pythons living in our house. We lived on an insufficient diet at times because we had to eat tinned food a lot as we had no efficient cooling system to store perishable items. We cooked on an old fuel stove, bathed with a sponge each night and washed our clothes in the nearby river. Also, we carried our drinking water in plastic bottles from the river to our house so we had fresh water daily. I knew what living a tough life was like. I learnt from a young age to be strong, independent, and resourceful.

Apart from having to deal with these external influences, I had to deal with the intense isolation of living in a remote area. Making new friends, hardly seeing my dad except during the school holidays and adapting to a totally new life. Remember that I was seven years old when this happened. I am sharing this with you because it is not the circumstances that create us, it is how we perceive them and ultimately deal with them. I could have ended up either dead, have chosen to give up, or not move forward and achieve anything of value in my life. I chose to turn these challenges into blessings and go out and create a life truly worth living. It is quite often the challenges and heartaches in life that push us forward to excel. And that is my desire for each and every one of you. That you excel in whatever endeavours you choose for yourself. This I have to say is not easy, but well worth the effort. I know it was for me. Eventually, at the age of fourteen, my twin sister, younger brother and my mum moved to Sydney. To be closer to my dad and get a better education, because excelling at school academically was extremely important to my parents. I loved being closer to my dad too because I missed him terribly. Life then became a little more normal.

In fact looking back, my childhood and teenage years really prepared me for life. My perceived challenges and difficulties certainly had its blessings. And ironically enough I was extremely grateful for my childhood. My childhood was anything but normal, though, at the age of fifteen I simply stopped talking about my life. Mainly because people looked at me so strangely when I talked about myself. I believed they thought I was either lying about my life or that I was just too weird. It really hurt.

As a result of this, I became really great at asking questions and extracting information from everybody else. I never really shared about my life with others. This art of learning to ask questions really served me well later in life, especially in business. Most people don't even take the time to listen to what people are really saying. This was an enormous blessing for me. For anybody that is in business, or any job for that matter, they too know the art of asking questions and listening to what their clients have to say. It is crucial to the outcome of any sale in whatever form that may be.

I guess that is why I now want to share my life with others too, simply because I have remained quiet for so long. I also want to really help others through the lessons of my own experiences. My unusual childhood led me to begin to look for more answers as to why we are the way we are. What defines us as people? And why do we create the lives we live? For years, I have studied philosophies and transcripts written by the great teachers throughout history, read countless self-development books, attended workshops, listened to CDs, watched DVDs, etc. You name it, I did it.

From a young age I was always attracted to self-growth and I embarked on a journey of self-discovery that would eventually culminate to my purpose. Which to me was serving others through business and self-development? I decided to take those teachings and apply them to my life and thus help others do the same.And because of this I have been able to help others through tough challenges in their lives and also assist them in their business and personal endeavours.

I knew from a young age that I had a purpose, it was inherent in my being. A deep inner voice that kept talking to me, but did I listen? No mostly not. I dismissed the intuition I was born with and thus created a lot of challenges for myself along the way. Instead of feeling sorry for myself, well most of the time anyway, I realised that was simply part of my journey. There are blessings in each and every event in life. I now wanted to put that to good use. My life is a gift, as is yours.

Our journeys are different but we all have a wealth of knowledge within us. The best way to access this knowledge from within is to find yourself a mentor and learn skills to assist you along your journey. This is why I spent so much time studying human development and finding mentors along the way. And this helped me enormously. And still does, for my quest for knowledge only increases each day.

As an adult, I sit here reflecting on the days of my youth and I asked myself, how did my childhood experiences help me overcome the challenges I now faced as an adult. How did it define who I am now and who I would eventually become? One thing it certainly did was create a very strong desire in me to not be governed by anybody else. This is within reason of course since we all have to answer and be accountable to a higher authority in some form. This was in all areas of my life but one, in particular, I want to touch on. And that is my vocation. My independence as a child clarified for me very clearly that I did not want to work for somebody else.

I began at the age of twenty to become an entrepreneur. I remember after finishing my HSC having a few odd jobs here and there, but nothing really satisfied me. I got bored quickly even though I was very good at my jobs. One of the jobs I had been working for a large women's clothing retail chain in Sydney. I was there for nine months and rose quickly in the company. I worked my way up to be second in charge of the two largest stores in the country. To me, it was like being in jail. I was not allowed to talk to the staff, I had to stand in one section of the store and not move anywhere else.

I had to wear the clothes whether I liked them or not, which mostly I didn't, and basically smile and be friendly to everyone even when they were rude and rotten to me. Having to bite my tongue and not defend myself almost killed me, as I was a very outspoken individual. I always believed in standing up for myself. There was one day in particular, which was a defining moment in my life. I remember standing on the floor feeling miserable looking over to the door that led outside. I stood there and looked at it, and said to myself (since I wasn't allowed to talk to anyone else) the door is right there and I can't walk out! There were no bars on it, but it was a prison nonetheless. That was it for me. The next day I spoke with my area manager and quit.

She looked at me and said this one sentence, which I have never forgotten. "I knew this was coming, and if you ever need a job, ever, you always have a job here. It's a tough world out there but always know that you can come back any time". I remember thinking to myself... I don't care how tough it is out there, I'm going out and I'm doing it myself. To me, it is far easier than being stuck here working for someone else following ridiculous rules that I hated and feeling empty each and every day doing mundane things that I couldn't stand.

I knew that I would never walk back through those doors again and accept that job offer, and nor did I. After that day I never looked back. Was my entrepreneurial journey easy? Absolutely not, but as I said earlier my childhood had certainly prepared me for the challenges I now faced as an entrepreneur. Anyone who is in business knows exactly what I am talking about? It is challenging at the best of times. I attracted a lot of opportunities in business and tried many new things over the years. Some were successful, and some weren't.

Each one taught me new things about not only business but also about myself. It takes enormous determination and strength, knowledge and skills to run successful businesses. I've now had over twenty years of experience in business and that has been an interesting journey to say the least. What I want you to realise is that no matter what life has thrown at you, it is preparing you for your purpose and future events.

Take a look at your experiences and use them as stepping-stones to face whatever obstacles and challenges you may be having in the present moment. Instead of beating yourself up about your past and your so-called perceived mistakes, learn from them. Gain the strength you need. For at one time you once believed you couldn't overcome the challenges you were facing. But did you? Well, you're here now aren't you? So obviously, you got through. You found a way, as did I.

As I first mentioned, my childhood experiences made me strong, independent and resourceful. Thankfully they did because it helped me through some very dark days in my life. Being an entrepreneur is extremely challenging. Not only did I have to make my business work and make money, it came with a lot of responsibility and accountability to others. I had investors to consider and employees to look after. Also, wages to pay, company expenses, criteria to meet to the ATO and ASIC and other governing bodies. It wasn't just me I had to look after and this created a lot of pressure, especially when some of my businesses failed. I have attracted money, people and business ventures globally. I have failed so many times, been stabbed in the back and kicked out of a business I started. I've lost loved ones, friends, money and ideas countless times throughout my life.

I have cried myself to sleep each night for so many years that I often wondered if there were any tears left to shed. You never really fail if you keep getting up and trying. Most of the wealthiest and most famous people on the planet failed more times than you know. However, society mostly sees their successes. Let me tell you they did fail, many times, as have I and so will you. That is life. So get used to it. Take the so-called failures and learn from them. We learn more from our mistakes rather than our successes. If you do this you will eventually succeed in whatever you desire. My tough childhood taught me to never give up and keep trying no matter what.

And for this, I was grateful, for if I hadn't taken those lessons and learnt from them I may have given up long ago. Dark days were certainly around me throughout my life and as I stated earlier I experienced some very turbulent times. My belief in myself plummeted because of some of my failed businesses and my self-worth as a person hit an all-time low. What is self-worth? Self-worth is the value we place on ourselves. Why was my self-worth so low?

Simply because I kept looking at all the failures I had experienced instead of also honouring my successes, and this was a very unbalanced perception of who I was. And I was selling myself short. I wasn't honouring the good things about myself in life and in myself personally. I actually spiralled down further and created a vicious cycle for myself. I attracted more negative experiences into my life because I was focusing on only one side of who I was. I will go into detail a little later about the energy we give out and why we attract the things we do. For we all do this at some point in our lives and there are ways to help you through this.

Why do we have such low self-worth? It is my belief that we are indoctrinated from such a young age of who we are supposed to be. Society injects values onto us and expects us to live and be a certain way. It is no wonder why we get confused and lack self-belief. We listen to the opinions of others and live according to what they think we should be. Instead of honouring who we are, we keep looking at our failures. And who we are is powerful. There is only one you. Why be someone else? You are perfect the way you are. We all just want to be loved and appreciated for that. I have noticed that we seem to spend so much of our time trying to be something or someone else. In the end, we don't even know who we really are. It seems to be ingrained in us from such a young age as to who we should be. Subtly over the years we become a living facade of what others believe us to be, hiding deep within us our own unique beauty. I did the same. Hence my lack of self-worth.

We seem to be afraid of who we are and we let the outer negativity affect our true identity. That is one of the biggest reasons as to why some of my business failed. I was listening to outside opinions of what I could and couldn't do and I lost faith in who I was as a person and also as an entrepreneur.

Lack of self-worth often stems from being altruistic. Giving to others, never receiving for once simply because we don't believe we deserve a good life. From what I have noticed, religion and society teach us to give rather than receive. We grow up believing that we are worthy and humble and 'good' for doing this. That's what I grew up believing. What a fallacy. There is no harm in giving. I believe very strongly in that but what I lacked was having the ability to receive. That is just as important. It is important to be both altruistic and narcissistic.

Give and receive in fair exchange. This is exactly what a good business consists of too. A fair exchange of goods and/or services for money. This was a lesson I seriously needed to learn, or should I say apply, for I already knew this. There is no honour in poverty and giving everything away. Nor is it fair to take all the time either. It should be an equal balance of both. For the more you have the more you can give. That is why I went into business for myself. To not only help myself create wealth but also help others do the same. Really think about this. I want you to see the value in what I am saying here for it is one of the most important things you can do for yourself and others.

This principle relates very strongly to money too. Most people are consumers. Low self-worth births consumerism. Consumerism results from a strong need to fill a void or emptiness within. Most of us look for a quick fix, we shop to make ourselves feel better. Or we spend it on mind numbing substances to alleviate the pain we carry in our lives.

This may temporarily alleviate the feeling of emptiness but actually, what it does is exacerbate the feelings of low self-worth and creates a larger void. Hence creating a vicious cycle that never ends and becomes bigger and bigger. We have to keep spending to make us feel better. Most of the time it gets us into debt because of it.

Can you relate to what I am saying here? In my case, I didn't spend money on myself. I spent it with other people. Or rather, I gave it away and lost lots of money through some of my business endeavours. In fact, I almost went bankrupt at one stage. All I did was dismiss and diminish my own wealth and power and ended up in extremely low positions at times.

The blessing here was that I had the tools and strategies to be able to turn this around due to my personal development over the years. This is why I am sharing this with you now. Those lessons I learnt in life I really began to apply so I am sharing some of them with you now.

As I began to realise that my energy and belief in myself was powerful, things around me started to change. I kept persevering in business and started honouring the power I had within and opened myself up to the opportunities that were around me. I changed my energy and as a result, I changed my circumstances. For our outer world is merely a manifestation of our inner world or thoughts.

I spent many hours writing lists of all my achievements over my lifetime. This helped me see that I had both sides, of both failures and successes, because as I stated I was focusing so much on my failures. If you are feeling down about your life then I strongly suggest you make notes of all the wonderful things you have experienced/achieved in life. This helped my energy change and I began to resonate on a different level.

And it will for you too provided you do the work suggested here. For thinking something is not enough, you have to act on it. And by writing things down you are now making it more tangible. If you leave it all in your head it simply remains a fantasy. That is why writing down your goals and vision is extremely important. In addition to this you need to back it up with action, otherwise things never self-actualise. And that is the mistake a lot of people make.

Everything around us is a reflection of ourselves. What we attract into our lives is a manifestation of what we feel about ourselves. This is very powerful when we finally realise this. And it strongly relates to self-worth. We create our own destiny. It's not around us, it is us. Society teaches us that we are victims. Victims of circumstance, and that we have no power. I used to believe this until I started studying the laws of the universe that apply to everything around us. They exist whether we honour them or not, so I decided to honour them and use them to my advantage. Start to realise that YOU create your life, no one else, YOU. This however, is not as easy to apply, as you would expect. It's well worth the focus and energy and work. You might as well use it for your own personal power and gain from doing so. The more responsibility you take for your own life the more power you have. When you have the power you are a master of your life. If you blame everything on your outer experiences you take away your power and remain a victim. Being tossed around by life's challenging forces.

It's your choice which path you chose to take. I would rather accept responsibility for my life and become a master of my life, not a victim of it. And I hope you do the same. Take complete responsibility for everything that happens to you. Don't blame others or make excuses. Take some time out to see where you have created your circumstances. Yes, other people need to be accountable for their actions but then so do you. You cannot change other people, it is simply a waste of time (how many of us have tried to do that with no degree of success?) but you can change yourself. And once you realise this fully, things around you start to change.

We create everything in our lives, simply by honouring that in itself, it allows us to open up to the limitless power we have within. If we can create hell on earth, then we can certainly create heaven. However, don't be fooled. For both really exist. Both heaven and hell. And there is no escaping this, it is designed that way to make us grow. Our job here is to honour this, accept it and see it as part of our journey. Decide where you wish to 'play' in this game called life, and not be a victim of circumstance, but rather be a creator of your life.

Everything in the universe is energy. Everything you want is energy. All energy has a vibration and emits a frequency. Every thought has a frequency and our thoughts are extremely powerful. These thought frequencies can be measured scientifically. Your innermost dominant thought, something that you continuously think about will eventually become your outer tangible reality.

Provided you back it up with action. What you think about continually you actually attract into your life. Think about what you want as the end result. Think of it in such a way as though you have already achieved this result, whatever that may be. Tap into that feeling as though it is here and now. Not as if you are going to get it or achieve it, but as though you already have it or have achieved it. In fact, look at it as though it's already done. There is no such thing as luck or coincidence. Everything we attract into our lives is a result of what we think about and feel about. Your outer world is merely a manifestation of how you feel about yourself. What you see in others exists in you. Your world is a reflection of yourself. Start with your thoughts, back it up with action and keep persevering and you will eventually attract the things you want in your life into your outer tangible reality.

Stop for a moment and have a good look at what you think about most. What are your thoughts telling you about yourself? How is your life manifesting these thoughts? Are you getting what you want, or are you getting what you don't want? These questions are very profound when you start to really look at them. As Dr John Demartini states, "the quality of your life is based on the quality of your questions" so I suggest you start asking better quality questions. It really does make a difference.

I would like to now go into a little more detail as to why my tough childhood years helped me to later become an entrepreneur. How asking better quality questions along the way helped me learn how to turn my perceived failures into blessings. You may also remember that I mentioned that our life is helping us fulfil our purpose and all the events along the way are actually assisting us.

Well here is another example as to how my earlier years helped define me as an adult. My childhood inner belief systems of feeling different and ugly created a void in me. Actually, this later turned into a blessing because I ended up creating my own fashion business selling women's clothes online. My void turned into a value.

And my uniqueness in fashion and how I wore my clothes helped me stand out and attract opportunities in this area. Women always asked me where I got my clothes. I started wearing the clothes I had for sale and, as a result, sold many pieces simply by just wearing them out and about. My void as a child created an opportunity to make money later as an adult.

What is a void you may ask? A void is an emptiness within. Something that needs to be filled. And we all have them. In fact, we need them. For our voids create values. A value is something that is extremely important to us and we spend all our time trying to fill these voids.

How do we know our values? The best way to determine your values is to look around you. Grab a piece of paper and write these 3 questions down, just to make it simple. Write at least 3-5 examples to each question. By doing this, you begin to really 'see' what is important to you because most of the time we lie to ourselves about what really is important to us. If you can do more, great. The more you do, the more benefits you gain from this exercise. This exercise is really well worth doing, so please take the time to do this. Finding out what our values are is one of the most important things you can do with your life. For everything in your life stems from your values. And I mean everything!

1. What fills your space? This simply means what do you have around you in your home/office? Is it books, clothing, beautiful furniture, photos, sports equipment, kids toys etc.

2. What do you spend your time doing?

3. Where do you spend your money/ what do you buy?

Whatever the answer is to these 3 questions is what you find most important. It is there staring us in the face always. My void turned into a value that made me money through business. Perhaps your voids can be also turned into moneymaking opportunities like mine did. My uniqueness and ugliness as a child pushed me to better myself in the way I looked. Thankfully I turned it into an opportunity to make money. I encourage you to take a look at this in yourself, where are your voids? For you could be sitting on a potential gold mine if you can turn it into a business opportunity like I did.

Previously I mentioned we all have the same amount of hours in the day and it is how you use those hours that determine how fulfilling and successful your life is. Prioritising your day is extremely important. If you don't prioritise your day it will be filled with time wasting circumstances that zap your energy and drain your resources. A great way to help you prioritise your day for maximum results is to write down each night the 5 top priority things you need to do each day. Every day push yourself to actually do these top priority things. If you don't do all 5, roll the ones left undone into the next day.

Make sure these are completed. After a while, you will begin to see that you actually get things done. Also, see how important they are to you, and also see what you don't get done. If you find that you can't get all of these tasks done, and they are still important for you to do them I suggest you delegate them to others and focus on the remaining tasks that are most important and inspiring for you to do. This really helps you get on with your day and helps maximise your time for optimum results. By prioritising your time effectively, you also start to feel better about yourself and your self-worth goes up. Setting goals and then actually achieving them is important to your self-worth and ultimately creates a more fulfilling life. This may seem really obvious, but you would be surprised how many people don't actually do this. Sadly, as a result, people really beat themselves up because of it. That is why finding out what your voids and values are is extremely important. Most of the time we kid ourselves into thinking we are something we are not and end up feeling like failures. This is because we have false expectations of who we are. Prioritise your day and really focus on what you love and need to do. Focus is essential to success. If we spread out time and energy everywhere we really don't get much done. But with precision and focus, we tend to achieve more. And make this something that you love to do. Life is meant to be lived to the fullest. We all deserve to have amazing lives, filled with opportunities and experiences.

Don't limit who you are and what you can achieve. Shoot for the stars and believe in yourself. Start believing you deserve an amazing life because you do! At the beginning of this chapter, I asked you one question. Keep this question in mind always. Ask yourself this question everyday and you will start to become aware of how you are living your life.

Please don't get to the end of your life and look back and think...If only I did this, and look back with regret. Look back and say to yourself. "I lived an amazing life!" Live a life of limitless potential. It's your choice, so my advice is just to go do it. I'm going to leave you now with one of the best quotes I have ever heard. Each time I read it, it brings me to tears. I am leaving you with the hope that it touches your life in the way it does mine.

It is from Nelson Mandela's inaugural speech.

"Our deepest fear is not that we are inadequate. Our deepest fear is that we are powerful beyond measure. It is our light, not our darkness, which frightens us most. We ask ourselves, who am I to be brilliant, gorgeous, talented, and famous? Actually, who are you not to be? You are a child of God. Your playing small does not serve the world".

There is nothing enlightened about shrinking so that people won't feel insecure around you. We were born to make manifest the glory of God that is within us. It's not just in some of us, it's in all of us. When we let our own light shine, we unconsciously give other people permission to do the same. As we are liberated from our own fear, our presence automatically liberates others. "

My hope is that by letting my own light shine, it allows you to do the same.

Chapter 8

My Inspiring Story

By John Ifergan

2001, that's the year I got divorced from my wife. I went through a terrible time where I analysed again and again what went wrong. I analysed what I said, what she said, what I should have done what I shouldn't have done. The more I thought the more confused I got and the more depressed I became. When we were together I didn't know how to control my emotions.

I used to answer without calming the situation down, I overreacted to her outbursts, instead of leading and having a clear path, I used to blame her for everything. I never listened to her or cared what she thought or how she felt. Before the divorce, before the relationship really took a turn for the worse, my Ex had a miscarriage and that led to further deterioration in our marriage with each of us blaming each other. As you can imagine the situation got worse and worse until it was unbearable and eventually we had to part ways.

After the divorce, I was in a serious case of denial with where my life was heading. No matter what people told me I never listened, I thought I knew how to handle it when I didn't and I made things worse. I was arrogant and not willing to compromise and help myself. I didn't realise it at the time but I was lost, I went out excessively to forget my problems and disappointments. I drank a lot and smoked. I knew I was depressed but I would never admit it. I always said to myself it's not that bad, I was always in denial. I know now that in order to fix a problem you first have to admit you have one.

This went on till the 31st of July 2009 when things changed drastically. I remember that evening so vividly that it feels like it was only yesterday. At the time, I didn't know it but it turned out to be the greatest gift. That night we were out, me and a few friends. I ran into an old friend I had not seen for many years and he said he wanted to tell me something. He took me aside and said John, no offence mate but you are becoming round.

I said what do you mean? He said don't be offended but you have put on a lot of weight. I said really, he said yes! I am not being nasty he said, I am just telling you the truth. I said thank you and we parted ways. I could not stop thinking about what he had said to me. It completely consumed me and took over all my thoughts. I couldn't think of anything else but that. Was I really round? Had I really let myself go that much? I can tell you that when an old friend tells you with all sincerity that your round, you need to consider making drastic changes to your life.

Once I got home and weighed myself I was nearly 106kg and I'm 5'9 in height, you've got the picture. I looked myself in the mirror and saw my big stomach, and burst into tears realising I was overweight, only now I could see it. I promised myself then and there that I would do whatever it took to lose the extra weight that I had stacked on. It was a defining moment that changed the course of my life forever.

I actually admitted it to myself that I have a real issue and I needed to take decisive action to avoid becoming obese. At the time, I also realised that my divorce was my fault as I did not take responsibility and I used to live in the blame game. As long as you do that you will never be able to rectify the issue. I realised I was an angry person, I hated so many people and for no real reason. At that point, I broke down again and I realised all the harm I was doing, I was actually hurting myself, and it was self-inflicted. The next day I bought two books. "How to stop worrying and start living". By Dale Carnegie and "The power of the subconscious mind". By Joseph Murphy. A friend recommended these books, but I never looked into it as I thought I knew it all.

Little did I know that these books would completely change my perspective on life? After buying the books - I rang a friend of mine that is a personal trainer. I told him my height and weight and I asked him how much do I have to loose in order to be fit and healthy? He said 20kg, at that point I told him the promise I made to myself that I will do whatever it takes, no matter how long it takes, I'm going to get fit. He said don't talk John. Just start running for 1-month 1km a day five days a week. 2nd month - 2km's a day, five days a week. And the 3rd month 3km's a day, five days a week. He also said don't live in the world of instant gratification that most people live in expecting immediate results but to be realistic and things will happen for you, I promise.

Don't drink and smoke for 3 months he went on to say, if you keep that up I will help you. Until then do not contact me as most people say they will do this or that and never do.

Every night I slept and I visualised myself running more and more, the more I thought about this the more I got emotional and the more I ignited my will power. I could feel a new sense of power and strength and desire come into me as if I was a new person. I never felt like that ever before, it felt amazing. I really loved it, as it gave me more and more confidence overtime.

I did what my friend told me to do to the letter. I ran for a month, 1km 5 days a week. It was hard but I kept saying to myself, keep going and I repeated my own mantra, again and again, I am strong, I am capable, and I am a winner. Next month I ran 2km's a day and again every time I repeated to myself, again and again, I am strong, I am capable, I am a winner! And the 3rd month I ran 3 km a day and again every time I repeated to myself, again and again, I am strong, I am capable, I am a winner! After 3 months I rang him, and he said to come in now and he wanted to see me in sports clothes.

I went immediately to his gym. He looked at my legs and my body and said to me bluntly you are the only one in the last five years that I said what to do without any supervision and did exactly what I said to do. I am so proud of you John. At this point, I burst into tears, but they were tears of joy, he said to me you have what it takes to let me write you a simple program. And follow it without fail, no excuses like it's too hot or cold. I don't want to hear any excuses because it's for you okay. Are we clear?

I said yes we are clear! Now follow it and in one year you will be on top of the world. Here is his simple program. Run 4 times a week between 4-6 Km each time. No bread - No cakes - No sweets - No Soft drinks - No Beer - No smoking -No fried foods - No KFC or McDonalds. Drink water and more water. They were all the things that I use to get stuck into on a regular basis. It didn't matter I was feeling better than I ever had and I was sticking to my guns no matter what, I was going to do whatever it took to get back into shape and to regain control of my life. That was it, no excuses, I was prepared to take my fitness to another level. I increased my running gradually and I kept repeating my affirmations that I learnt.

I am Strong.

I am Powerful.

I am a Winner.

At the beginning that was strange but after a few months, I loved saying it. Many times it brought me to tears because I really felt Really Strong really Powerful and I knew I was a Winner and within one year I was running more than 10 km's a day. I went to running competitions for a running club, "Sydney Striders", and the people there were very helpful. I asked one guy at Sydney Striders what inspires him and who motivates him? And he said, Terry Fox! I said who is he?

I had no idea. Terry who? Look him up he said, and I promise you will always be inspired even when you are exhausted and you think you can't do it. I looked him up on YouTube and saw many videos of Terry Fox. He was an amputee that had cancer in his leg and had to have the leg removed. He ran a marathon on one leg from the east coast of Canada to the west coast. He raised money for the Canadian Cancer society. The more he ran the more media attention he received.

This is a man that ran in heat and over winter in freezing temperatures of -20 Degrees. I was watching his videos online. I could feel his pain and struggles although mine were less. I felt saddened for him but at the same time inspired by his bravery courage and his inspiration. Again and again, I watched his videos online and nothing was going to stop me from continuing my goal of getting super fit and feeling alive again.

One day Terry Fox couldn't run, he was taken to the hospital, a doctor diagnosed him and found cancer had spread to his other leg. That day a TV station in Canada decided to make a telephone hotline to raise money on behalf of Terry Fox and the cancer society. The whole show they had people bring in and donate money to the Cancer Society. The telephone went wild! That was in 1980 and they raised one million dollars, can you believe it! In those days, it was a massive deal. Since then every time I think or feel I am tired or not in the mood I remember Terry Fox, he is now my anchor for motivation.

At the time I used to run from Rose Bay to Double bay (the eastern Suburbs of Sydney). Every time I reach the police station at Point Piper on the way back, I used to feel exhausted. I remember I used to repeat to myself again and again. How much do you want it? I want it! How much do you want it? I want it! Again and again, I would repeat those words until I had tears in my eyes. This simple mantra inspired me to keep going and going and going. I dreamt of running at night and I visualised how great I looked and felt. I kept it up for two and a half years, I ran usually 11KM in around 57minutes. One day I ran and I felt like a gazelle, half way through my run I clocked in at 27 minutes 05 seconds.

I knew I was around 2 min ahead of my personal best, I kept pushing and around the 8km mark I was around 2 minutes 40 seconds faster than my personal best. I said to myself I might die but I am going to break my record and I finished with a personal best of 54 minutes 45 seconds. I looked at my mobile three times and I burst into Euphoria of tears and joy. It took me 20 min to recover as I was overcome by all my emotions of the past and present plus the exhaustion of the run. After I calmed down I rang my friend the personal trainer, I told him what had happened to me. He said "Today you won!!!" Did I, really? What do you mean? He said you won against yourself!! Very few can do that.

I will never forget "That Day" and those words until the day I die. You are the elite of elite, that can master your willpower and strength, he continued to tell me. It was amazing, I remember that day, the 21st of February 2012, I will never forget it. When I die I will remember the 21st of February 2012, it was the day I took control of myself, the most amazing thing that I remember until now and I remember it every time before I run. I thank the almighty for giving me the strength, will power and desire to do it. I keep running now no matter how hot or cold the weather or the time.

At the same time, I joined salsa classes and learnt how to dance salsa, it was so much fun. I met another runner there by the name of Robert. We went for many runs together, usually 10-12 Km's. He was better than me, faster and younger. He inspired me, he talked to me and motivated me to keep going. I was telling Robert how much I ran, his enthusiasm and inspirations pushed me further and further.

I became the man I dreamt of being of all my life. A man of belief and confidence, I had never experienced those traits at this level before. The confidence and the belief that I received were amazing. I could feel it in the way I walked talked and breathed, not to mention so many people that knew me said I looked amazing! By then many people were asking me what I did and how? I forwarded them the simple program my friend gave me. Although as my friend said, most people talk and don't do anything.

You have to have belief, patience and perseverance. If you are missing one of these components you will never succeed no matter what you do. After doing everything I did, I am in the belief that this is correct because if I didn't believe in myself and my ability to it, I wouldn't have the patience or the perseverance. I would not be here writing about my story either. As the saying goes, if it doesn't challenge you it doesn't change you. Change is one of the only constants that we experience in this life. Is the question, are your challenges changing you for the better? That is a question I recommend you ponder and reflect on because the answers could well set you on your way to changing your life.

After pursuing my new passion for running, I came across an article on the net about a Danish woman who was coming to Sydney to run a marathon. In fact, she was doing 7 marathons in 7 days in 7 continents. Wow, what a feat I thought. I knew I needed to run that marathon with this Danish woman. I contacted her and she was telling me she wants to be the first person doing this and she needs people to join her so she has proof of completing the marathon. We organized the exact location of the run that started at Brighton Le Sands and went all the way to Cronulla.

We did a few big laps of the main street to complete one way 21.1km and back to Brighton Le Sands, all up 42.2km's, a marathon! The date was set and we picked her up at the airport and met the other Runners at Brighton Le Sands. So I decided to run with her and a bunch of other runners that joined us. I couldn't run all of it, I ran half a marathon and it was an amazing feeling. Before the run, she was interviewed on Fox Sports and they showed all of us on fox sports as well. It was amazing to run with her and fellow runners. WHY??? I hear you ask. Because I could feel the joy of it, the sense of excitement and achievement was exhilarating.

All the while I had been studying the book "How to stop worrying and start living" and I realised that my mind was cluttered. I was worried about things that never would happen and it used to make me so anxious. The book taught me how to prioritize my worries, what is real what is not. How to give importance to some issues and not to others so I know what is important and what is not. By reading so many books, I also realised that a lot of TV programs are not good for our own self-imagine.

The media and the news are so negative and it has a profound bad effect on our minds and that can cause fear and depression. I stopped reading the papers and stopped watching the news on TV as it mainly focuses on negatives and it wasn't adding value to my life. When I want to know what's going on, I read on the net a little bit. I know that too much is detrimental to me and I stop as soon as I feel like I'm being overwhelmed. I have a friend that works in the media and he told me not once but twice that they do not publish good news on purpose. Simply because bad news creates more drama, more drama means an increase in ratings and, of course, that means an increase in revenue for the networks.

I am sure you get the picture. I really believe that a lot of people are depressed today and don't want to admit it. I know this for a fact as I live next to The Gap at Watsons Bay. At least five times a week people try to commit suicide, first the police come then the ambulance. Then it's the fire brigade to retrieve the body, it's so sad but it's a fact. I have a friend who is a doctor and he told me how many patients are depressed and ask for all sorts of medication.

Thinking if they take this or that all will be fine when it won't. It goes back to people living in a world of instant gratification and this is partly caused by the media. All the ads where people think if they do this or that or buy this or that all will be fantastic in seconds. When in truth we really have to work in order to achieve anything meaningful. You can't be a great athlete if you don't plan to train. You can't be a great engineer or architect or anything without putting in the time and the effort and the practice.

After I studied that book "How to stop worrying and start living" I read and studied the power of the subconscious mind by Joseph Murphy. This book gave me an insight into how my mind works and how I sabotaged myself without even knowing it. This book gave me vision and insights how to change my thought patterns and how to focus on the good things in my life rather than the bad. It showed me how to have gratitude and compassion for others. Over time this made me happier and happier to where I focused on what worked rather than on what didn't. What we focus on expands is a universal principle that I utilised for my own happiness.

I highly recommend these books to my clients as so many people struggle with these issues. At the same time, I meditate four times a week to be calm and to think of nothing, yes nothing. It is hard at the beginning but over time, you can succeed if you put your mind to it. It makes you calm under pressure and you are able to handle things that others can't. You are able to see things that others don't as they are in a heightened state of emotions. Therefore, over time, you become a leader as screaming or yielding to uncontrolled emotions solves nothing in life. After battling with people and with myself, I was sick and tired of making myself a victim. I realised the biggest battle in life is 'What goes on in our own head'. What I learnt the hard way is if you really, really want something you can't wait for people. Most people will let you down, that's why I love running.

I can do it anywhere anytime and I don't have to wait for anyone. At this point my transformation was complete. Thank you God for helping me. As I changed my life I made it my mission and life goal to help others achieve even more than I did. It took me so long to do it and if I had guidance from day one it wouldn't have taken me 5-6 years, it may have only taken me 18-24 months. I know what I went through and I can make it easier faster and more enjoyable for you. You won't procrastinate or give up like more than 95% of people that say they will do this or that with most giving up within 4-8 weeks. It's my job to help you motivate you and inspire you to be the best you can be.

I know that I have to keep it up so I can stay fit mentally, physically and emotionally. This way I can inspire others to take action and achieve more, become more and become the person they really want to be.

Today I work with people and teach them it's not enough to want something. You have to combine faith, patience and perseverance. The more emotions you put into your dreams and desires and the more will power the better chance you have to get what you want. Your story my friend has not been written yet, get out there and do something different. If not, one day you will wish that you had. Even if you think you may fail it's better to try, than give up. Most people don't even start and the great thing is the more you do it the more momentum you will get. Over time you will be more inspired to continue living healthy habits. You will be surprised how much you can do once you get started. Don't wait for the perfect time place or people, it will never happen. Look at yourself in the mirror and say I will do whatever it takes and I don't care how long it takes because I am a winner!

I am strong, I am capable, and I am a winner!

Chapter 9

Grow after every climb

By Vanessa Tran

"When we least expect it, life sets us a challenge to test our courage and willingness to change; at such a moment, there is no point in pretending that nothing has happened or in saying that we are not yet ready. The challenge will not wait. Life does not look back. A week is more than enough time for us to decide whether or not to accept our destiny."

~ Paulo Coelho

Looking back at the challenges I faced, I felt as though I was travelling through a dark tunnel of obstacles in an underground railway, where I only got to rest and see where I was, at each illuminated station. Many times when I was faced with a challenging circumstance, I felt like the victim. I felt sorry for myself and kept saying "Why me?", "Why I am so unlucky?", "It's not fair!" I believed every negative remark that my mind threw at me and ended up crying over it. There were times I was so depressed that I even considered taking my own life. Thank goodness, I did not have the courage to go through with it.

After reading and attending personal development courses, I started to see each problem as a challenge, a chance to adapt to a new situation, a chance for me to solve the problem and learn from it, a chance for me to stretch out of my comfort zone and grow further in experience and mentality.

I've learnt with every challenge we face, we have two choices.

1. To face it anyway and find a solution to overcome it or adapt to it. At the same time, we become more experienced and hence develop to be greater person or;

2. To feel sorry for ourselves, dwell on it, get disgruntled about life, feel depressed, give up and accept defeat.

There are a series of challenges that have made me a better person today and made me see life in a different perspective.

My first biggest personal challenge was at the age of seven. I found myself with my grandmother, youngest aunt, my mum and my 6 year old brother (3 women and 2 young children), sneaking out quietly in the night, leaving my grandfather behind all alone in our four-storey house. My grandfather elected to stay back just in case we failed in our mission.

We were at the beginning of our escape from the after math of war, under a new communist government. My grandmother, a successful Chinese business woman, planned our escape by sea after she heard repeated news on the radio, announcing of a new anti-Chinese policy. My family had enough of the harassment to ethnic Chinese by the communist government.

My grandmother heard news about other people who fled Vietnam, ended up in a transit country, Malaysia, before they found refuge in Canada, United States or Australia. She saved enough ounces of gold to pay for our tickets on a 21.5m wooden boat for our departure as refugees. I was too young to realise that it was a big challenge for my family, to make their biggest sacrifice to leave their wealthy lives, their love ones and belongings behind, in exchange for an unknown journey ahead, to hopefully settle into a Western country. Fleeing Vietnam to settle into another new home country was secondary for my grandmother. She had escaped before from a war in China, to reunite with my grandfather and start her new life in Vietnam. So she saw it was a better risk to take, to leave Vietnam with the hope to find freedom, safety and security in a peaceful western country.

The journey on the sea with 351 wealthy refugees squeezed side by side, from the front to the back of a wooden boat, was a big test for my family and me. We faced many obstacles on our quest to find a new homeland on the sea. Our only hope for survival was the dream of a better life in a Western country. Left with only my youngest Aunty, I was somehow separated from my grandmother, mother and younger brother after we boarded the boat.

We battled seasickness, hunger and dehydration. We were attacked and terrorised by two different bands of pirates. They robbed every passenger and my family's valuables mainly jewellery, gold and diamonds. I witnessed a pirate forcing a jade bangle off an elderly woman's wrist. He thought her scream of pain was a scream of resistant, so he clobbered her head with a torch. I was petrified as I watched what unfolded in front of my eyes. Conscious that I had kept my Auntie's ring secured in my mouth away from the pirate, I dare not opened my mouth nor swallow. A day later, the elderly woman was dead. The captain refused to throw her body overboard with the thought her spirit will guide us to our new homeland. So we had to withstand the stench of her decaying body until we found land.

After the pirate attacks, the only valuables left from my family were those sewn obscurely in the hem of some clothes and towels. My grandmother who heard stories of pirate attacks on refugee boats, cleverly prepared for our journey by hiding the valuables in the hem of such items.

We were desperately starving and dehydrated. After 3 days and 3 nights on the sea, the captain navigated our boat to find land settling on a Malaysian Military island.

Our short life on the Malaysian military island was another challenging experience for us, this time on land. We lived in tents on the beach. During our short stay there, my brother was so sick that every time he coughed, he coughed out blood. I thought he was going to die. I thought I was going to lose my only sibling. There was no medical facility around.

Although we stayed on the camp for a few days, the condition of the camp was horrid. I remember feeling repulsed every time I used the open toilet on the beach. I would see maggots in hundreds or thousands crawling around. It was an excessive transition for my family from a luxury life in a four-storey house in Vietnam to a survival camp.

We were transferred to a refugee camp on an island known as Bidong Island. Life in a refugee camp was tough. We lived under a makeshift shed made of salvaged timbers from wrecked boats, plastic sheets, tin cans, and corrugated iron sheets. We shared our open shed with many other refugee families. There was no privacy. Our space consisted of a big bed made of a thin plank of wood. Our latrine was a small bucket with a can next to a squatting toilet surrounded by planks of rusted corrugated iron. We also washed ourselves in the latrine. We were fed on mostly vegetarian can food especially peas. It astonished me on how many different cuisines my family could make from can of peas. As clean water was rationed, we had to source alternative water from a well dug into the ground. The water was filthy every time there was a tropical rainstorm.

Every now and then a new refugee boat would come ashore and share about about their horrible confrontation with pirates. Some unfortunate women were either kidnapped or rapped by the pirates. There were stories about other unfortunate people were drowned or worse barbarically killed at sea by the pirates.

After sometime, I was able to adapt to the life in the camp. Though conditions were tough, I have rarely witnessed my family complaining, especially my grandmother. Her attitude was, complaining was not going to change the situation we were in. So just accept the circumstance, adapt to it, and create opportunities to make the best of out of it.

There were times when there were joys amongst the hardship and survival conditions. I remembered my first fascination when I first discovered a new fruit, a red apple and awoken with wonderment by the taste of it. I recalled our outings by the beautiful beach where we flew the kites we made, bathed or played in the clear crystal emerald sea with caution not to step on sea urchins. I often followed my grandmother and Mum to the hilltop near the makeshift temple to do Tai Chi in the early mornings.

Though as a child I did not acknowledge it at the time, for my family, my grandmother was our courageous leader, breadwinner and guardian angel. She was an amazing woman. With a little bit of gold jewellery and a lack of spoken language on the island, my grandmother was able to start a business making and selling savoury white radish cake (a business that she prosper from in Vietnam) in the island's open market.

My grandmother was a fearless woman. What she set out to achieve, she always did. She was a great model for our family. When she passed away at a very old age of 92 year old, it took me a while to grieve over her. At the same time, I knew deep down inside, she had left a legacy of a fearless adventurous life in our family for us to follow.

The process to call Australia our next homeland was a long process. We had to join the long queues to go through a number of procedures. This included applying for migration to certain countries, to being interviewed by immigration officials from that country for resettlement.

I adapted to refugee life on the island after living there for a year. Somehow within me, I wanted to desperately leave the camp to our new homeland. Every time there were announcements from the speaker, I would wish hard that they called my family's name next, to leave the camp. One fine day, while I was sitting on an old rotted wooden bench just outside our shed, a bird pooped on my head. Straight after that, I heard our names called out to leave the refugee camp. I was ecstatic. I ran to find the rest of my family regarding the announcement. Years later, I heard it was universally known that getting pooped on by a bird is "good luck". I was not certain whether it was really "good luck" or just coincidence, whatever the case, I was glad the bird pooped on my head that day.

We were transferred to another refugee camp in Kula Lumpur Malaysia. The refugee camp was purely for people who were migrating to Australia. We were kept confined behind prison walls, away from the outside world. We lived under opened space units, each shared with a few families, sleeping on the floor. We shared common toilets and showers. We were fed better with unfamiliar food such as cow milk and bread. We had to be fed with nutritious food to bring our health to a required level.

Our ticket out was when my grandmother's health check received the tick of approval. It took my family approximately six months before we could leave the camp. I remembered the excitement I felt, when we were on the bus out of the high prison doors of the refugee camp. My excitement accelerated when the bus drove along the streets of Kula Lumpur towards the airport. I finally saw civilisation for the first time since we fled from Vietnam. I was astounded by my first sighting of an aeroplane that was going to take us, in comfort, to our new homeland we dreamt about, Australia.

Looking back today, our escape from Vietnam, that led us to our challenges on the sea and living conditions in two very different refugee camps, was a blessing in disguise. Though I was quite numb at times and I was just a kid who followed my family around, the whole journey has ingrained deeply in my heart. It motivated me to build a better and prosperous life for my family and me. It has made me appreciate the basic things in life and to be grateful every day for what I have. It has made me appreciate every day the following specifically:

1. Our life in Australia – We see it as a heaven on earth.

2. The opportunities and help we received.

3. The Australian government who helped the refugees to transition into life in Australia. Looking after the local residents with so much welfare benefits especially our ex-prime minister, Malcolm Frazer.

4. Freedom, democracy and capitalism.

5. The abundance variety of food that we have, so I hardly waste any food.

6. The fresh air and beautiful nature.

7. Charity groups (especially Salvation Army) that helped us when my Mum could not afford to buy clothes and toys for us.

The tough journey to Australia was a huge transition from a wealthy life. In Vietnam, our family relied on my grandmother's business and wealth to live a very comfortable life. The escape had fully taught us about our independence from my grandmother, especially for my mother.

The challenges have taught me about responsibilities. While I studied hard at school to learn English, I also helped my Mum with house chores and sewn garments into the early hours of the morning. The hardship we faced gave me the strength to persevere and not give up on our dream of a wealthy life.

Being a refugee has tested our ability to start afresh with very little and find joy in a harsh environment. It has taught us about preparing for the challenges that we may face ahead. According to my Mum, if we were to leave Vietnam and go straight into Australian life, we would not have settled easily into Australia as we all lived a wealthy life under my grandmother's wings.

My life was engulfed with more challenges as soon as we landed in Australia. I discovered there were other people of different sizes, hair and eye colours that I have not seen in Vietnam, especially bright blond hair, blue or green eyes and tall nose.

We lived in a government funded hostel that housed refugees migrated to Melbourne, which helped us, transition into the Australian culture and life. It was ironic for me to understand that in this world there was a government that gave to its people compare to Vietnam, where the communist government took from its people. This experience had always made me feel grateful and blessed that we have a democratic government, no matter which party is in control. They provide people with so many welfare benefits, more than many other parts of the world that I know about.

While transitioning ourselves in Australia, we were finally able to check how my grandfather was doing alone in Vietnam. That's when we discovered a young man, who was our family friend, murdered him. He knew my grandfather was living alone. He planned a robbery during dawn to steel from my grandfather. When my grandfather tried to stop him, he ended up killing my grandfather. The sad news was, as there was no direct family present in Vietnam to place charges on the young man, he was freed. The news disgusted us knowing we could not do anything about it for my grandfather.

After leaving the safe haven of the hostel, my family had to make a life of our own independently from scratch. We lived in a small two bedroom flat near the hostel. After my Aunt got married, my grandmother decided to move in with her. They moved to another suburb that I could only travel to by public transport to visit.

My Mum was left alone to care for my brother and me. She had to work two jobs, working as a factory labourer on weekdays and at a farm on the weekend to pay the rent and make ends meet. My brother and I quickly learnt to take care of each other and help my mother when she brought work home. I stayed awake up to 5.30am to help Mum finish her work by a given deadline. We made our own lunch, went to school ourselves, and fed ourselves after school. We helped our Mum with house chores; however, I did most of the chores.

I had to confront racism every now and then while walking along the streets. I had to confront racism and bullying both in and outside of school. I could not discuss this with my Mum, as she was always busy working. It made me very depressed from Primary to Secondary School with the thought that I didn't belong in Australia, the country that was meant to be my peaceful new home when we escaped Vietnam. Over time, friendships have helped me to forget the racism and bullying. As time passed, I became stronger mentally to tolerate the calling of racist remarks. I just focused on continuing where I needed to go without getting distracted or disturbed.

My rage over the racist attacks did get the better of me on one particular occasion. I lashed out at the bullies when my cousin moved to our primary school. Being the new little Asian kid on the block, he was constantly a target. I could not bear seeing my cousin being the victim. I snapped and chased one of the bullies and wrestled him down to the ground. That experience made me tougher as a person and we became less of a target from racist harassment from then on, at least in primary school anyway. In high school, I somewhat grown up and changed quite a lot in dealing with bullies. I would just ignore them and when things did occasionally get out of hand, my close friends would intervene and eventually those bullies changed. They became friendlier in the last years of high school. I believed the bullying was one of the main underlying motivations for me to succeed in life. Rather than being depressed about my situation, I chose to focus on making my life more successful than those bullies and to make a difference to other people's lives in the process.

"I realized that bullying never has to do with you. It's the bully who's insecure." - Shay Mitchell

My next new challenge was my relationship with my father after he reunited with us. We were separated for 10 years. My father left Vietnam to escape from the War when I was just 4 years old; he was just in his twenties. I could not remember what he was like except for the description that Mum gave me. We were desperate to migrate Dad to Australia and reunite him into our life, so I could have a father figure again. I wrote a letter to the best of my English ability and sent it to the government. I even visited a local parliament member often to ask him to help escalate Dad's migration approval. Thankfully, after a number of attempts, we received news that my father was given the stamp of approval to migrate to Australia.

It was an awkward reunion with my father at the airport having been apart for that long and I felt no bond with him. But I was glad that our family had reunited at long last.

As Dad settled into our lives, I started to see a different side of him. He was not the father I imagined him to be from my mother's description. He was depressed and cynical, temperamental, never satisfied with his work or anything.

There were often quarrels in the house between my father and Mum. Every time he shouted with rage at Mum, my brother or I would jump in front of him to fight him off. My childhood dream of a happy time with my father turned into a recurring nightmare. I was afraid that one day he would hurt us as he easily went into an uncontrollable anger.

My hatred towards my father intensified one day when I stopped my father from hitting my Mum. He ended up slapping me on my ear so hard that I heard constant humming in my eardrums. I felt I was about to go deaf and my crucial Year 11 exam was just days away. I had to live with the pain and infection in my ear for some time while I struggled to study and sit through my exam. There were many times where I contemplated suicide during my parents' constant fighting.

After Dad adopted the Christian religion, Dad's temperament calmed down tremendously. Throughout the countless quarrels and fights, I saw Mum forgive and forget and things were back to normal again, until the next quarrel. Most of the quarrels were around Dad being lazy and around money. The quarrels had somewhat driven my desire to become wealthy to avoid the arguments. On the reverse, I think it somehow drove my brother to give up on life with no desire to succeed. The great challenge of living with my father had motivated me to one-day give Mum a life she deserves for handling him. I adore her more and more for her patience. I also learnt to be a better caring parent and learnt not to inflict pain on my children.

The quarrels between my parents had made me resent my father for many years. The resentment diminished after I attended a self-development course (that healed and released my pain from my childhood caused by my parents). I started to understand why my father was the way he was, why he was disgruntled about life, especially when he was forced to leave his family to become a soldier in the Vietnam war.

Through the course, I learnt to accept & forgive my Dad. The seminar inspired me to call him about that specific incident where he slapped me on the ear before my exam. I told him I started to feel cold towards him from that time. When I heard my Dad's response over the phone, tears welled up in my eyes. He told me that he was very sorry that it happened, although at the time anger gotten the better of him. Then something he said that wiped off the hatred toward my Dad. He said I am his daughter and he would not harm me. I started to see his disgruntlement was built up from the experiences in the war and the living conditions in Hong

Kong, far away from his own family, where he could not cope, as he had never had any hardship in his life before.

My father was the only son, so my grandmother pampered and protected him from any hardship. (Traditionally amongst most Asian families, a boy is the most treasured). However without notice and preparation, he was forced to fight in the war. He was not prepared for this when his life was effortless. With grandmother's help, he escaped Vietnam alone, bounded for Hong Kong. He had to live in a harsh Hong Kong environment and struggled to keep his employment. He built his life there, miles away from his own family, his wife and two young children.

I've learnt to forgive my Dad and let go. I've learnt to understand my children and to understand them from their perspective. I've learnt not to overly protect and pamper my children. If I don't expose them to many experiences, they will lack the experience to know what to do in any environment. I am still working on this today.

The above series of challenges above have deeply built my desire to achieve financial success and freedom. That goal led me to study hard in my early days to get myself to university and obtained a professional career in Accounting.

My goal intensified after I had my first child and read "Rich Dad Poor Dad", a book that my husband gave me to read at the time. I realised that relying on climbing up the corporate ladder in my accounting career was not a solution. I had to find other alternatives. That was when I was introduced to property investment opportunities. It's unique how the universe works, when you set your mind on something specific, the HOW, shows up. My jaw dropped when I discovered it only cost me approx. $20/week at the time to invest in a property. That was back in late 1999. So we decided and took action to invest in a property a few months later. It was a great decision.

That property we bought was recently valued close to a $1 Million and generating us a passive income. That same property gave us the financial ability to invest in many more properties which generates more passive income for my family.

With my mind set on building up our investment properties, an opportunity emerged. Almost a couple of years after I had my son, my friend approached me to work with her husband's company. When I saw the wealth she had built and the amount of investment properties she owned, especially the new car she drove into my driveway (I am a luxury car fanatic), I got excited at the opportunity. I was enthusiastic at the possibility of entering into a property investment company to further my investment knowledge.

We were assisting investors to build their wealth using property as a vehicle. At the same time I was continuing to build up my own investment portfolio. There were many up moments as there were down moments. On the up side, the meetings were focused on self-development. The directors did a great job to encourage us to become big dreamers and pushed us to go beyond our comfortable boundaries.

The environment was very positive. Any negativity was not tolerated. I was surrounded by investors in a competitive environment where everyone wanted to succeed. I was given opportunities to manage a team, train new recruits, host and speak in seminars in front of a few hundred people. All these opportunities challenged my fear of public speaking, but overtime I became a better speaker, trainer and manager. I received acknowledgement from guests, new recruits and my team. With all the opportunities that were available to me, I stepped up. I took the challenge and became a better confident person.

Whilst working with the company, I faced some other undesirable events that really tested my strength to move forward. Before I joined the company, I told a friend about it. We agreed to join as partners to work on our clients together. After some successes and receiving many attentions for our successes, my friend decided to break the partnership up. I took it as a betrayal. I thought she didn't want to share her success with me and wanted the spotlight for herself. I took the break up badly. I watched her take off with greater success, receiving recognition for it and even received a promotion. I felt lonely and depressed. One late night when I left the company after a seminar where my clients did not show up, my mood took the better off me. I tripped over a stair and fell face down over a couple metres onto the hard concrete walking path. I felt some blood dripping off my head like a leaking tap. I also felt an excruciating pain creeping in from my right elbow. I went back into the office and luckily the blood came from deep scratches on my forehead. However my elbow was swelling up and the pain had intensified. I decided to drive myself home. I drove home in tears feeling sorry for myself. As it was already late, my husband and my little toddlers were asleep already. I went to sleep hoping my elbow would get better. The swelling got worse and the pain became intolerable during the night. Next day after a doctor's visit, I found out that I had a fractured right elbow and had to wear a plaster on a sling for 8 weeks minimum.

As a right-hander, having a plaster on my right arm that disabled me from using that arm and hand, challenged me in my role as a Mum. I had to resort to my left arm and hand, to care for my 4-year-old daughter and especially my toddler son. So I started using my foot to replace my right hand especially when I had to change nappies.

Although I was temporarily one arm short, I was not going to use it as an excuse to give up and leave the company especially after the partnership with my friend had broken up. I attended the meeting and continued working. I was very blessed my parents cared for my kids when I needed help. I became very hungry for success and lost my balance and time with my kids and family.

As my clients were working during the weekdays, I mainly saw them on weeknights or weekends. At times, I found myself at a client's house up to 2am either on my own or with a consultant under my management. On commission, there were times, I put in many hours and did not make any money within a month or two. When my earning was low, I faced many more rejections. When my earning was low, my parents and my husband told me to quit and go back to my professional accounting career.

I had my family members criticise me as a bad Mum who spent too much time at work and neglected her children. My emotions were determined by the amount of money I made. Despite the constant reminder to quit, my loyalty to my friend made me fearful to leave, as I didn't want to disappoint her especially after she told me one time that she could not sleep when she heard I was planning to leave. My loyalty to the company kept me sticking with it when there were signs the company was falling apart. I saw directors and top consultants leave. I was offered new roles with the possibility of earning more money still on commission and ended up still chasing the dollars.

While struggling in my career in real estate, my property investment journey was struck with obstacles after obstacles too. Some of the obstacles were the disagreement with my husband. Ten years had passed since my husband and I set our financial goal to retire on a passive income of $100,000 per year from property investment. That goal became my own goal, as my husband was happy to settle for half.

My husband and I had quarrels over the bad investments we purchased blaming me for the decisions I made on them. One day, I could not take the quarrels or the blaming anymore. It happened after my husband forced me to cancel a course that I wanted to take to gain further knowledge to achieve my financial goal. Instead of fighting with him any further, I gave up on making any decisions to purchase any property and handball the decision to him. Years passed, I saw the property market rising, I did not see my husband make much efforts to search for any property. Every now and then, with my itchy fingers I would search the Internet for properties and suggest them to my husband. Though he attended some auctions, the market took us out of the suburb that we wanted to invest. Frustrated by the lack of action, I decided I would not rely on my husband if I wanted to achieve my goal. I will make my own money to allow me to achieve my financial dream.

I saw an email that invited me to a free 3-day seminar from an author I admired dearly and have referenced many times in my training to new recruits. I was in a dilemma whether I take the Friday off work and upset my co-manager or go to the seminar for the weekend. I decided that midnight I would go. That decision was one of the best decisions I made. I felt I was released from a cage during those three days with T. Harv Eker. I came to understand that my root cause of my financial limit. That one seminar led me to where I am today, a co-founder of my own real estate business.

My challenges and strong interest in self-development courses, has taught me many valuable lessons: -

1. Setting goals are important. It gives you a clear direction where you want to go. It gives you the reasons why you are pursuing the goals.

2. I've learnt loyalty does not pay when the environment is against my personal values and I hence I become unhappy.

3. In pursuit of my goals, I have to be courageous to upset people (as long as I did not harm them). I learnt success comes more easily when I am happy and fulfilled.

4. Rejection is just a "No, I am not ready to receive what you are offering yet". So don't take it personally.

5. My energy is a reflection of how I feel and how I feel is a reflection of how I think.

6. I've learnt rather chasing money; I just need to focus on adding value to other people's life and money will come.

7. When times are tough, I just have to make a decision to dust it off, pick myself up and keep moving forward towards my goal.

8. Family is number 1. Kids grow up very quickly. I regret the lack of time I spent with my children while they were toddlers to earlier primary school age. However I cannot do anything about the past. I can only control my time with my children and family in the present.

9. Finding a balance in all areas of your life is important to a fulfilling life. One leak in an area of your life, will lead to leaks in others.

10. Staying positive and never giving up on your dreams.

11. If you are feeling lost, keep asking yourself why and be truthful with yourself. Seek help in finding your true self or higher self through self-development courses.

12. There is always a solution to a problem. I just need to keep looking for it or ask for help.

13. Team spirit and staff morale are important for a company. A company's success is a reflection of its people and its environment.

Although the challenges I personally faced so far in my journey may not be big challenges compared to others, I have gained so much knowledge from the experiences to prepare me mentally to deal with certain circumstances. I found that after I made a decision and stuck with it, the universe did its strange thing to deliver the solution, the HOW.

When the HOW shows up, it is my part to take action, otherwise I will still be in the same place. While taking action, there may be obstacles that challenge me. Those challenges are there to test me to find my strength and become a better person. I know when there are obstacles I am not alone. I can ask for help. I can seek for solutions. I can talk myself into gaining the courage to deal with the obstacles and to resolve a challenging situation.

Like the saying goes, "when there is a will there is a way". I discovered that the hardships I had faced had made me a tougher, resilient and a patient person. Throughout it all, I learnt to persevere with my goals and never give up!

Chapter 10

Inner Riches!

By Elaine McGuinness

At the end of 1999, I developed a sore throat and had to be hospitalised when I started vomiting and felt very unwell. I developed a high fever that didn't respond to antibiotics. The glands in my neck swelled up to the size of golf balls on each side. I had never felt like this before. I developed neck stiffness and also went off food.

All of my tests came back negative. I asked a doctor what was wrong with me and he said I had tonsillitis. As a nurse, I partially accepted this "diagnosis", because I had never seen glands so swollen in the neck before. While in the hospital, I felt aches and pains going through my body and I felt weak and strange. The doctors tested me for glandular fever and this was negative also. I was puzzled about what was going on in my body.

After a week, I persuaded the doctors to discharge me on New Year's Eve, even though they were reluctant to do so. I still felt weak, but wanted to go home anyway. I thought I would be back to normal in no time, but that was not the case. For the next two years, I suffered physically, as my body was out of balance and my organs were not functioning properly.

I felt fatigue at times, so I had to learn to conserve my energy for doing certain things before it became used up. I also experienced fevers, swollen neck glands, headaches, and pains going up my spine, along with rashes, weakness, fatigue, pallor and heavy legs. My sleep pattern was affected and I got pressure headaches in my central forehead. I was not depressed. These things were happening in my body and I didn't know why. I saw many doctors who didn't know what was wrong with me, so I had to search for my own answers.

After two intense years, I went to see an endocrinologist (a gland specialist). He repeated some blood tests and found that I had glandular fever all along, caused by Epstein-Barr Virus. That meant it was still in my body! He was reluctant to diagnose me with anything in particular but did say that I should not work anymore night shifts. These made the fatigue and sleep cycle worse.

In the years that followed, the symptoms subsided at times, but never completely left. My whole body felt out of balance and I used to feel exhausted at times. After a while, I realised that the medical profession could not help me and so it was up to me to help myself. First, I needed to understand what was going on. In 2002, I graduated with a Bachelor degree in the Humanities, majoring in psychology. Psychology didn't give me the answers I was looking for. This search for understanding what was going on in my body changed my whole life. It also changed my perception and understanding of who I really am. As Wayne Dyer says "When you change the way you look at things, the things you look at change." I knew it was up to me to find my own answers.

The more I focused on self-help and self-empowerment, the more I came across tools and techniques that gradually helped me to shift the illness out of my body. I became fascinated with the mind/body connection. Various books I read provided the information I needed at the right time that expanded my perception also. Slowly, over time I realised that your inner world creates your outer world and not the other way around. The book The Secret gave me a lot of information about the law of attraction initially. As I gained more personal understanding, I became even more curious about how the universe operates and where I fit in relation to it.

In 2004, I started training in martial arts. This taught me the discipline of the mind and body, as well as persistence and determination. After a training session in the "dojo", I would feel more energised than before I went in. I was not going to let this beat me.

I continued to get fevers, rashes and frontal headaches. For this reason, I started researching the pituitary gland that lies in the forebrain behind the central forehead. Then, I gradually learned how the brain worked in relation to illness. I've learned a lot more since about the brain and how to tap into its power. I knew that glands produce hormones and that hormones control the organs. The pituitary gland is considered the master gland of the brain by the medical field and it controls all the other glands in the body. One of my blood tests showed that my prolactin hormone, produced by the pituitary gland, was twice as high as normal levels. Why was this?

I learned that the pituitary gland is controlled by the hypothalamus in the brain, which weighs up situations in the environment. "Could my thinking be causing this?" I said to myself. I discovered that the hypothalamus has a function of detecting danger in the environment. The amygdala takes over if the perception of danger is considered a threat to survival. Then, the pituitary gland stimulates the adrenal glands on the kidneys to produce the stress hormones adrenaline and cortisol. This well-known "fight, fright, flight response is controlled by the hypothalamic-pituitary-adrenal axis (HPA). In cases of post-traumatic stress disorder (PTSD), the initial trauma has not been processed fully and stored as a memory. As a result, hypersensitivity for triggers of stress develops. This leads to a chronic state of stress in the body that is over-stimulated by adrenaline and cortisol. Too much cortisol depresses the immune system. When I proposed this theory to my doctor, I knew he didn't understand.

Research shows that an illness can develop two years after a trauma. In my case, my father had died two years before the onset of symptoms. I was getting somewhere at last. Too much adrenaline in my body explained why I experienced chest tightness, chest pain and palpitations. I was admitted to hospital a few times thinking I was having a heart attack.

My heart was perfectly normal as shown later by tests, which was a relief. The fact that I had too much cortisol explained why my immune system had become suppressed, why I was getting fevers and also why the immune blood tests were abnormally low. That was also why I got Epstein Barr virus and Brucella virus in my body. These viruses, in turn, caused myalgic encephalitis (ME) and chronic fatigue syndrome (CFS).

My immune system was struggling to function normally and in its efforts to overprotect me, it actually attacked my body instead. My ability to absorb nutrition became affected also, as my gut did not function efficiently. I learned that in some cases of ME, the gut becomes "leaky", where it lets in larger particles of food into the blood stream. This, in turn, causes an auto-immune response, where the immune system attacks the body. I started getting pains in my ankles and wrists, I consulted with a rheumatologist who confirmed that the joint pains could be auto-immune.

Autoimmune conditions occur when the immune system becomes so overwhelmed, it works harder as a result. In the process, the immune system attacks the body it is meant to protect. This leads to further burnout and exhaustion. I felt that nobody understood what was going on with me.

At the time, I felt powerless, as I thought I had no control over it.

Since then, I have learned that it is up to me to be the hero in my own life and to control my life from within. This process happens as you let go of the layers of conditioning and programming that do not serve you anymore. In the process, you move closer to your authentic self on the inside and the limitless power of your inner being.

This is one of the most valuable lessons I am grateful for. It was through my suffering that I was forced to learn what would make me better and to see things in a different light. There are no victims, in reality, only victim mentality. There are no problems in reality either, only our perception of events and the meaning we assign to them. All meaning is context related and we give our own personal meaning to the experiences we have in life. Each person's perception of the same event is different for this reason. We put our own twist on it, so to speak.

Now I see that illness as a blessing in reality. It taught me so many things on the physical, mental, emotional and spiritual level. I realise that there are no limits to how much you can learn about yourself. Self-discovery becomes a fascinating journey that becomes a quest to find your treasure within. The deeper you go, the richer your treasure.

Instead of resisting illness, look for the message it is trying to teach you in your body. By fighting against illness, you only give it energy and that makes it stronger. By accepting everything in your body and changing your perspective, you can move out of a state of victimhood. This happens over time as you learn to give yourself the unconditional love you deserve. One important thing I have gained from all of this is that my true power comes from within. I can empower myself by tapping into the source from within at my heart centre.

Over the years, I started setting challenges for myself, as I knew I had to let go of my "stuff". As Bruce Lee said, "Use what is useful and discard that which is not." In 2004, I undertook an endurance challenge in the Himalayas of Nepal with the charity Concern.

On this expedition, we camped out in the mountains off the beaten track in the most beautiful spots I have ever seen on earth. The highest altitude we got to was around twelve thousand feet high. I realised that experiences like this made life worth living, in spite of what I was going through. Nobody understood the pain and suffering I endured, so I gave up telling them. Instead, I decided to conquer my fear no matter what. It was up to me to move from a victim mentality to being the hero in my own life. I was finally transitioning from letting life happen to me to creating my life through me instead.

I still wasn't fully sure at the time of the message my body was trying to give me. Now, I know that the human body has its own intelligence. Your body is an instrument that you can use to feel what is right for you in life and what isn't right for you. Call it your gut feeling or inner knowing. Intuition is another name for this inner guidance system that helps you decide what is right for you in life. Over time, you can grow your intuition as you become more centred and whole on the inside. I now realise how much ME/CFS has taught me in relation to the body, mind and spirit that I didn't know before. In the process of searching, I became a truth seeker over time, until I finally realised that my inner truth is what sets me free. It was about ten years before I got a reluctant diagnosis of Myalgic Encephalitis (ME) from another endocrinologist, who wouldn't put it in writing. She couldn't give me a cure either. I now realised that other people must be going through this same thing that was not being acknowledged by the medical profession. It was very much a grey area with all the doctors and specialists I encountered, when I was looking for answers on the outside. It was frustrating at times when I got no answers or help. I had to keep going to find answers for myself.

Early in 2006, I decided to go on a skiing trip to Austria and the highlight was to go paragliding. I flew with my tandem pilot "Mike" after taking a "leap of faith" when I ran those five steps off the mountain. In that moment, I had made the decision that this was my statement for leaving my old life behind and moving forward with the life I wanted.

By this time, I had developed the fierce determination to do whatever it takes. I wasn't going to give in to a mediocre life of being at the effect of an illness and having to adjust my life to fit in with it. I had learned to push my boundaries and as I flew through the air, the palpitations in my chest subsided when I took in the amazing view. We could see a hundred and twenty kilometres around the Alps.

The sun was setting below in the valley and every mountain took on the hue of violet as the sun's golden rays streaked through the valley. It was an unbelievably beautiful sight that became imprinted on my brain. That was one of the most beautiful things I have ever seen. Over the next two years, Mike and I flew over many mountains in Europe.

Paragliding became normal over time, the more I flew. Flying thousands of feet high in the Alps gave me a completely different perspective on life. Things on the ground seem so small when you can see the whole picture. In the years that followed, I used that leap of faith as a metaphor for my life. I was beginning to realise that I was stronger than I thought I was and that I could use my body to get more out of life. This fuelled my passion for adventure and meaningful experience even further.

Eventually, back in Ireland, I passed my Para 1 test after I learned to fly solo around the Wicklow Mountains. It was exhilarating and I felt relaxed as I imagined my pilot "Mike" was there with me. I had done this myself and I was proud of my achievement.

During the twelve years I had ME/CFS, I found that being able to rest and get proper sleep helped me a bit. Any stressful events usually made things worse, so I knew I had to avoid those kinds of situations. I also knew I had to focus on getting better and not to become identified with the illness I had.

I empowered what worked for myself by learning more about it. In November 2006, I went on another endurance expedition to China with the charity Concern. During this time, we again trekked off the beaten track in the mountains surrounding the Great Wall of China. Each evening, we arrived at a new camp and a delicious hot meal prepared by the mountain guides. This was truly living I thought. I felt so grateful. Later, I realised that having gratitude in life can help with healing. On rare occasions, I would have a break from the symptoms, where I could rest, eat and sleep normally. My energy levels would come back to normal. I became conscious of the energy I stored in my body and began using my energy consciously. If I didn't, my voice became hoarse and my knees became weak when my reservoir of energy was used up.

In October 2007, I went to Thailand and got to spend two days, with five other people, inside a closed monastery of Buddhist monks. Two Buddhist monks were assigned to teach us about meditation and their way of life. They were poised and gentle while appearing physically strong and mentally alert. The monk's bodies seemed to follow their minds, as they walked and moved in a graceful fashion. I learned so much from them in that short space of time. At one stage, after we came out of meditation, I heard one whisper to the other "perhaps a seed is being sown here".

Buddhism is a way of life I learned and not a religion. For the next few weeks, my skin glowed and I felt energised. Shortly after this trip to Thailand, I went to India on another expedition in the Himalayas with Concern. The mountain guides (Sherpa's) were highly educated and very wise. As we trekked higher into the Himalayas, the conversations I had with the leading Sherpa were usually about spirituality.

A lot of what the Sherpa said resonated with me as truth in itself. I became curious and wanted to know more about the spiritual side of life. At this time, I was experiencing longer breaks between episodes of

ME symptoms. I noticed how I became exacerbated by certain events that I perceived as stressful. Stress, or my perception of it, seemed to set things off again.

In 2008, I commenced training as a life coach, to learn more about the mind and empowerment. In 2009, I started attending various seminars on self-empowerment and had many breakthroughs. I was starting to feel better at last, but my sister's death in April 2009 brought on the ME again full blast, all of a sudden. In the same year, I qualified as a certified co-active life coach. I knew I needed to learn more about the subconscious mind. In September 2010, I commenced studying as a clinical hypnotherapist. In December 2010, I got my black belt in Taekwondo martial arts. In 2011, I graduated with an advanced diploma as a clinical hypnotherapist and Hypno-psychotherapist. During 2010, I also got certified as a neurolinguistic programming (NLP) master practitioner and Reiki master.

My experiences with Reiki, meditation and hypnotherapy showed me that there was another dimension to my being when I looked within. I was onto something at last! I had changed unconsciously to myself during all my training and afterwards, life seemed different in a more expansive way. I had learned how to experience deep tranquillity and serenity inside myself, as I went deeper and deeper over time. It became a fascinating journey within. I learned that I could actually reach my subconscious mind and change my programming by using the tools that I learned. This was profound! I could actually reprogram my life now and be in control of my destiny.

With empowerment from within, I realised that this is where my truth lies. I had been seeking answers from outside about how I could get better. It was only when I started looking within, that I could let go of my past as I perceived it then. You can always recreate the story of your life and it's meaning for you. All meaning is context based. By changing the context of my life story, I knew I could finally change its meaning for me. I was never a victim. I had become the hero in my own life with a warrior spirit that had passed the initiations set by my higher self. I was being guided all along and I was never alone.

Over time, I realised that suffering is a choice and I knew that only I could help myself to recover. This self-awareness led me on a journey to self-realisation and health. At some stage, I stopped referring to myself as someone who had ME/CFS, as I continued to stretch my boundaries. The more empowered I felt, the less I would experience flare-ups or symptoms in general.

I focused on alternative therapies and spiritual healing. I realised there was much more to learn, as new understandings and experience enriched my life even further. I immersed myself in personal development seminars with thought leaders and I became ferociously curious about learning in general. I practised yoga also, where I could access inner peace and calm as a personal experience.

In overcoming ME/CFS, I have found my path in life. I have lived full out as much as I could when challenged. I also witnessed my fierce determination and strength to overcome and move beyond any challenges that arose in my body and my life. I had always looked for ways to help myself, even at my lowest points of exhaustion. That's one reason why I also turned to spirituality and spiritual healing.

To feel whole and complete from within brings with it the balance of the mind, body and spirit. If the spiritual aspect of your nature is ignored, then that will reflect in your life also. To be at one within yourself is to be at one with all that is on the outside, including people. With Oneness, you recognise that each person is a soul that needs love. I became a trainer for Oneness University when I spent a month in India in October 2014.

All behaviour is for the fulfilment of love, whether giving or receiving, consciously or subconsciously. When you realise that you are not a victim anymore, you can let go of judgment or blame, as you take full responsibility for your own life. Gratitude for the riches you gain means you want to pay it forward by being in service to other people. You receive first on the inside so that you can share this with others on the outside. This is the gift of life and the riches that come from within in making this world a better place to live in. When you overcome challenges in your own life, you want to help others free themselves from their own suffering also.

In February 2012, I started writing my first book called Unleash Your Authentic Self! And I finished it exactly a year later. My intention now is to help other people feel empowered from within just as I have been. I know I would never have ventured beyond my comfort zone as a truth seeker if I had an ordinary life, without its own challenges. Now I realise that all my challenges are opportunities to grow and evolve even further.

Today I am healthy and my blood tests are normal. I am grateful for everything that happened, including ME/CFS and I wouldn't have it any different. What may have seemed unpleasant at the time was indeed a blessing. I was being guided to find my own truth and no other people's truth. Now, I can say that my health has returned and I have normal levels of energy, sometimes super normal!

What has changed? My perception of my surroundings comes from the inside out. My inner state of mind determines how I see what is around me. Self-awareness and conscious choice allow me to live consciously in every moment.

What has this experience of ME/CFS taught me? It has taught me to let go of what does not serve me. This also means forgiving for my sake and not just other people's. Forgiving frees you up when you let go.

ME/CFS has also taught me to be grateful in a more conscious way for the little things in life and the big things, of course.

Being grateful opens your heart to receive more of the same. Being grateful for what you want aligns you with it so that it manifests in your life with belief. I have also learned to believe fully in my purpose in life, which is helping others to be empowered from within. With belief comes expectation. The Expectation is what predicts results in life. Also, what you focus on is just as important. When you know what your intention is for your life, just stick with it. The paradox is you also have to let it go while trusting that the universe will give you what you need. A good belief to have is that the universe conspires in your favour. What you believe becomes true for you in reality. Your belief creates your reality.

The most profound learning I have had during this time is to look within, instead of outside for direction in life. It is important to move out of your head and your identification with you thoughts. Your thoughts come and go. You are not your thoughts.

At your heart centre, you connect with your inner source and the unlimited power there. From your source, you express your authentic self and the truth of who you really are. As you gradually learn to live with more courage and authenticity, you let go of the layers of fear built up over a lifetime. That way, you move forward on the fast track to the life of your dreams. When you have conviction and passion for what you do, you have all the motivation you need for getting anything done. Your inner guidance leads you in the right direction. Whatever feels right for you usually is right for you.

The more you get to know yourself on the inside, the more you can discern what is right for you on the outside. In the process, you let go of judging and free yourself to give and receive love instead. By loving yourself first, only then, can you give it to others. You can only give what you already have within yourself. When you love yourself unconditionally, you also accept yourself for who you are. As you go deeper in self-discovery, you realise there is no limit to how deep you can go.

Then you know that discovering who you really are is the journey and not the destination. There is always more to learn on this journey of riches. That's what makes it so fascinating. When you are learning, you are growing and evolving. Learning is for life.

When I look back at taking that "leap of faith" off the mountain in 2006, what stands out for me are three key points that have helped me in life ever since. Those three keys made it possible for me to take that leap of faith at that time, and many more since then. The three key points are as follows:

- I have one hundred percent belief in what I am doing. There is no room for doubt, fear or questioning what I am doing when I know it feels right for me.

- I feel one hundred percent safe with full certainty, no matter what is going on outside of me. I trust my inner guidance and follow my "gut".

- I have fierce determination focused sharply at the moment. This gives me power at the moment, as I stretch my comfort zone into new territory. I have the pure determination to keep going while knowing all is okay.

Jumping off that mountain was such a powerful defining moment in my life and it has stayed with me ever since. In that moment, I let go of all fear and embraced everything fully in that moment. In return, I got countless riches and my life was never the same again. Many doors have opened ever since leading into new dimensions and experiences in my life. My life has expanded on all levels as a result, for which I am eternally grateful.

Gratitude is another way of bringing more of what you want into your life. It's the same with forgiveness. You forgive for your sake in letting go, so that you are free to move forward in your life. With your new found keys of belief, safety and fierce determination, you can open many doors to a brand new life of your dreams. Yes, dreams can come true and you can make it happen, by becoming the hero in your own life. You can let go of being a victim as your walls of conditioning and programming come crashing down. These were built from the time you were a child. Now, you don't need them anymore and it is time to dismantle what is blocking you from your authentic life.

The more you remove the barriers, the more people get to see the real you. The more you express your true self, the more you can create the life you want. As your control grows from within, you are less influenced by other people. When you discover that you are the cause of your life, then life happens through you and not to you. You are not at the effect of others' opinions or actions anymore. While people behave the same, you can respond now instead of reacting to their behaviour. When you feel grounded in who you are, your own roots give you solid footing. You can imagine you are connected with the earth itself and the vast resources inside. You are a child of the universe. You are in the universe and the universe is in you. You are made of the same stuff as the universe and are connected to it for this reason. Can you imagine the immense power you can tap into on the inside?

Your moment of power is now and you create your reality in every moment of now. If you ruminate over the past or anticipate the future, you are not present in the present. There is only now. In the moment of now, you can change your perception of your past. You can see the good and where you got your strengths. You can also see the patterns and intelligence behind everything that happened to bring you to where you are today. Without the challenges, you would not have learned to feel the richness in each and every experience.

Each experience teaches you more about who you really are and that's what wakes you up to your own self-realization. When you start becoming self-aware, you realise that this is the reason you are here on earth. In becoming awakened to your own inner truth, you can harvest the riches as you journey deeper within. Your journey of riches means that you move ever closer to the treasure that you truly are on the inside. There is not a destination to be reached, because who you really are is a journey in itself. Your journey to your authentic self gives you riches along the way.

By focusing inwards, you are moving away from distractions on the outside. The more you look within, the more centred you become. When centred, you can rely on yourself for your own truth. The truth shall set you free is inscribed on a stone tablet in a church beside one of the Alp mountains. I visited there in 2007 after a paragliding trip through the Alps. I had always wondered what this truth is that sets me free. Now, I know it is your inner truth that sets you free. As you journey deeper into self-discovery, you realise that there are many dimensions to your being.

You are not your body, your thoughts or your personality. So, who are you? By asking this question, you become aware that you do not have all the answers already. As you peel off the layers of conditioning and programming built up over a lifetime, you gain the new freedom of self-expression from within. With this new found freedom, your life and all your potential expands on the outside at the same time. You realise now that you are limitless, as are all the possibilities in your life.

As you journey deeper within, you experience more synchronicity in your life. The universe conspires in your favour, as certain people show up, situations arise and events happen that guide you on your journey. As you align your energy with what you want, it is only a matter of time before it manifests into your life.

Thought alone does not achieve this, nor wishful thinking. When you feel in your body what it is like to have what you want already, along with intense emotion, and creative visualization, you are attracting your heart's desire to you. When what you want is linked with serving others with humility, rocket fuel is added to your intention. If your intention is not genuine, then the universe will know. You are the creator of your life in every moment of now. When you use the three keys to having one hundred per cent belief, feeling one hundred per cent safe and having fierce determination in the moment for manifesting your intention, you become unstoppable!

You truly are a powerful magnificent being. Believe it! As you develop your warrior spirit, you get to fight the good fight where everybody wins. There are no sides; no them and us. We are all in this together as one. In Oneness, there is no competition, only collaboration and sharing. In reality, there is only connection and not separation. With Oneness, the focus is on community and helping each other.

The old ways of separation and individuality are an illusion. While it may feel real, according to our senses, at a deeper level, we are all connected energetically. What kind of world would you like to live in? Each one of us has a part to play in the collective whole of humanity. You too can make a difference. According to Einstein, "Your imagination is more important than knowledge." Your imagination is more powerful than you realise.

Now is the time to become both the director and actor of the movies you project from the inside out onto the screen of the world. You are part of humanity and you affect the whole, as the whole affects you. You are an active participant in global consciousness in the same way. By following your purpose in life, you can find true fulfilment and happiness.

You can make a conscious decision now to make a difference and leave a legacy to the world. What legacy do you want to leave behind to make the world a better place? Here are some questions that may help guide you to find your own truth for your purpose in life:

- What do you want to be remembered for?

- What imprint do you want to leave behind you?

- What gives meaning to your life?

- What are you passionate about?

- What riches have you gained from the challenges in your life?

- How can you be in service to others, using the riches you have gained in life?

- What do you love doing that helps others?

Your journey of riches includes finding your purpose, mission and vision in life. Your purpose includes anything that helps others when you are in service to them. Your inner journey affects your outer journey in life. When you follow your purpose, you become more certain of what you are here to do. Your mission is how you do this and your vision is the big picture of where you are going. You can take steps to your vision of what you want to create, one step at a time, one goal at a time. It's the same with setting goals.

Each goal is your signpost as you move closer to the ultimate goal of your life, the big picture. Knowing what's important to you in life is what you value. Living your life according to your values makes the journey much easier and gives you the motivation to keep going. It also means you have inner integrity and full coherence with what you are doing when following your purpose for what you are creating. By fulfilling your values, you are also fulfilling your happiness needs. It's important to tend to your needs first before you take care of others. It is not selfish, because the more you are at one with yourself on the inside, the more you can express your truth. My inner truth and learning are my real riches. May you also find your inner truth and free yourself from within.

The source has always been there at your heart centre, where you can access unlimited power in your life. May the source be with you as you journey to further riches in life! Namaste.

Chapter 11

Life's Non-Negotiable

By Narelle Henry

It is with great pleasure and privilege to be asked to contribute a chapter to this book about sharing life's journey. If anything I share can assist another in their life journey then that is what this is all about. We all have individual aspirations and wants, we all have different ways to achieve and meet these. We all experience obstacles and challenges but sometimes we can feel that we are alone in experiencing these challenges.

In this chapter I share some of my obstacles and challenges and how I overcome them. You will notice that you can relate to these challenges, they are things we all need to overcome to achieve our aspirations and needs. I hope you learn new insights on ways to overcome them and to continue on your life journey.

I am a 46-year-old woman, married with two boys, I am a daughter with three siblings and I am a business owner. I recently sold my business of 15 years and it was serendipitous that on the day it was sold I was asked to contribute a chapter to this book. As one chapter closes another opens and this was literally the case for me.

Challenges that you have overcome:

In contemplating this question I thought best to outline my challenges in three separate areas:

ISSUE OF CONTROL

1. Internal factors

2. External personal factors

3. External business factors

Internal factors:

I describe internal factors as things within ourselves, which we can change. As much as they can have an enormous impact in assisting us to achieve our aspirations and needs alternatively they can act as a barrier to us in achieving our aspirations and needs.

Limiting beliefs

We all have certain beliefs about many things but the beliefs we hold about ourselves and our connection with others has the power to increase or decrease the time taken to achieve our goals. I held so many limiting beliefs, here are just a few:

- Only smart people can be rich

- Only beautiful people can be happy

- Only slim women can have a truly loving relationship

- You have to have money to make money

- Money makes you selfish

- Money makes you arrogant

- People want to pull you down

- Successful people are just lucky

Self-belief

Self-belief is the greatest asset you need in order to achieve the goals you want and overcome the many obstacles that life throws our way. Developing self-belief is an ongoing challenge because as you establish new goals you are setting yourself new directions, down paths not yet travelled.

FEAR

Fear creates so much worry and anxiety, it is paralysing to the attainment of your goals. Fear can rear its ugly head out of nowhere. I believe that we are not fearful of success but we fear failure so it's often easy to not try than to try and say I failed.

External Personal factors:

Life balance

I am a woman with two boys aged 20 and 11 and have been married for over 20 years. The thing I am most proud of is my relationship with my sons and my husband and I have done an excellent job, not a perfect job by a long way but excellent one all the same. Getting the life balance right is a very real challenge, one that still challenges me to this day.

Intimate relationships

I have been with my husband for over 27 years and married 23 years and I know when our relationship is going well then I can do anything. When we are in a bad patch my energy and enthusiasm seem to alter in a negative way and I take myself to a place where just getting about can feel like slogging through the mud. This is when I'm most unhappy, hence, the need for me to ensure significant focus on this relationship to ensure I can stay on track in achieving my desires.

Relationships

I come from a large extended family and grew up with cousins, uncles and siblings around all the time. Family celebrations were very important and missing one left me feeling disappointed. We moved from Sydney to the Mid North Coast 17 years ago so making all the family celebrations became very challenging.

Physical fitness

Being physically fit is known to be essential for your overall health and your wellbeing. I believe that regular exercise and a sensible diet is an important aspect in assisting me to achieve my goals. (I still need to reduce the consumption of fabulous champagne and wine from my diet, I am far from perfect).

I embarked on a fitness program and clean eating diet several years ago, which resulted in weight loss and increased strength and fitness. I have participated in several fun runs and look forward in completing my first half marathon later this year. I have used exercise as a stress management strategy as it is difficult to exert yourself physically and also think about your worries or challenges. For me, it is a time when I shut down my mind and just focus on the task at hand. There are lots that can be said about the importance of our physical and mental health. It is an area I am very interested in exploring further and worthy of a whole book on its own.

External business factors:

Organizational and Planning skills

Developing effective organizational skills is paramount to my business success. I do have a natural tendency to want things organized. This business factor for me was one of the less challenging aspects, but I have included it as I feel it is non-negotiable. Finding the best way to get organised is an individual thing but the need to be organised is common to all successful people.

Business skills

I went from working in a government agency to running my own business. My business was in line with the work I was doing for the government so I was considered an expert in my field. I knew nothing about running a business nor had I invested any time or energy in learning about business until it became crystal clear that unless I did start to invest in my business skill set my business would not be successful.

Financial planning

Ensuring sound financial planning for your business makes sense, we all know that, but achieving it can be challenging for some like me. Developing budgets and having the discipline to stick to them is essential (I have a tendency to spend oops!!). It is important to always know your balance sheet and knowledge is power. I was always fearful of knowing my balance sheet, which leads to several problems with cash flow and debt management.

Consistency and Discipline

Maintaining consistency takes discipline. By consistency I do not mean to imply doing the same thing over and over but be consistent about critical business processes. Such as consistency in planning, consistency reviewing your balance sheet, consistency in your sales and marketing strategy. It took me time to understand and realise just how important this is particularly when your business reaches a level of maturity and success. You can forget what it took to get there and you can experience a drift away from those very things that made you successful.

Staff Management

I was very passionate about my business and had an expectation that anyone who worked for me would share the same passion and enthusiasm. It didn't take me long to realise that whilst my staff had a passion for the field in which we worked they were not passionate about the business being a success. Creating a work environment that contributed to staff morale, staff engagement, staff investment and staff reward became key aspects of my staff management philosophy and hence my business success.

Customer management

Without customers, there is no business. I had such a strong view of how my business services could change the lives of the most vulnerable people in our society i.e. the disabled, the aged, troubled youth and children. I believed that every organisation would see clearly what was on offer and secure our services immediately, it was a no brainer. Was I mistaken! I went from working for the government with non-profit organisations to establishing a for-profit private company targeting not for profit organisations? My passion blinded me from being able to disassociate from my services and associate with the customer. At the time I was accused of trying to make money off vulnerable people and that I would be back knocking on the government's door for a job. My approach to presenting, selling and marketing my business needed to change and change we did to overcome the objections that we were being presented with. As the old saying goes the customer is always right.

Marketing and Public Relationships

In the early days of my business, we secured work through reputation and word of mouth. The investment in terms of both time and money was very limited in the areas of marketing and public relations. I think this was largely due to the negative response we received when we first launched the business and also we had no real budget. What this meant was that we were operating reactively and responding to work requests without any real strategic planning. At the time, we were in a position that we could not afford to knock back work and whilst we had an idea of where we wanted to go it occurred in an ad-hoc fashion. I soon came to realise the very importance of ongoing marketing and public relations activity consistently applied across the business.

Partner support:

As stated, I have been in a relationship with my husband Ken since I was 19 years old, I am now 47 that is a long time hey? We have two sons, "touch wood" who are healthy, happy, have good peer groups and they both have goals for their future selves. As a wife, mother and business owner I could not have achieved this outcome without Ken's support. When we met and got married we could not have known where our lives were headed. We both had good jobs, bought a house and had our first son, life was not easy as we were living from week to week. Most people are at this time in their lives.

I had an opportunity for a job transfer from Sydney to Mid North Coast, whilst I hesitated Ken was all for it. Within two weeks we packed up our house, got tenants into it and were living in beautiful Port Macquarie. This is where we remain to this day, it has been the best move we made. Soon after the opportunity to start my business came up. I discussed this with Ken, I was so full of fear, fear of leaving a very secure and well-paying job, fear of the business failing and fear of losing our house. All the things we had worked so hard for. I will never forget what Ken said to me, he said "Narelle you do not need to be afraid, this is a great opportunity and if it fails you are more than employable and we will not lose anything". I am embarrassed to say that I know without a doubt back then if the situation was reversed I would not have been so supportive and it would have taken some convincing. He has such great belief in me and that feels wonderful. Now I can't go on without also sharing that there are things I have undertaken in my quest to make things better that I have not had Ken's support with that I have pursued anyway. Some have worked out and some have not. We have a very passionate relationship, we love and fight with passion. It is never boring and at times exhausting.

My relationship with Ken has been one area that has received less focus over our children, over my business and over my own fitness goals. There are several reasons for this but I have changed my focus and my relationship with him has become even more of a priority. It has been both interesting and at times funny as we work on mending areas in our relationship that have been fractured. Being a fly on the wall in our couples counselling would make fantastic viewing, we will get there, it just may look different to what I expected.

Mentoring and coaching

I have always understood the importance of good mentoring and I have always had a healthy thirst for knowledge. I sort out professional mentors when I first started working I would work out who was considered the best. I would ask to meet with them, send them my reports to get their feedback. I was tenacious in this near to the point of annoying my mentors.

I figured that they would appreciate someone wanting to enhance their knowledge and improve their services so I kept at it. I got lucky and got to experience some great mentorship whilst working for the department aiding in my own professional development and reputation. I continued with mentoring with my business and at various stages of my business life I have had business coaches. These coaches varied based on what I felt I needed at the time but each one contributed significantly to my knowledge and I worked to implement their recommended business strategies.

One of the important things I learnt from my mentors was to keep reading and so now I challenge myself to read books regularly and I subscribe to many articles. This assists more to be at the leading edge of new business ideas and strategies.

Mistakes

The word mistake has been given such a bad wrap it has a negative connotation. I am not really sure why but I have been comfortable in making mistakes. I have an attitude that mistakes give us the opportunity to learn how not to do something and that is powerful. I know I will continue to make mistakes and I even prepare myself for them. I will say to myself that I'm not sure how this may work out but I will catch the point where the mistake happened, identify it and know not to repeat that again.

Being surrounded by people who believe in you

I am very grateful for the people in my life and this needs to start with my fabulous parents. I have never for one second of my life ever doubted their love for me and this brings me such great comfort. My parents were very supportive and provided encouragement and advice at key points in my life and still do to this day.

I have two of the best sisters possible, it really is a case of blood is thicker than water and they are very proud and supportive of me as well. They may not always agree with me but their love and support is unwavering. My sister husband's is also another fan, we have shared some intense moments around smashing limiting beliefs with amazing success, for that I am grateful. My in-laws are a great support to me and my family, well they were tireless in their support assisting us with balancing childcare and work. Our sons think their Nan and Pop are just the ant's pants.

My brother and sister in law have given me some of the best times, it is always filled with much laughter and good cheer. I have a gorgeous bunch of nieces and nephews and now one great niece. I am very proud of everyone of my family members and love spending time with them as well. I have way too many friends to mention them all as I just have

1 chapter of a book, not a whole book. Friendship to me is very important.

I love socializing with my friends and I have remained in contact with many for over 30 years. I just love that fact. Over the years friends have been my sounding board, my complaining board and my advice board. Thanks to all of you for that and oh yeah my drinking partners as well. My two boys bring me so much joy and I know that they are very proud that I am their mum. Thanks for believing in me and for loving me, without that I would not be able to do the things I do. I have already mentioned the critical role Ken has played, having a partner that has a strong belief in you is essential. I am one lucky and grateful girl and I must never forget that.

Creating a successful mindset

All the above factors lead into creating and having a successful mindset. Maintaining positive thought processes will lead to positive outcomes. Now we all know that this is true and there are numerous motivational quotes all on the same theme. However how do you do it when you are under stress, when you are feeling overwhelmed and when your ability to think clearly is impaired by fear. I have created some quick and effective strategies to get me out of thinking negatively during these times. I have written a number of great scripts that I say to myself, keywords and phrases that immediately move me from fear and anxiety to belief and excitement. I have created very effective visualization techniques that when implemented correctly and consistently will overpower the negative thoughts whenever they appear.

You need to develop a successful mindset if you want to lead a successful and happy life, whatever that is for you. Just like studying for an exam or training for an event you must invest your time in developing and improving your mindset, i.e. you must practice these techniques consistently in order to have consistent results.

Most profound learning during this time

There are so many learning's but if I had to pick what for me is the most profound it would be "What you focus on you get and what you do not focus on you do not get". This fact has shown up in my life in so many ways both professionally and personally. Let me outline the impact professionally.

My business achieved some great milestones, the biggest being awarded the National Small Training Provider Award. Winning the NSW award was something I really wanted to achieve. I had been state finalist the previous two years, to win that and then to go on and win at the National level was amazing. It is like the logies of training, there is no more prestigious award available to training companies. We worked hard and we did deserve this award and it was an exciting time for the whole team.

I took the pedal off the metal afterwards, thinking I had made it. I had somehow believed that everything would now work out just fine. I chose to focus on anther business opportunity with a couple of start-up ideas, one I was taken for a ride, like a $30,000 ride…ouch! The other, I'm still trying to raise capital even though it has been several years in the making by the time this book is published. It will either be launching or dead and the financial cost has been significant not to mention the time element as well.

Taking my focus off my main business resulted in significant decline in company sales, thus creating significant cash flow issues. At the time, there were also legislative and operating standards changing (these things being out of our control) which greatly impacted on the viability of my business model at the time. I changed the business model from an employed staff group to a pure contracting model. The business model that I created was viewed as innovative and progressive but the execution was lacking due to my lack of focus. The impact was significant, it was a very stressful time for all involved both professionally and personally. We also had a government contract worth over a 1/4 million dollars put on hold for over a 12-month period. I had not predicted the delay and had already invested in resources to deliver. It wasn't a good position to be in. I had already invested in the project and I had no other work to take the place of this contract, placing further stress on my bottom line. To say it was a tough time is an understatement.

Additionally, the contractor I had established an arrangement with had very little entrepreneurial skills and the numbers they were putting through never reached the requirement to make the model viable. My success mindset and self-belief were really tested at this time, I was being hammered from all areas. On the up side, I got plenty of practice using my mind and visualisation techniques to help me get through and stay focused. Myself, my team and my husband all got through it resulting in a company approaching me to purchase my business. Whilst it was not up for sale I knew it was worth looking at their offer. After 15 years owning this business I felt ready to let it go and move onto to other things and the offer suited me. I was very excited about the next chapter in my business life.

This was such a profound place to be in, after navigating the business through a very rocky period. Now let me share with you the profound impact the following statement had on my personal life. "What you focus on you get and what you do not focus on you do not get". I have previously indicated that my focus on my relationship with my husband Ken had taken second place, he would rightfully argue it was more like the tenth place. When this happens obviously it creates fractures and if you do not notice them and take action to address the issues the fractures get worse.

We experienced lots of heartache during this time, we both behaved poorly and made poor decisions. I am very sorry about that. We now, however, have jointly decided to focus on each other and our relationship. I doubt we will ever have a peaceful relationship but it's dynamic, passionate, fun and unique. As long as we stay focused the journey will be rich to the end.

Three key points that helped me:

Core values:

Staying true to your core values and course correcting when necessary.

Determination:

Understanding that consistency is critical and using a running analogy that life/ business/success is not a sprint but more like an ultra-marathon you need to pace yourself and stay focused on the end goal.

Planning:

Having effective planning skills I have found to be invaluable and whenever I am feeling overwhelmed is says to me go back to planning. After I do this it always makes me feel in control and not overwhelmed.

I have just sold my business and embarking on a new chapter in my business and professional world. I am going to take all that I have learnt from the previous 15 years in business and take that into a new business venture that I am creating. It's very exciting and hopefully impacts the lives of many people.

One of my aspirations for the future is that I'm planning to provide others some insight into what is possible if they want it enough. I want to be able to provide business and life coaching to women of all ages, teenage girls to women in retirement. I have a strong belief that we create our experience. Before every feeling and action is a thought and if we improve our thoughts we can immediately improve our experiences without having to change much else.

I would love to assist women to achieve their aspiration, however big or small. I want this process to be practical and personal. There are some life coaching programs that promote saying you can have all the abundance in the world if you follow their program. The problem with this is that it is their program based on what they want to achieve in their life and what they think makes people happy. What happens is people sign up believing that they will achieve abundance and soon realise, as it's not based on their values and true desires, they do not achieve abundance and then it feels like they have failed.

I believe strongly that the human spirit loves to contribute to others. My program will allow women to examine themselves fully and to gain a comprehensive understanding of what their needs and wants are. They will be able to identify the stuff in their life that is assisting them to achieve their wants and needs. Also, the stuff that is impeding them from achieving their needs and wants. Once identified the person can undertake the necessary steps and plans to achieve their life needs and wants.

I hope you have enjoyed reading this chapter and have gained some useful information that can benefit you in your life journey. For me, I am just revving up and the best is yet to come.

Chapter 12

Love Yourself First

By Adam Todd

There is no way to repress your experiences of pain, fear, and anger without repressing your love, joy, and inspiration as well.

Like a lot of great stories, this is a love story and how channelling the power of emotions can take your life to new heights. Emotions are powerful. People get married for them, kids are made, wars are started, and creative arts are inspired. Some of the greatest songs have been powered by the real life experiences of the artist. Love is a powerful emotion that can make you do amazing things, some positive and some negative.

At the start of the year, I really dedicated my free time to improving myself as an electronic music producer. I bought a new computer and new music making software. I knew there would be a big learning curve with how to use the software. I saw this as a challenge I was ready to endure. I organised four, three-hour private lessons with a tutor to accelerate my learning. I also dedicated my free time to mastering the software. Many weekends were spent in 8-hour blocks just working on making tracks. I could hear my tracks getting better.

My friend who runs Discovery records released two of my tracks on his digital label in June as part of a various artist EP called the "Navigator EP". I was really excited about that and thought 'I was on my way'. Making music is a real passion for me and I love getting lost in the creative process. I really feel that being creative is a great way to spend your time and one of the principles Wayne Dyer preaches is to *"not die with your music still in you."*

When I started out as a producer I knew I wasn't where I needed to be to take my music to another level. I just kept making tracks, trying new ideas and new ways of doing things. Each time I tried I learned. I dedicated time to it. One of the things a personal trainer friend told me is that in sports you have to put in at least 10,000 hours of practice to improve as a player.

He learnt this from the AIS soccer program he was involved in. He went on to say how Australian kids generally take longer to attain the 10,000 hours of practice compared to children living in nations that excel in soccer. This contributes to Australia's inability to be a world leader in this sport. I had that concept in mind and applied it to my music, I just keep plugging away to get my 10,000 hours in. I had to really manage and prioritise my time in order to put in the hours.

Trying to master music production was just one aspect of my year. Basketball season had started and I was playing well and my team was winning. Around April though, I met a girl that would add romance, excitement and challenges of my life. There was a strong attraction between us. We would engage in flirting and conversation at the gym. My friend at the gym even commented, "Would you stop flirting with her?"

I said cheekily, "She's flirting with me!" We started messaging each other almost daily, and every day was exciting getting to know each other. The weekend would come around, Friday night and we were constantly messaging each other. All the time I'm thinking, "Where is her partner?" as I knew she was currently in a relationship. She would spend more and more time at the gym and I would make sure I would talk to her.

The chemistry was strong. It was one Saturday night that she opened up a little more. She said she was not happy with her relationship and hadn't been for a long time. She also admitted to having feelings for me. I was developing feelings for her too. She left her relationship a week after she revealed her feelings for me. He moved out and we started dating. The passion was intense and we were falling in love. Every weekend we would spend together. It was really great and so passionate.

In hindsight, though, the only problem was it was all too quick and she really needed time to move on and heal from her previous relationship. Although she didn't want to be with him, she really enjoyed the mutual friends and the lifestyle that came with it. Not only did the relationship end, but also pretty much her whole life, as she knew it ended. With them parting ways, they also parted finances, and her money situation became very tight. Her lease was going to end soon so she had a lot of outside stress to go along with the emotional stress she was experiencing. She was fighting a lot of internal battles and this affected our relationship.

Someone with this type of stress is not going to have much love to give. I was kind of like "We can do this. It'll work out." And I ended up going over the top in my showing her love and she ended up saying she doesn't feel worthy of it. As these issues came up and she began to doubt what she had done. I could feel the doubt and we talked about it. I could feel our relationship was in trouble. I wanted to make it work. I could feel her sometimes wanting out and sometimes wanting to stay with me. With feeling this emotionally insecure in the relationship, I became very sad and quiet. I had opened my heart to her as she had to me. Now I could feel mine was going to be broken and smashed to pieces. As probably everyone knows it's not a pleasant experience. I didn't feel emotionally safe to love her.

I'm not one to hide my emotions either. If I'm upset you can tell, and as a personal trainer, I need to be upbeat and energetic. No one wants to get trained by a depressed trainer, so I would really work on putting myself in the right emotional state. I did this a few ways. One way was through keeping up my exercise. As a personal trainer, I need to be in shape and I enjoy working out and being fit. A lot of people in relationship trouble hide and stop their exercise, but exercising actually improves your mood. Just moving your body helps improve your mood. Often, I would have trouble sleeping because my mind was just thinking about her and whether it was going to be over?

If I didn't sleep well, I would still do my training but it would be at a lower intensity. Another thing I did when I was having trouble sleeping, and this was probably the biggest tool, was to turn on my night-light and start writing in my diary. I was wide-awake anyway and I needed to do something. The writing was something I hadn't done in a while and I felt like these thoughts that were looping in my head needed to be written down and out of my head. I needed to get in control of my thoughts.

What would I write is, what is the problem? What is the worst-case scenario? I would ask myself if I could handle that. And I always said yes. I can handle that. As a PT, I'm often giving advice to others on all sorts of things. By writing in the diary, I was able to have conversations with myself, ask myself questions and give answers. This was so important because my self-esteem and relationship with myself were being affected.

The diary writing really helped me. If I was really feeling down, I would put on happy songs and sing them really loud in the car. By using my body this way I was able to create energy and get me in a state where I would be able to be around people and train them. The reality was, I just wanted to hide from the world. I felt unloved by her and not good enough. Everyone's worst fears are that they are not enough and that they won't be loved. I felt this way at times.

I was constantly playing positive material in my car. Things like Tony Robbins' "Get the edge", Brian Tracey's "The psychology of achievement" or Zig Ziglar's "View from the top". This is important because I believe that input equals output. With that much emotional pain in my life, I knew I had to constantly put positive input in. The energy I was getting from the relationship was up and down, many great moments but the majority was negative energy. By using positive input along with my self-coaching diary entries, I was able to manage my emotions and keep myself going.

I also talked to my friends. My friends know me to be a happy, energetic person and could tell I was upset and when they ask the usual question, 'How are you?" Instead of lying like we all do and say, "I'm good." I would say "I'm feeling a bit down because…I'm feeling insecure because"… Some would offer advice, some would just listen.

This really helped as well. I didn't feel ashamed or embarrassed to show I was feeling emotions that could be viewed as 'weak' emotions. I know everyone goes through this, everyone has times of weakness, everyone needs help and I'm not afraid to show vulnerability. I even watched Ted talks about being vulnerable. It was insightful. One of the things I learned was that if you shut off the negative emotions of anger, sadness, pain, fear, you also shut off love, joy, hope, and inspiration. I knew I needed to process and talk about these feelings in order to get back to my natural happy, positive, inspiring self.

When you're in a relationship it's constantly on your mind, particularly when you don't feel safe. Questions constantly running through my head: 'Why can't it just be like the beginning?' And all through this I have to suck it up and do my best to be an inspiring personal trainer. It was very important for me to manage my states. The truth is she was going through her own issues and I just fell in love with her and got in the way.

Eventually she checked herself out of the relationship. I was really upset and hurt, but I had a deep belief and confidence that I'd get through it and return to my happy self. I had this confidence because I've been through a few lost loves before and was able to bounce back, so I knew I could do it again. Like I said, one of the things that are important is getting your feelings out. Getting them out takes time though and I had to go through the pain of lost love. I can remember being really upset on the weekend cause that's when you've got the time to think. I felt like crying but couldn't get myself too.

I knew if I had a good cry it would help release the pent up emotions inside of me. I started playing some emotionally sad songs I like and eventually found one that really struck the right chord and the tears started flowing. This moment I remember clearly, it was an Avril Lavigne song. I played it on repeat, too many times to count, each time as loud as the last just to make sure I got out all of the pent up emotions. I remember, despite the flowing tears, I knew it would be good for me. I knew it was feelings of hurt inside of me coming out. I believe when researchers say that pent up emotions is a cause of disease and cancer. I believe you have to process them. After 20-30 mins of crying I'd had enough. In emotional times, you don't really feel like eating but I put a little bit of food in me, got in my car and drove to Mt Lofty in Adelaide.

I like to run up Mt Lofty and I did that. I ran it in one of my fastest times ever! I got some exercise, got outdoors, back to nature and by conquering a challenge I felt good about myself at the moment. I would go for 2-hour walks. I remember the first one. I was still sad and thinking of her and I wasn't my happy self. Usually, I enjoy being alone, and my own company, but I was still emotionally hurting. I was still living in my head, grieving over lost love, living in the past just looping memories, and I remember challenging myself. "What... can't you smile? I bet you can't laugh" And straight away this got me to smile. I remember it being my first smile for days. It was the building blocks to strengthen my relationship with my 'self' again. I challenged myself more that day and I remember I ended up walking about 10km up and down the beach. I could feel my relationship with my 'self' building up again.

I would do incantations like Tony Robbins teaches. Repeat phrases over and over like, "I can get through anything" or "Anything is possible." On another of my beach walks, I thought about all the girls throughout my life that I had feelings for at one time or another, all the way back to Primary School days. I thought about how each of those relationships ended and what I had learned from them. This also helped me put this current pain into perspective.

In the moment, it's very painful, but years from now it's going to seem insignificant. I started looking at my Saturday nights at the beach as an uninterrupted date with myself. Just as if I was taking the girl out and spending quality time with her, I was taking myself out and spending quality time with me. I really had fun nights out on my own. So much to the point that I would've rather been out with me instead of her.

A few quotes I came across are "You cannot be alone if you like the person you are alone with." And "No one deserves your love and attention more than you." I think it's essential to just spend quiet time alone to process feelings and thoughts. It's easy to distract yourself with TV, movies, going out, food, drugs, but I'm not into that. I just had a deep knowing that I would get back to myself by being alone with myself. I kept writing in my diary, what was happening, how I was feeling and saying positive affirmations.

As a basketball player of 30 years, my ankles have seen a lot of injuries and suffered a lot of wear and tear. During one game, shortly after I got together with this girl, in a play, I landed on a ball that was just off the court and sprained my ankle. I thought it wasn't that bad because the next day it was kind of sore but OK.

The pain and the swelling got worse. Looking back now, I see it as my karma for playing my part in ending her past relationship. Their relationship was ruined and my season was ruined. My heart was broken and now my ankle was too. This was difficult to deal with. Every step was a pain. 6, 7, 8 weeks passed and it was still really swollen. I had all this emotional insecurity going on and every step I took, there was a physical pain too.

It was a really difficult time because playing basketball is really a form of therapy for me and I wasn't able to play. My team was playing the best season in their history and it looked like I would miss the rest of the season with an injury. I thought it was just a sprain but it was taking longer than usual to heal. Finally, I got my ankle checked out with an ultrasound and eventually an MRI. It turns out I had completely torn a ligament in my ankle that needed surgery to fix. Partially torn another ligament and stretched the tendons. There is also major cartilage damage and fluid in the joint from previous ankle injuries and 30 years of playing the game. I wondered if I would ever be able to play basketball again. This was very upsetting.

Really the only way through this was to have faith in the universe. I'm being stopped from playing basketball for some reason. It's up to me to turn this into a positive and find the bigger meaning. Maybe that made me focus more on my ambitions of being a music producer.

And to look deeper at my current relationship, maybe it allowed me more time to develop spiritually. Or embrace the healing qualities of walking along the beach, or to develop more compassion as a personal trainer to people who have injuries. I was able to keep my fitness and my training despite the injury. I would do more bike riding and leg exercises that didn't involve much ankle movement while doing more upper body training. I know the lesson is there for me. Trust in the universe. I continued to work hard on my fitness and be an example to people that injuries and pain don't have to stop you. It made me a better personal trainer.

I was getting myself back to my old self. I was healing my heart, but out of the blue, she calls me. She just wants to chat, she wants a friend, like

I said she had her own problems and issues going on, she needed a friend. Deep down I still loved her and cared for her so I took her call.

What eventually happened is we talked many more times on the phone after that and actually our friendship, honesty and understanding of each other grew to levels that it wasn't at before. We would discuss things we hadn't before and our relationship grew again. I was excited about this and thought maybe we could get back together. In this new found level of communication, we felt like we could tell each other anything.

One of the things she told me is she didn't like my house. She said it's too much like a man cave. I thought, "I'm a man. I live on my own. What do you expect??" She didn't like my leaking toilet, or the cracks in the walls or the colour of the walls. I set about to improve my house with the hope of her coming back and being impressed and in the process helping us get back together. Love is a powerful motivator. It also made me look at what was really important in my life. When I was really grieving over the lost love, I realised that none of the material possessions I owned were making me happy. None. Not even my beloved Air Jordan's.

'Happiness is all determined by what meaning you give to the events that happen in your life. '

I set about getting rid of a lot of my possessions that were just clogging my house and my life. My journey towards becoming a minimalist had begun. Any possessions or clothes or books I hadn't used for over a year I gave away to the Salvos or to friends. As a huge basketball fan, I had all these basketball newspapers and cards, posters, videos that I put in the bin. All I wanted was to love her and be loved by her, none of these possessions meant anything more than that so I got rid of them.

And without realising, I was making way for new stuff to come into my life. I watched Ted talks about living a minimalist lifestyle and it really inspired me and affirmed I was doing the right thing. I even questioned where I lived and owning my house. Do I need a house? I questioned everything. Nothing mattered but love. Getting rid of possessions was a process because the council bin is not huge. I would fill my bin every week. It took a consistent effort of making sure it's full. It also took a few attempts to get rid of some beloved pieces of clothing and shoes. I'm a big basketball fan and had quite a few pairs of Air Jordan shoes that I sold. Many of my friends were like, "What da fuck is wrong with you?" I knew they were not serving me in any way. I never wore them, they were just clogging up my cupboard. I sold two pairs for $540 and bought myself a new controller to make music with. This money was tied up in these shoes doing nothing and I converted into something I use almost daily now.

My house needed new gutters so I got that organised. I choose a new colour for the gutters which meant I had to paint the roller door and the underneath part of the gutters all the way around the house. This was a big job. All the time I'm working on the house hoping she'd come back. All during this time I'm thinking of her and why is she calling me?

What does she want? Does she like me? Does she want to get back together? My heart had a big wall around it at this point. It didn't feel safe to open up to her again. I didn't want the pain of being broken again. I wanted the amazing feelings of being in love again. Getting the cracks in the house fixed was something I thought I could do on my own.

I watched a few YouTube videos on how to do it. Three of them said 3 different things. I thought I could do it. Once I started, I realised it was going to take a lot more time than I was prepared to put into sanding and puttying. I was talking about my house with my friend at the organic food shop that I shop at. A lady was in there listening and she says my husband fixes roofs and walls, here's his number. I was like "Is he a good dude?" she says "Yeah, I married him" lol. I called him up and he came around to look and quoted me an affordable price and I said yep let's do it. The universe came to my rescue. It put the answer right in front of me and I acted on it. Trust the universe. I also knew a guy that used to go to the gym I worked at who worked in a paint shop. I hadn't seen him for ages, I call him up out of the blue. He says it's his last day at work tomorrow. I called him at exactly the right time. I bought the paint through him and saved about $250. Again trusting in the universe.

With my love interest, we continued to have really open discussions on the phone most nights. I wanted to get back with her. I wanted her to be into me again like before but from our phone conversations I realised that wasn't going to happen. Our relationship had morphed into this grey relationship of being really close and attached to each other, but not officially together and with no clear boundaries. This created a lot of pain and jealousy. The way she acted was like she wanted to be with me, but then she didn't want to be with me. She didn't want anyone else to have me.

I thought I could keep my heart guarded and play this game, but I couldn't. I'm someone who shows and feels my emotions. My heart opened back up to her but I didn't feel emotionally safe. This would again play on my mind daily. My mood was up and down. This love game was affecting me again. When her lease was up, I helped her move into her new house. Instead of living 5-10 mins away she was moving 30-35 minutes away. I knew this would change the relationship again. I was prepared to make the drive but I wasn't convinced that she was. Also, her birthday was coming up. She said for me to not get her anything.

I said, of course, I'm going to get you something. On the night of her birthday, she came around and I cooked her dinner and gave her some gifts, but all throughout the night the vibe was off. I could tell she wasn't fully present. I could sense something was off. This really got my mind going and again I didn't feel emotionally safe. All I could do was continue to write in my diary and try to keep the relationship with myself strong. I could sense she was going to end us again. She had been acting kind of distant that week. Later that night she tells me she wants to be "Just friends" again.

My feelings were crushed. I was sad and emotionally unstable. I didn't know what "Just friends" meant. I felt like she just used me. Used me to help her move. Used me to get some birthday love. I really felt like she didn't care about me at all. I was angry, I was upset, I was grieving, but I had to heal. And again it wasn't all about me. She had her own issues going on and felt it was the right thing to do for her life. I felt kind of relieved because at least we had some boundaries to our relationship now. I had great confidence I could heal again.

I went through all the same strategies to heal. I kept up the journal writing. Getting my thoughts down. I know I give good advice to others and myself, and I made sure I had conversations with myself. I was also very aware of what media I was exposing myself to. Input equals output.

What this means is, if you're exposing yourself to violence, killing and hatred in your entertainment and news then it's going to negatively affect your subconscious mind and how you feel. I would play Tony Robbins, Zig Ziglar, Stephen Covey, Brian Tracey and Wayne Dyer tapes in my car and in my headphones when I went walking on the beach to fill my mind with positive stuff. This really helped me too. Input equals output, so I made sure I "hung out" with some of them each day.

One of the things I heard was from Wayne Dyer. He said, *"Be attached no-where."* And this is a great one *"I am diluting myself into a belief that if I can't have or can't do this or that thing then somehow I will become immobilized."* This helped affirm that my happiness is not dependent on her and her opinion of me. For me to be happy, I am in charge of that. I have to fill my life with things I enjoy. I also heard him say this *"I am not really attached to you at all. I am merely diluting myself into the belief that without you I will not be happy. I leave you free to be yourself, to think your thoughts, indulge your tastes, follow your inclinations and behave in ways that you decide are to your liking."*

Quotes like these really affirm that you are in charge of the meaning that you give to things and you are in charge of your own happiness. You don't own anyone.

I listened to Tony Robbins and he was talking about selecting the right partner for you. He said to ask yourself these questions. "Can they do the job of being your partner?" and second, "Will they do the job of being your partner?" "And will they do the job long term." And when I asked these questions, I thought she can do it. But will she? No. She didn't do it before, she wasn't going to do it later. I needed to focus on moving on and getting myself back to my positive self again. We continued to talk on the phone after that and even then it was like we were together but not together.

Still a small part of me was hoping that it was going to workout between us. A large part of me was like it's never going to work. You can't change people. She still had her own issues to sort through. Recapturing the magic wasn't going to happen. My self-esteem was up and down with the greyness of our relationship. I continued to write positive affirmations in my diary. I would write stuff on how I wanted to be. I would write *"Be loving, be forgiving, be caring, be open to love, choose happiness, I am worthy, I am enough and I am loved."* Stuff like that, over and over so it gets ingrained in my subconscious. Love taken away leaves the pain behind. It leaves a hole in you emotionally.

I was very conscious of filling myself up with forgiveness to myself for ignoring my needs and also forgiving her. She was doing the best she could with the knowledge she had at the time. It's very easy to fill yourself up with anger and resentment when going through these moments. But doing that is like drinking poison yourself and hoping your enemy will die from it. I kept affirming that I forgive her and I forgive myself. I had faith in the universe that all the pain that I went through was driving me to the next level in my life. The journey is the reward.

I used that love/pain to fix up my house. It is now painted inside and outside, all the cracks are fixed. It's probably in the best shape it's been in since I bought it and I'm now in a position to think about getting a housemate in to help with the mortgage. This would've never happened if I didn't fall in love. I'm a minimalist now. I don't buy anything I don't need and I really look at giving things away now. I prefer empty space in my house than the crap I don't even use.

I had a bunch of old records that could be worth something. I sold heaps of them and I had this Bon Jovi record I could've sold for a little bit of money. I just gave it away to someone who really wanted it. I got 2 free movie tickets and I gave them away to someone I just met, just to make their day brighter. I would rather spend my free time alone at the beach anyway than be in the movies.

She ended up taking her friend for her birthday. My attitude now gives stuff away and more comes toward you, then I give that away too. My relationship with self-became really strong again through my diary entries. I would write things in my diary like *"This may be your last day on earth. Make the most of it. Live in emotions you choose."* This would help get me out of thinking about all the good and bad times with her and wanting her back. I would write, *"The future is not guaranteed. The past cannot be changed, all you have is this moment right now."* And I would do my best to embrace that thinking. I would also write, *"The opportunities you get today, may not be here tomorrow, and may not be here next week or next year. You have to live right now."*

All this stuff helped me. That's not to say I was completely healed of the emotional grief and the broken heart. That still takes time. I would visualise my heart and get a picture of what kind of health it was in and would visualise little versions of myself with their tools working on healing it.

I've had a lot of conversations with people about their relationships and some people tell me they can't cry, or their heart has a big wall around it and they don't let people in. Or they distract themselves from feeling their feelings. I made sure I dealt with them. If I needed to sit in silence and write I did that. If I needed to go to the beach on my own I did that. If I needed to cry I did that. If I needed to talk to a listening ear I did that. I'm not afraid to be vulnerable and ask for support when I need it. It's a sign of strength.

I would actually search out people who looked like they were struggling more than me and help them. A lot of people can end up with depression, and filled with hate and resentment. I made a conscious effort to fill myself up with love and forgiveness. My attitude is to fill myself up with so much love that it flows over to everyone whose life touches mine. A great lesson is to turn a negative into a positive. Your relationship with yourself is the most important and longest relationship you will ever have. Nourish it. Develop it. Make it one of deep love every day. This is done through journal writing, taking silent time with yourself. Doing loving things for yourself such as exercising, feeding it the best organic food, avoiding putting chemicals in it, being creative, spending time doing the things you love, taking yourself on dates. I even started meditating, which is another positive to come from my broken heart. What would you do for the person you love? Most people say anything. This is the attitude to have towards you. I learnt that you feel you're best when you are giving yourself time to express your creativity, when you're giving to people and when you're growing as a person. It's important to look for opportunities to do that. Give yourself time to be creative and paint and write and make music. You'll be surprised what magic you have inside of you that comes out.

Lessons

1. Control what you can control.

2. The more you try to control, the more stressed you'll be.

3. Be unattached.

4. Turn a negative into a positive.

5. Write in your journal, thoughts, feelings, what happened, why, coach yourself, be the parent.

6. Affirmations.

7. Be wary of what you are exposing yourself to.

8. Communicate with friends.

9. Be vulnerable, feel and process the feelings. Unprocessed feelings can lead to cancer and other diseases.

10. Have a good cry, get it out of you.

11. Visualisations, you tend to visualise the good times, if you know a person or situation is bad for you, visualise you moving away from them.

12. Ask yourself quality questions, "What else could this mean?"

13. Trust in the universe, trust you're moving towards something better, the next lot of lessons.

14. What lessons must be learned from this situation?

15. Relationship with self, you deserve your love and attention more than anyone.

16. Don't make emotional decisions.

17. When you're happy with yourself, everything is good.

18. Spend time being quiet, meditating, embrace silence.

19. Fill yourself with love and forgiveness.

20. Life is lived between your ears. Control what meaning you give things.

21. Be grateful for all the good in your life, things could be a lot worse.

22. I would rather sit in silence and heal than distract with TV.

23. Get rid of material possessions, be unattached, what really matters?

24. Self-assess your happiness, ask people to tell you honestly if you look happy.

Chapter 13

Life Is Beautiful

By Valeria Astorga

Humble Beginnings

I was born in Chile to an average, middle-class, working family. My parents met in Antofagasta, the largest town in the region and in 1958 both had moved to the capital Santiago. They lived on a shoestring budget as young university students away from home. As it happened, my mother became pregnant with my oldest sister, an event that precipitated an unforeseen wedding. In her state my mother abandoned her architecture degree and married my father, becoming a full-time mother. As the bills and the family started to grow, my father, still an undergraduate engineer, found employment with a mining company located in the fringes of the Atacama Desert.

As a junior engineer, my dad's salary was enough to feed us all. Meals at home were simple, fresh meals cooked from fresh ingredients. We mainly ate fresh food grown locally and bought in the local market or at the street corner shop. Chilean homemade food always had veggies and either rice or potatoes, with once a day a piece of protein, either meat or pulses. We often ate seafood brought from the villages at the nearby coast or deliciously warming and nurturing chicken soups, lentil dishes and especially delicious for us kids, my granny's homemade cakes. My mother remembers that at that age I already lectured her about what was healthy food.

I was a very sensitive child that had bouts of crying for no apparent reason. Whenever that happened, they tried to find out the reason for my mood change but could never fathom what was wrong. I would then cry endlessly until I fell asleep, with my mother or my Gran by my side.

I have always wondered if these were early signs that my mood was affected by some foods or other environmental factors.

All Hell breaks loose in my world

I was seven years old when we moved back to the capital Santiago. It was the year 1970 and the first socialist president had been democratically elected in Chile. It was a very exciting time in the country, full of possibilities and enthusiasm. President Allende was my family's hero, we admired and loved his gentle and kind nature, his vision and dream of a just and fair country for all Chileans. My father, a socialist, had completed his degree and was a young mining engineer by then. In 1970, he was offered a management position in one of the recently nationalised large copper mines, one hour South of Santiago, due to an unexpected shortage of mining professionals. A void created when US mining corporations withdrew their staff after the copper nationalization. My mother found a job at a government legal firm and with the new income my parents bought our first home.

All seemed great in our life until all hell broke loose in the family and around us. My parents separated in the midst of great political turmoil. The right wing political factions in Chile were creating fear, chaos, food and petrol shortages, repeatedly undermining Allende's Socialist government. The country became very unstable, the food was rationalized; to get powdered milk, bread, pasta, canned meat, oil and sugar we had to queue for hours at a time. Veggies became like gold, and meat or fish were only available occasionally.

Life wasn't so secure anymore and uncertainty became part of our routine. On 11th September 1973, my sister, brother and I boarded our school bus as we did every day. When we arrived at school there was a state emergency with chaos and fear being palpable. We were told that that school was closed for the day, a military coup was happening and we had to go home. My mother came from work to collect us from school and we went back home.

I remember only the feeling of shock, confusion and fear. We listened to the radio for news and soon after 9 am, heard Allende's "Last Words to the Nation", his last discourse before being killed defending the Government's Moneda Palace. I can still hear his last words coming from the radio and to this day I remember that moment with an immense sadness. The days after the coup we slept at home on mattresses on the floor, just in case, a stray bullet hit our windows. There was a curfew and at night we could hear gunshots, horse's hooves and hurried footsteps on the street outside.

Our life stopped, the city stopped moving and breathing, workplaces and shops were shut. I remember hushed voices when my parent's friends came hurriedly to drop some food for us. In the turmoil, my father went missing from the mine and we didn't know what had become of him. *Around* the end of September, when things had calmed down a little, I was sitting on top of the fence in our garden, looking into the street.

At some point, I saw a bearded man approach me from the right and he was smiling at me. At first I felt fear and surprise, then it dawn on me that I knew that face. My heart skipped a beat and I shouted *"Daddy!"* My dad smiled openly and said *"my little daughter!"* I jumped on him from the fence and he carried me into the house. I couldn't let go of him, I was mad with joy! My father told us that he had left the mine fearing for his life on the day of the coup, heading to the Andes Mountains. There he walked for days towards Santiago, hiding from the military and the police until he had finally arrived back home. That day is one of the two most joyful, happy memories of my life. Only days later I lost my father again. My dad handed himself to the authorities following my grandfather's advice, believing that nothing would happen to him.

Much to my grandfather's shame, shock and sadness, my father was imprisoned for political reasons. Luckily in a jail in a regional city, not in the main Stadium of Santiago, where many political prisoners lost their lives. My father never spoke about his time in prison and we never asked him. Three months later, on Christmas Eve 1973, an army officer appeared at the prison where he was detained with orders to release prisoners.

He gave my father an ultimatum to leave the country within 48 hours, so my grandfather bought a plane ticket for the following day. On the 25th December 1973, my mum and his three kids (aged 13, 10 and 7) went to the airport to see my father fly into exile. Thus, I lost my father for the third time. The next two years are a haze of my memory.

My mother lost her job after the coup and was banned from finding another job afterwards, so she rented our house in Santiago and we relocated to live in a granny flat in northern Chile. Sometimes in this hazy period, my 7-year-old little brother was sent flying unaccompanied to Finland, where my dad was living in exile. So he disappeared too, from our life.

Moving with Change

Early in 1975, my mother decided to migrate elsewhere to look for better opportunities and a job, for a life free of fear. By the month of August, my mother, my sister and I had landed in hot, exotic and strange Morocco where my mother's boyfriend had taken exile. As a young 12-year-old female, Morocco was an interesting experience. My girlfriends at school were getting ready for arranged marriages when I wasn't even thinking about boyfriends. Even though sometimes I felt lonely and set apart from others, I felt better than in Chile, there was the world to discover and that kept my mind busy. I loved going with my mother to the Kasbah market, full of people, smells and colourful goods.

One of my persistent memories is the image of our dining table fruit bowl. The bowl was around 70cm in diameter, a woven dish we had in the centre of the table, topped to the brim with mandarins and other fruits of the season. Most of my memories of that time are of a happy nature, with much curiosity for the culture of the country. Our quality of life improved and so did our food quality. Meals were prepared most days of the week by Fatima, a young Moroccan woman that worked at home which I remember with much affection. She cooked wonderful fresh meals with Moroccan tastes like couscous, tagine and lamb stews, all delicious and with plenty of veggies. My health improved significantly at the time. I have no memories of sadness or moodiness, in spite of feeling bloated many days and experiencing my first period. I thought having a bloated and sore tummy was normal for some teenage girls. Even though I never felt physically comfortable and I hated having a bloated tummy.

Being a skinny teen, I never questioned why this was happening to me. Even my mother, who called me *"aguatona"* (large tummy) as a loving nickname, didn't question these symptoms. In 1977 my mother, my sister and myself moved to Spain, after an unfortunate incident that led to the end of my mother's relationship with her boyfriend. The way it ended meant abandoning the house in haste and never returning to gather our belongings. It was as if the exile from Chile had repeated again, at a family level. My mother moved to Menorca as she had landed a temporary job at a seasonal tourism hotel, and my sister and I followed her.

The three months we spent in Menorca were amazing. My mother worked and lived at a beach hotel, whilst my sister aged 16 and myself, aged 14, were boarding in a family house at the nearest village, Ciutadella. Those three months were total freedom for my sister and me. We slept at our hippy friends' houses, ate when we were hungry and mainly lived on *horchata* (a milky drink made of chufas) or *cafe con leche* and *ensaimada* (a heavenly sweet pastry typical of the Island) for breakfast, meatballs in tomato sauce sandwiches for lunch and whatever we could grasp for dinner. We lived care freely and had lots of fun.

The island was stunningly beautiful, very small and with wonderful beaches with azure waters. The community was caring and safe so we were somehow protected and cared for by my mother's friends and our friends. It was a fantastic time for us.

The monster shows its ugly head

When the summer ended, the tourist numbers dwindled and hotels started to close so my mum decided to move to Barcelona, in search of work and stability. This is when my life changed dramatically for the worse. We arrived in Barcelona and here we were, an immigrant Chilean middle-aged mum with two teenage daughters and a very large suitcase with all our belongings. On a 6-month temporary visa and my mother's will to make a life in the city. That time was a struggle for the three of us. Barcelona still had the scars from 40 years of General Franco's dictatorship and the city looked soot-stained, tired and vanquished.

The grey buildings needed repairing with very old streets, centuries old. My mother's savings allowed us three months of breathing space until she found a job openly bluffing her way through the hiring interview. Although she had never seen a phone switch in her life and with two young daughters at home, at the interview she emphatically said, *"Yes, of course, I am an experienced phone switch attendant! Yes, I can work any shifts"*. She got the job and we settled, my mother learning quickly to manage a 4- star hotel phone system.

She worked from 2pm to 10pm with my sister and me going to secondary school, trying to meet friends and learn Catalan, the language spoken in Barcelona. My schooling went from bad to worse and after the second failed attempt to have a boyfriend I went straight into the blackest time of my life. I developed allergies to everything and got sick with hepatitis, a legacy of one of the fleeting boyfriends. Coming back from the hospital and recovering from hepatitis, my first major depressive episode unfolded.

I guess that the entire traumatic experience from the military coup in Chile, losing my father, my country and my friends all compounded and depression showed its ugly head. My diet didn't help a bit, mainly based on wheat, dairy and sugar. With depression, I spent my days and nights in my bedroom, which I had painted black. I also replaced the carpet with a black one and the bed cover with a bright red sheet. I kept the shutters closed, day and night. I lived in the dark, unable to face daylight. I felt exhausted, out of contact with everything and in so much pain that my heart felt as if it was physically torn apart. I was full of incredible emotional pain and I only wanted to sleep to avoid feeling, being aware of my emotions. As soon as I was awake, I felt that I didn't want to be there, nowhere. I was drained and I had no energy to live anymore. Sleeping was the only way to protect me from thinking the blackest thoughts. This state of mind and body lasted for a period that seemed like a very long time.

Several months later, I slowly came out of the pain to just feel numb. At the time, neither my mum nor I really identified that I was clinically depressed or wondered what the cause might be. We didn't think about getting help, we couldn't afford any expenses not covered by the public health system. We didn't even think to ask the doctor if there was any access to a psychologist or psychiatrist. Mental health wasn't a word or subject that anyone spoke about. The common belief in Spain at the time, I am talking about 1979, was that if you needed a psychologist you were mad and no one admitted the need for one. It was shameful. Neither my mother nor I knew that depression could have a physical cause and we didn't even think I had depression. We thought it was all emotional and that it was part of life. There was nothing you could do but live with it, except suffer and keep going. So I dragged myself around, trying to live life and wondering why me. Many years later I discovered how wrong I was by having these assumptions unchallenged. In my forties, twenty years later, I discovered with regret that I could have done much better if only I had known what I know today about depression, nutrition and mental health.

There is always a cause

My mother has always been one of my best friends. I told her almost everything, we laughed and cried together, we fought sometimes, not that often. I always asked her opinion on what to do when I had a problem. At the time of that first depressive episode, she was desperate with worry, especially because she didn't know how to help me. So we had a serious talk about my situation and how I felt and decided that it was better for me to go back to Chile. In 1980, aged 17, I flew back to Santiago to live with my grandmother and auntie. My auntie had separated and had very limited income, in Chile there aren't universal benefits for anyone.

When I realised their situation and not wanting to be a burden to my Gran and auntie I accepted my grandfather's invitation to live with his family. His situation was totally reversed. My Grandfather, his wife and two children lived in a beautiful neighbourhood in a wealthy area of Santiago. My grandad had successfully developed mining businesses on a small scale and was quite well off. When I moved in my grandad was very happy. They provided me with my own bedroom and enrolled me in a special secondary school for troubled teens where I was to study all the secondary school subjects condensed in one year. The class was full of nerds and mischievous kids and I made friends with both types. I loved being with my nerdy and intellectual friends and I would go to parties with the mischievous lot.

All in all, I had the best of both worlds and lots of fun. My studies went well, I felt happier even though my health wasn't great. I still had hives permanently which I managed by learning not to scratch myself or by scratching so badly that it hurt, which at least masked the itchiness. I felt bloated with most foods, I didn't know anything about food intolerances. I just assumed it was just my stomach and had to live with it.

After a while I moved to live with one of my intellectual artistic friends from school, meanwhile completing my studies successfully so my secondary school was finished. At the time "my" depression had settled into a constant dark grey cloud over my head, some days lifting a bit, other days were worse. The 'black dog' was always around, lurking. I had bouts of depression in an emotional rollercoaster, which I blamed on my hormonal cycles. I believed "we women are like that, right?"

A year and a half later, in January 1982 I went back to Barcelona, to start my Biology degree. I wanted to be a marine biologist and have adventures like Captain Cousteau, a hero of my childhood. During those years I lived with my boyfriend, I went out partying some weekends and studied during the week. I was never addicted to anything except sugar and dairy. Again I had friends at Uni that were nice and nerdy and the weekend friends that were nice but used drugs and drank far too much. So I smoked marihuana and hashish occasionally with the effects of having the silly giggles immediately and anxiety afterwards... My boyfriend had started using heroin and cocaine during his compulsory military service three years earlier.

At the time, his addiction was affecting our relationship. To the point that one morning, after a cocaine-filled partying night and a vicious fight, when we were both coming down off it. I fled the house we shared to never return. Since then I have a strong fear and gut-based aversion to fights, drugs and alcohol. They became synonymous with violence and dependence. The good side of that experience is what I learnt from it. I strongly dislike the fuzzy head I get with alcohol and the exhaustion the following days. Besides the negative effects it can have on relationships.

Equally, I have never touched drugs again, for the same reason. Drugs are not worth destroying my health, sanity and relationships. Much later I discovered that life is so much more beautiful without any of it. There is so much to enjoy, so much beauty even in the simplest of days, so much adventure to have without the need of anything else. Literally I can say that I am high on life and nature's beauty, nothing defeats that wonder.

Three years after that experience, I finished my Biology degree and got married fifteen days later with a young British man. I had met him in Africa whilst visiting my father, who was at the time working for the United Nations Development Program as an economy-mining advisor to the Tanzanian government. My husband was ever so gentle and a quiet man. He was considerate, loving, hardworking, patient, supportive and very nice, nice to live with and plan my life with. His family loved me and I adored them, they were caring and accepting, they put up with my lack of English speaking skills graciously and patiently. Our marriage was a good one, we never had a fight and we were loving and caring to each other. We bought and renovated an apartment in Barcelona, which we sold later to buy a house one hour and a bit away on the Northern coast. When I finished University and whilst looking for a job I was offered a position as a Ph.D. researcher.

I accepted the role, becoming a wetland ecology researcher. All the while, when I was supposed to be happy and ecstatic with all the good things that were happening in my life, my marriage and my Ph.D. But I felt flat, sad and many days unmotivated. Finishing my Ph.D. in Biology was a mammoth effort that took me nine years. Getting up was many days a struggle, I always felt tired and with unclear thinking, with a hazy head. I was still hooked on sugar and bloated most evenings, so I started restricting my diet to avoid it.

During those years, I became aware that not everyone lived with depression. I thought that depression was related to not being well in my head. I went to psychologists and psychiatrists they taught me good tools to manage my life better but didn't help with my feelings of depression. I spent a lot of money on therapies that helped me to accept living with depression.

I learnt that other people also had it and that it was not madness or going crazy. That it happened to some people due to their life history. I accepted depression as a personality trait, something I couldn't change. After eleven years of marriage, I divorced out of sadness, even if nothing much was wrong with my marriage. My husband was still the same caring and gentle man. In a rash decision, I sold my budding gardening business I had started after finishing my Ph.D. and got a job as an environmental auditor.

Nine months later, having met a Chilean man and believing love was the answer to my permanent sadness, I decided to move back to Chile. I was looking for something or someone that would make me happy when nothing did. Marriage, men, studies, career, business, friends, family, nothing made me happy. I thought, *"Maybe if I go back again, I will be happy"*. I just wanted to feel my heart again, to feel it pumping and if not happiness, at least, peace.

There is a joyful life at the end of the tunnel

And then, one day in Chile, a door finally opened. I guess I was ready to learn and ready to change. It was the year 2000. I had moved back to Chile and had found a good job as a researcher. I lived in a nice apartment and had started life in Chile as a single professional woman. My workplace provided for subsidised meals at a canteen close to our headquarters, so I ate there nearly every day. They provided freshly made, wholesome Chilean food, so I ate good, healthy meals. I always loved eating veggies, fish or lean meat, plenty of salads, bread and butter and my weakness, milk based puddings.

I still felt bloated many days, but went to the gym nearly every day and started to get fit. One night some people at work invited me to welcome a German expert that would be working with us. At the dinner, the expert in question was seated at the end of the table and looked aloof and extremely bored, he didn't seem to be enjoying the attention of the people or the food, and he was definitely different. On the following weeks, he usually went to lunch alone, keeping to himself, having a limited knowledge of Spanish. I tried to keep him company, as I knew how lonely one could get when being shy, in a new country and with limited language skills. We started having lunch together, some days, then every day. He was not only an Environmental Engineer but also a Naturopath.

During our lunches and dinners together, he explained about food allergies and celiac disease, about dairy intolerance, about natural energies, about inspired living. We fell in love and spent most of our free time together. He introduced me to Tai Chi and Kung Fu, to climbing and trekking. With him, my exercise time skyrocketed. I started exercising at least 10 hours every week. I practised Tai chi and Qi Kung every day, I went running, cycling and climbing and loved it. Following his advice, I became a "raw foodist". I ate 90% of my food intake raw for almost 2 years. My meals consisted of tonnes of green leaves, including herbs like parsley and coriander, lettuce, spinach, escarole, dandelion leaves, anything green, leafy and edible, wild or cultivated; nuts and seeds, fresh and dried fruit, plenty of it, for breakfast, lunch and dinner. I stopped eating cereals, meat and dairy almost completely. Some weekends we treated ourselves to cooked meals when we went away to the Andes to walk or climb.

The new lifestyle and diet changes had dramatic effects on my health and life. During the initial months, I was bloated constantly. Until I learned what fruits and leafy greens to combine and which to eat on their own. With time, my stomach and bowel started being able to digest all that fibre, flattened and I became regular with my period for the first time in my whole life. I didn't experience bloating and discomfort anymore.

Instead, I was fit, energetic and happy. It was so liberating! My energy skyrocketed and my allergies disappeared. My skin and my hair were lustrous and healthy. My eyes were so bright and shiny that people commented on them. My moods improved so much that depression and anxiety disappeared, for the first time in my life! I could feel stressed, sadness or anger when some things happened, but not the deep consuming "blues". The best of all was my thinking. For the first time in my life, I felt intelligent and a quick thinker. My brain felt as clear as a mountain lake in the morning. It was absolutely exhilarating!

Australia

Fast forward two years, I was living in Australia, on the Gold Coast. Bojan and I had separated after 4 years living together but we were still good friends, even if I was very sad and angry at times. I was hurting, blaming him for my hurt and my anger. My diet suffered, I was eating cooked food and dairy again. I started reacting to some foodstuffs, to foods with colours or preservatives, corn, peanuts, other fatty foods or too many sweet foods.

Those times I would get depressed or anxious, shaky and vulnerable. The feeling was horrible and it was hard to face normal life in those days. It was really weird, one minute I was perfectly okay, balanced and peaceful, the next I'd be having suicidal thoughts. I'd be scared of what I was feeling and thinking. I discovered I was reacting to tiny traces of rancid oils, especially on nuts. Those times I would call Bojan for help and cry my eyes out. He patiently listened to me, calmed me down and coached me.

I started meditating and writing about what was happening in my head. As a result, I realised how dependent on men I had been my whole life, expecting them to make my life better, full, funny, secure and safe. I didn't believe I could do that alone. Bojan said that I needed to spend time on my own, to wait until I was better to start dating again.

It was important that I have a loving relationship with myself before engaging in another one. I listened and followed his advice. At the time, I had moved from my job as a sciences tutor with a correspondence school to work at a holistic health clinic owned by Bojan and Dr. Price. I started as an assistant to reception and admin and escalated my way up the ladder. Simply by way of taking responsibility for whatever wasn't being done.

I studied nutrition, completed my master practitioner training in Neurolinguistic Programming (NLP). I started meditating and spent much of my free time alone. I would read personal development books, listening to personal development audios and writing. Gradually I started to feel better and I improved my diet, incorporating plenty of raw foods again, lean protein and nutritional supplements, especially amino acids and vitamins. I was exercising at least 7 hours per week and started dating, gently, with no pressure. Three years after landing in Australia I was feeling pretty satisfied and contented with my life. Even though I still had bouts of tiredness and sadness, generally after eating foods, hidden in apparently harmless meals, like a commercial salad dressing added to restaurant meals.

One day I was at the beach with another NLP coaching graduate. We were testing techniques for coaching and talking about depression, what it was, why it happened. Trying to explain what the experience of depression meant for me. I had an amazing thought that really surprised me, a wow moment. She asked me: "What would happen if you were not depressed (when you are)?" I immediately blurted out: "Well, I wouldn't be able to hide from my problems! I would have to see whatever is that I don't want to see, I wouldn't be able to hide my head in the sand!" I realised then that I had been using depression all my life to hide from emotions.

When the emotions I was feeling were too much to me, when I couldn't solve whatever was creating those emotions. I was without solutions or resources to face those problems. It mostly related to feeling angry or utterly frustrated and without choices. Unable to change what was happening, it was easier for me to go into depression than challenge myself to go beyond the emotion and learn or do whatever I needed to learn or do to solve my problems. I mean, it was easier because I didn't know any other way. When I discovered my disempowerment, I was shocked! Every time I had to face a difficult decision in my life I went into depression. I was using being depressed as a strategy to avoid feeling helplessness, which was very painful and I didn't have an alternative behaviour. After this realisation, I became aware that I used depression as a strategy to confront life or rather to avoid life. Just like the matador waves the cape, turns around and proudly ignores the bull.

The only difference is that in my case, the bull always ran me over. I realized that I also used depression to avoid making decisions or have an opinion that could contradict someone whom I loved. I was terrified of conflict and I was terrified of voicing my choices, for fear of rejection and for fear of hurting my loved ones. Instead, I was hurting myself. After that experience I put into practice to ask myself "What is depression solving now?" or "What is depression covering up that I don't want to see or I don't feel empowered to face?" whenever I felt the blues. I started using those moments to dig into my emotions and have honest conversations with myself. I started listening to my thoughts and acknowledging what I was feeling. I knew the depressive feelings were due to a reaction to a food colouring or food preservative or rancid oil or a blood sugar imbalance. I spied on myself, developing awareness of the moments when I felt depressed or anxious. I started using these experiences to heal my past and my present relationships, especially with myself. I started being loving, compassionate and understanding of myself.

The hardest part of it was being forgiving and forgiving myself for the decisions I had made with their consequences. In the meantime, I had become the health clinics' Operations, Accounts and Admin Manager. I learned a vast deal about health and natural healing, healthy lifestyle and happiness. I was meditating almost daily, I went to the gym one hour every day, and I went running and swimming 3-4 hours every weekend.

I bought organic fresh food, I ate and drank only healthy food. That's when I had an epiphany. I walked to my balcony overlooking a majestic fig tree and I stretched looking into the sun. Out of nowhere, a huge surge of happiness, of tingling bliss, of ecstasy took over me. It was like a wave from my feet up to my head and arms, it filled my chest and my heart. It was so pure, so blissful, pure ecstasy! I will always remember it, how delicious the feeling was, I was in heaven, truly. It was mine, it was me, I was happy, truly, truly happy. Finally, I knew what real happiness was, true joy!!

From that day on I know that ecstasy, natural joyful bliss is possible and it is possible for everyone. Nowadays I still have to exercise, have awareness and remember that I am well trained to do "depression".

Sometimes I realise that I am heading that way when I am tired and irritable when I am having negative and angry thoughts about everyone and everything. I stop and look at what I am eating, how I am sleeping, what lifestyle I'm creating? I ask myself questions: "*Am I hiding from confronting a relationship issue? Who or what I am angry with? Am I eating healthy food or becoming complacent and "standard"? Am I sleeping well enough? Am I stressed? Am I exercising enough? Too much?"* These questions help me to manage my emotional state. I always check what I am eating, that's my first item on the list. Sometimes it is just like *"Oh! I had too many nuts."* Or I realise I have been eating too many carbs or yogurt again, or too little protein and fats and my blood sugar is becoming unstable. I correct the imbalances and I feel peaceful and centred again.

Recently I had a battery of medical tests done on me. The holistic medical doctor found that I am celiac (gluten intolerant), which probably explains why I developed an autoimmune thyroid disorder leading to my thyroid being almost totally removed. I don't take thyroid medication, except for iodine and nutritional supplements now and then to maintain my TSH, T3 and T4 within normal levels. I have also learnt that my cravings for sweets are a symptom of serotonin deficiency. Known as the happiness molecules and that I need a high protein diet to provide enough building blocks for those molecules. Nowadays I avoid gluten and most dairy products and I eat generally healthy foods. My genetic make-up, including celiac disease and dairy intolerance and their consequences on my thyroid and immune system, could have contributed to me doing depression when I was a child and especially in my teens.

If my mother and I had known my life might have been a very different. Still, this is my life and the things I have learned have led me where I am now. Depression has been a learning path and still is a useful albeit painful tool. Now I am a nutritionist and I tell my story to whoever is ready to listen. I can't let other women live lives half-lived and not tell them what I know.

They can also be happy, they can be their happiest and most fulfilled selves. I know that depression can be at least well managed and that *happiness is possible.* It starts with eating delicious, healthy food, taking care of one's health and loving oneself with understanding and compassion.

Chapter 14

To Make a Difference...You Must Be Different

By Anthony Peluso

I remember as an 8-year-old kid, whilst at a birthday party, I came across one of the most bizarre pictures I had ever seen. I picked up an album cover (remember them) of a rock band that was playing through the speakers at the time. I saw four faces painted in white Kabuki makeup staring back at me and I thought to myself "WOW" what is this? From that moment, I knew that I wanted to stand out from the crowd and be different.

My journey isn't one of the rags to riches, where I came from a poor family with no money and struggled to get ahead. Growing up as a kid was actually a very cool experience and one I look back on quite fondly. My father and mother emigrated from Naples, Italy in the sixties and came over to Australia like so many others at the time ... to find a better life. They settled in Melbourne, Australia and were married in 1969. I was born one year later. I was the eldest of three sons growing up in the seventies and eighties. Most of my spare time was spent outside playing football and cricket whenever I had the chance. There were no computers or addictive technology. All of our social media was done outdoors, face to face with people.

My journey was more about wanting to rise above average and mediocrity, and wanting to be somebody that makes a real difference in the world. I wanted to stand out. I wanted to be different. I wanted all the attention I could get. Society does a great job of promoting "average" and "mediocrity" and playing small. It conditions us to believe that this is enough and it has cleverly created a "system" that the majority of us buy into, without even knowing it.

Both my parents worked hard and paid off their home in what is considered, even by today's standards as record time. Like most people that grew up in that generation, debt was a bad word and not something that sat comfortably with my parents. My father and mother worked real hard to provide for my two brothers and me. My father would leave for work each morning by 7am in the dark and get back around 6pm in the dark. He would work 6 days a week, getting home around lunchtime on a Saturday.

He ran his own engineering business, producing industrial fans and shipping them all over the country and overseas. He did very well out of this and went on to be very successful, even winning the prestigious Ethnic Business Award in 1996, the then Prime Minister of Australia John Howard presented him with this honour. Now retired for almost 18 years, he continues to reap the rewards of that hard work and investment. My mother was a machine operator for clothing manufacturing giant Hole-Proof and basically worked similar hours to my father except for Saturdays.

For a large portion of my childhood, my grandmother raised my brothers and me, which was very common for families in those days where both parents worked. Try getting a traditional Italian family to put their kids in childcare back in those days. Forget about it!

If there was one thing that both my parents taught me growing up, it was a strong and relentless work ethic. Whilst hard work alone does not guarantee one's success, without it, it's near impossible. Both my parents sacrificed so much so that we could have the life that we had growing up. Whilst I didn't understand or appreciate it back then, I certainly do now.

There was a downside to all of this, though. Because my parents worked a lot, there wasn't much bonding growing up - you know, that father-son stuff. We never went camping, we hardly went on holidays, fishing

... nope, none of that either. Other than watching my beloved Bombers (Essendon Football Club) play whenever Dad managed to get home before midday on a Saturday, and watching the Aussies play the Boxing Day Test and one-day games, we never strayed too far from the family home. We spent a lot of time visiting relatives and friends and also hosting them at our place. I didn't care too much, to be quite honest, about things like camping, fishing, as that kind of stuff never really interested me. I'd be bored after 15 minutes. I would be lying however if I didn't wish that my parents spent more time with us kids growing up.

Nevertheless, I knew both my parents were there for me and I couldn't be happier about being their son. As a father myself now to three beautiful and amazing girls, my wife and I make it a priority to make sure that we play a big part in their lives and provide them with a great support infrastructure and foundation. A child will never have a more influential teacher in their life than their parents. I also know that as a father, I will be the blueprint that every other man will be measured against, as my girls get older.

I had an absolute blast both in primary and high school excelling in sports (mostly football and cricket) and arts. Academically I always did well but began to see that much of what was taught in school would have very little use in the real world. Frankly, I could write an entire book on this subject alone and most likely will. Imagine a school where you could learn sales, communication skills, financial literacy, investing, marketing, business success and other entrepreneurial activities. It's not surprising to hear that a majority of the successful people in the world left school at a young age to go on and learn, funny enough, what they didn't learn in school. Our education system needs a complete overhaul if more of our kids are going to have any chance of success in the real world when they leave school.

Doing six years in high school and then another 3-5 years in college or university to learn very little about how the real world works is only going to perpetuate the current employment, economic and funding challenges most governments and countries around the world face today. Our current education system will not create the leaders and industry captains that our society so desperately needs more of. The survival and expansion of our societies, countries and global well-being sadly lie on the shoulders of too few men and women. The social aspect of high school, however, was awesome.

Away from school, we spent most of our weekends going to see bands, in discos, and the regular Saturday night party at someone's house. There were no drugs in school, very little fighting and other than the occasional racial digs copied and given to almost everyone, it was all pretty harmless stuff. I also liked the structure and discipline that went along with high school, even though at times I found this to be a real pain in the backside. Box Hill High School was an all boy's school so there was very little trouble that we could get into ... until Year 11, which is when girls first came to the school.

After I left high school I went to work for a company called Telecom (Telstra). I went for a job interview in the summer of 88/89, which consisted mostly of questions around what football team do I barrack for and how well I could handle a phone call. Nothing at all about my previous results or performance at school. I started as a Customer Service Representative three weeks later. I saw this job as nothing more than a stepping stone to bigger and better things and it wasn't too long before I started to work my way up the corporate ladder. Working for many years in a customer service role taught me a lot about what not to do when dealing with clients.

I was really surprised by how little care was given by some staff when handling a client enquiry back then. Most people were more interested in going to lunch or talking to each other about the weekend or what was on TV than making the client a priority. With a company the size of Telstra, you could imagine that I heard every single type of customer complaint and service issue possible. I took this on as a personal challenge and really enjoyed turning around a client's perception and creating an amazing experience for them each time they dealt with me. I did whatever it took to get the job done and always followed up with the client days and weeks afterwards. Some of the clients started sending me gifts of appreciation and would choose to only deal with me when they called in again. This is when I first began to understand The Law of Reciprocity that states, whatever it is that you send out, must come back.

The disappointing thing is that most customer service issues that arose could have easily been avoided if a little bit more care had been taken with hiring the right people and having these people take a more proactive approach to clients. This is easier said than done in a company this size, as the culture must start from the top and be driven all the way down. As the famous author, Ken Blanchard said: *"Profit is the applause you get for taking care of your customers and creating a motivating environment for your people"*.

Within a few years, I had worked in most of the business units within Telstra and built an extensive network of contacts and resources throughout the organisation. The last position I held in the company was that of an Account Executive in the Business and Government division, in Large Corporate Sales. I was responsible for growing the revenue within my patch and was given everything I needed in order to do so. I really thrived in this role and was first in each morning and last to leave each day. Working to a clock was just not even a consideration. I went in and was able to improve the bottom line of both my clients and my company through strategic and consultative selling.

I consistently smashed the quotas given to me each year and built a reputation within the organisation as one of the most successful Account Executives. I built amazing relationships with my clients, some that I still have to this day and many of these clients are now loyal Telstra advocates based on the groundwork my team and I put in all those years ago. This is also when I started to discover the art of selling and closing. There is no greater skill that human beings can possess than knowing how to sell and how to do it well.

I am always encouraging high school student looking at forging out their career path, as well as industry groups, staff members and my own family to master the art of selling. It is the one skill that is always in demand and very difficult to outsource overseas. Learn how to sell, and there is no ceiling on how much you can earn or where you can go. I could talk about this topic forever and have travelled the world and studied with the best when it comes to the art of selling. Sadly, it's a topic that is greatly misunderstood by both the seller and the buyer and one of the reasons why there is still too few great salespeople in the world.

It was in the summer of 2003 that my entire world changed. That Christmas I had gone into a bookstore with my wife and came across this book that I had heard so much about. To say that I was curious about the way this book was changing lives was an understatement. I figured I'd buy myself an early Christmas present and take this book with me on the holiday up in Noosa that we had planned in a few weeks' time. It was February 2003 and I remember sitting on the beach in Noosa with my beautiful two-year-old daughter Ava. There I was looking out into the ocean pondering the meaning of life. It was the first time I had taken a holiday in quite some time and the first opportunity I had to get off the treadmill of the corporate world. I remember so vividly looking into Ava's eyes as she lay on a beach blanket next to me.

I said to myself, one day, my daughter is going to look me in the eye and say, daddy, "What did you do with your life?" At that moment, I froze, as I couldn't think of how I would answer her. I thought to myself, is this all there is to live? Working 60 hours a week, 12 months a year for the next 30 years for a telephone company? Is this how I want to be remembered? Is this the mark I want to leave in life? Is this what I want to tell my daughter when she gets older? I knew in that very moment that I was destined for so much more. There was a bigger game in life that I had to play … a bigger game that was calling out to me. It was at that moment that I pulled out "Rich Dad, Poor Dad," the book I had purchased a few weeks ago. I read this book like a madman. I couldn't put it down. It was like being opened up to the world that I didn't know existed. I buried myself in this book the entire time I was up in Noosa.

I made the worst holiday companion you could imagine. I couldn't believe what I was reading. I read this book back to front on more than one occasion and had mind blowing cognitions as I turned each page. I started sharing it with my wife, I started calling my friends and family back in Melbourne and raving about this book and the transformation it was having on me. I was literally jumping out of my skin. How could these ideas and principles have been hidden from me all this time? Why hadn't I discovered these sooner? I knew that my life had changed forever. I could feel it. I was not the same person that I was a week ago. My language changed, my realities changed, my belief system had done a complete 180-degree turn. I remember calling up my boss at Telstra whilst I was up in Noosa and giving him my resignation. Talk about impulse. He kind of laughed at me and then asked if I had been smoking crack. For me, however, there was no way I could go back to working for somebody else after having discovered what I did in this book. It was like being in another world, I just couldn't go back.

At that time, I had also become a little disillusioned with the corporate world. I had lost my passion for the role at Telstra. I felt like I had gone as far as I could go in the company. The only way to go was up, and I certainly had no intention of getting caught up in the bureaucracy and political agenda's that were such a big part of Telstra back then. I wasn't interested in a sideways move so the only way was out. After all, I had been there 16 years and had seen and done it all. The challenge was gone. I was in a rut that started affecting my own performance, my clients, my staff, my company and myself. It would not have been fair to anyone if I had stayed. My company and my clients deserved better. I handed in my formal resignation and had it knocked back a number of times by management. I was offered more money to stay, more incentives, a new portfolio and so on. I was flattered by the gesture but knew that it was time to move on. To hand over a portfolio the size of mine was no easy feat. I had some of the biggest corporates in the country.

Businesses that had complex structures and business units that spread out all over the country. I was also in the middle of some very high-level sales negotiations worth millions to Telstra so my transition and handover had to be managed very carefully. It took close to eight months for all this to be completed and in December of that year, after 16 years I finally left. Say what you will about Telstra, and I know it gets its fair share of bad press, but I believe it is one of the best company's in the country to work for. I am eternally grateful for the opportunities it gave me and will forever be in debt to that company. My time there was incredible. After all, it was at Telstra where I met my extraordinary wife, Lisa-Marie.

So with that chapter of my life now closed, where to next? As life would have it, earlier that year a friend of mine had invited me to a seminar workshop up in Sydney. The workshop was on property investing and property development. I had always been intrigued by property and whilst I had a few investment properties, I never had a great understanding of the subject. So I attended this four-day workshop in April that year at the Westin Hotel, Sydney with some friends of mine.

I remember arriving on the first day and seeing two beautiful red Ferrari's parked out the front of the hotel. I thought to myself, this is going to be a great day. As I sat in the audience and listened to these two property developers talk about everything that there is to know about the property it dawned on me just how much money one could make from property developing and property investing. These presenters were making more from one transaction than what most people make over a lifetime. The workshop was purely educational and did nothing but reiterate that I had made the right decision to start my own business. What intrigued me the most though was the deal making, the number of different property and business strategies that one could apply? I was like a kid in a candy store. I had found my new career path, my niche in life. I knew right there and then that I was going to make a difference in the lives of so many. The two property developers had made a difference in my life over the course of this workshop and I couldn't wait to get started.

I studied all the materials again and again, over and over, and it wasn't too long before I had purchased my first renovation project. I had developed such a passion for real estate and spent months putting a great mastermind team of people around me. Ranging from Mortgage Brokers, Tax Experts, Business Coaches, Solicitors, Builders, Conveyances, Property Managers, Real Estate Agents, Valuers, Bankers, Mentors and so much more. Anything I needed was only a phone call away. I still have most of this team with me to this day who have been by my side through all the ups and downs along the way. I'm also proud to say that I chose my team very well as these guys are regarded as some of the best in the country and the absolute experts in their field. A lesson that I teach today to all my clients is the importance of setting up the right team of people around you. Do not underestimate the amount of time and effort it takes to create financial freedom. It's almost impossible to do it on your own and you need experts in the areas where you lack the knowledge and time. You must have a rock-solid foundation to build upon before you start going out into the market and accumulating wealth.

The real life examples I've encountered of this being done incorrectly are too many to count and too costly to mention. In saying all this, my first renovation project was an absolute disaster. I lost just under $67,000 dollars. You see, the thing about having a mastermind team of experts around you is that you need to listen to them and not your ego (wanting to always be right). My transition from employee to employer was not what I had hoped. I found the going very tough to start off with. I now had the responsibility of being the sole income earner for the family whilst my wife was busy at home raising our kids. No base salary, no more guaranteed wage from the corporate world coming in each fortnight. For a while, this tested my character. The lesson I learnt was that going from an employee to employer requires a severe change in mindset and is one of the main reasons so many businesses go under in the first five years. You cannot expect to take an employee mindset into an employer role. After applying some strict policies to ensure that my future property renovation projects would not suffer the same fate as my first project, we were off and running again. Each renovation project we took on made more and more profit.

This was just when all the renovation reality shows were beginning to hit TV. I remember one project we were looking at acquiring in the suburb of Port Melbourne. It had to be seen to be believed. The front door was leaning to the left, as was the entire house. The kitchen had a hole in the roof covered by a garbage bag and the house was riddled with termites. I decided to then sit in my car and watch all of my competition, as they went in through the front door to inspect the house. I gave them two minutes at best before they would come storming out. I was right. Most of these people were riding on the coat tails of these reality shows on TV that was anything but real.

Nobody was prepared to take the chance on this project, as the work required would have tested even the best. Except for us, that is. We could see what others failed to see. Experience had taught me to look where most people do not look (which by the way is always where the big money is). We purchased the property on very attractive terms and within six months had made a profit of $355,000. One of the lessons here is to truly understand the correct estimation of effort it takes to get something done. Most people underestimate the effort required to start a business, to expand a business, and/or to undertake a renovation or development project.

This incorrect estimation can severely ruin one's dreams if left to perpetuate. We developed an amazing renovation system and built a great team around this system to the point where I could fully renovate (mostly cosmetically) any unit/apartment within two weeks. Total overhaul and looking brand new. We renovated houses (usually period style homes, 2-3 bedrooms) including an extension in most cases, in a period of three months. This came about after a lot of testing and measuring trial and error and understanding the correct estimation of effort involved.

The Versace look on a K-Mart budget we call it, and one that continues to be extremely profitable. In addition to renovating houses, we decided to start property developing and securing house and land projects across some of the hottest estates in Melbourne. This was extremely successful and something we continue to incorporate into our business today and also share it with our clients. With a $1,000 holding deposit, we were able to control $320,000 plus worth of real estate. We would settle on the end project value, take out the equity gained and go again on the next project - recycling the same equity over and over again. I must admit that lenders were a little bit more lenient back then. We built this again into a rock solid system, inviting family and friends to get involved and investors to come on board so that we could increase the speed at which we operated. Once we ran out of friends and family members, we set this up to take it to the market and built, what is known today as Wealth For Life Institute. A multi-million dollar business that specializes in helping Australians create financial freedom in simple, safe and secure manner.

Wealth For Life Institute has incorporated education, property acquisition, mortgage brokering, financial planning, property management and so much more, all under the one roof. A complete system, that if followed, works every single time. My greatest joy in life and my absolute purpose is to help others. Nothing gives me greater satisfaction and fulfilment than to know I was able to help another, be it financially, emotionally, spiritually or other. Our clients understand that we go above and beyond anything that they could ever expect or sign up for anywhere else. We treat them like family and give them an experience like no other.

I would always continue to learn and gain knowledge from as many people as possible. I only had one rule, these people had to be doing better than me (at least from a business and financial sense). I always made it a point to surround myself with people much smarter than me so that I could increase my learning's and, as a result, increase my earnings. I became a seminar junkie, attending anything and everything I could get my hands on. I went to business seminars, property seminars, money workshops, marketing and sales boot camps, mindset and personal development events.

I would travel as far as the USA, Singapore, and Thailand and all over Australia in order to be the best I could be. I gave up Saturday nights, going to birthday parties, football games, and some family engagements and basically did whatever it took in order to make it. I was looking to take my game to the next level. I felt like I had hit a plateau and wasn't progressing.

Whilst I was very competent on subjects such as real estate and investing, I hadn't felt that I had quite broken through yet in the area of business, money and mindset. What I learnt very quickly was that without the right mindset, all the rest didn't matter. You will never be a success in any area of life, in any field, unless you have the right mindset. Once you have the right mindset, the rest takes care of itself. You see, in life, how you do anything, is how you do everything.

I literally singled out BRW Millionaires and Billionaires that could help me in the areas I needed improvement on and went after them. I can tell you that these people were some of the nicest people I have ever met, extremely humble, generous with their time and so giving. Most of these people had many things in common, which I took on board, but the one trait that I hadn't expected was that they were all very spiritual. Now, I had no idea what that term even meant back then. All of them talked about their spirituality quite openly and regarded it as the cornerstone of their life and success. This did not resonate with me as I wasn't spiritual and couldn't really connect with any religion. I heard presenters talk about this in seminars, in books and on retreats, but it never made much sense to me.

This began to agitate me as I thought back to my upbringing as a Catholic. Now, whilst I respected all religions and faiths, I couldn't connect with any of these religions on a spiritual level. Maybe there's something wrong with me, I thought? Do I really need to be spiritual to be successful? I knew however that there was something that I didn't know yet and hoped I would soon find out. When it came to success and being the best I can, I was prepared to leave no stone unturned. You see, my biggest challenge in life has been moving from good to great. Good just doesn't cut it. Good is also the greatest enemy of Great, as the amazing author Jim Collins states. It's also where the masses all sit. Always comfortable, just surviving but never thriving. This is the average, middle class that most of the society buy into. You won't make a difference too much, playing at this level. I learnt that to make a difference, you must do differently.

It was a year or so later that I had a business meeting with a very successful friend of mine. At the conclusion of the meeting, my friend closes the door to his office, walks over to me and asks me, "What do you think about Scientology?" I was dumbfounded by the question, which caught me totally off guard. I said, "I have no idea, as I know very little about the subject, so I can't comment one way or the other". He turned to me and said, "Anthony, I think you would love this as I know you'll stop at nothing in your quest for greatness. Are you interested in having a look? I've been studying it for about a year" he said. Sure, I said.

When a dear friend, extremely successful, who has nothing but your best interest at heart and would do anything to help you, recommends something, with no other agenda, you should, at least, look at it was my view. I walked out of the meeting not knowing what to think and surprisingly enough when I mentioned it to my wife that night, she was all for it. That night, however, I refrained myself from doing any type of Internet research, as I didn't want it to cloud my judgment. I do remember however going to bed that night and thinking about something I had read a book recently by Simon Reynolds called "When they Zig you Zag". It simply states that if you want to be successful, look at what most people do, and do the opposite. I thought to myself, if so many people have an issue with Scientology then there must be some good in it as the masses seem to be against it.

I remember my wife and me walking into this place for the first time, thinking it would look like your normal type of church - a chapel, holy water to the right, crosses, etc. Much to my surprise, it reminded me of nothing more than a very big library. Books everywhere, quotes from the founder on the walls and a lot of people smiling. I have never known a place to have so many people smiling. I thought these people must really enjoy what they do here. My wife and I were given a tour of the premises by a lovely lady and were then left to our own. As I'm looking around, I became very curious and interested in what I was reading and observing. I thought, here's a guy that has the same mindset as me and here's a place that I can definitely connect with.

Some of what I was observing, I was already applying in my life and, therefore, could relate to it immediately. Some of it just absolutely floored me. Without any pressure to sign up for a single thing, my wife and I willingly filled out some paperwork, purchased a whole bunch of books and DVD's and after a few hours went home. It was totally different to what I had expected. I was very curious to say the least. I wanted to know more. As we were driving home, my wife and I looked at each other and said, this is it.

This is the missing piece we had been looking for in our lives. It now all made sense. I now finally understood why all other religions I had looked into didn't make any sense to me. Why I couldn't relate or use them in my life. On some level, the universe had something else planned for me. I went on to discover that its founder (Mr. L. Ron Hubbard) a renowned philosopher and science fiction writer, had put together a technology for not only spiritual freedom but business management, education, literacy, arts, music and photography, along with some amazing humanitarian and social betterment programs worldwide.

I had realised that for me, the bridge from good to great was all about mindset. I had finally found a workable system, a body of work that made sense. It turned the ones doing well, into doing even better. I was finally able to control my mind, as opposed to it controlling me. This for me had always been the greatest challenge and my greatest barrier to freedom. It is, by the way, a work in progress. I have never stopped developing myself across all different areas of my life.

Now whilst I know that there is a lot of controversy about this religion, I really couldn't care less. You see, I just refuse to fail in this lifetime. I will look for any advice or information that will make me better. A better father, a better husband, a better brother, friend, son, a better business leader and so on. These are the real riches in life.

Living in denial has no place in my universe. Clearly most of the education systems around the world and most of the advice we get from TV, radio, and newspapers are not good. Also, look at the people you hang around each day. One of the best things I ever did was to lose some people in my life that were bringing my family and me down. I realised that people are either going to lift to you up and support you, or bring you down and look to destroy you. You know the ones I'm talking about, those vampire personalities that suck all your time, energy and resource. They say one thing to your face and another thing behind your back.

They are negative, judgmental, lazy, unethical and extremely suppressive. Don't know who they are? Take a look at how the people you hang out with make you feel after you leave their presence. Do you feel good about yourself or do you feel angry and upset, getting into arguments with the wrong target soon afterwards? In most cases these people are closer to you than you think. It's a tough call, but if you want to attract the right people in your life, you need to get rid of the wrong people, and you know who they are. My life skyrocketed on all levels when I did this. It was the best outcome for everyone.

I have read every great book there is on personal development, business, sales, marketing, finance, money, health, marriage and relationships. My library at home literally has no walls as books hold up the roof from floor to ceiling. In my quest for greatness and overcoming the challenges I faced in life, I was prepared to go to the ends of the earth and study anything I had to in order to succeed.

I sure as hell wasn't going to let a word like "Scientology" and peoples misunderstanding of it, decide my destiny, my results, and my greatness. Now if your reaction to that word (or any word for that matter) puts you off, you may want to look inside of you a little deeper? It is, after all, just a word. Your reaction and judgment will most probably be based on gossip, innuendo, basic misunderstandings and what your family and friends think and may have heard. Let's face it, if you let one word stop you, you'll probably let most things in life stop you. Harsh but that's the brutal truth and my absolute experience. For me, I was just looking for something to take my game to the next level. I knew there was a higher force. I really couldn't care whether it was Scientology, Buddhism, or Christianity ... heck, I would have gone to and studied Willy Wonka's Chocolate Factory if that worked for me.

Quite frankly, I really didn't care what it was called or what anybody else thought. The fact that something works is more important than how it works or where it's from. If one is dying and goes to see a doctor who has the cure, are they going to say, um ... do you have something else? Of course not. You take it, get cured and move on. Sadly, there are people not doing very well in many areas of their lives, but their lack of willingness to confront this and take responsibility for it only prolongs the pain with the outcome being inevitable (i.e. financial struggle, broken marriages, dead-end jobs, bad health, and very little fulfilment in life).

The amount of powerful quality content that I have studied from L. Ron Hubbard, that is both rational and analytical, has helped me to improve my business, my finances, my personal life, my marital life, my kids and so much more. It sometimes blows me away, just how powerful this technology is and the results that come from it. I can't believe it took me so long to discover it. When a rational human being reads the information in a book from Mr. Hubbard, they'll realise there is nothing weird about it.

Some of the most successful businessmen in the word, real power players and opinion leaders on the planet, have been using Scientology for years to bring balance, organisation and expansion into their lives. The point I'm trying to make here is not that you should study some particular technology or religion in order to be successful, but rather to look with your own eyes and not listen to the masses unless you want the results and the life that the masses have. I encourage you to look, not listen. It's just that simple. Find what works for you and use it. Scientology worked for me and it certainly wasn't the only thing that worked for me.

Here's a secret that I am going to share with you that will change your life without a shadow of a doubt. This policy has helped me in ways I cannot even begin to go into. If you ask yourself the following question daily, your life will be unrecognisable in three months' time. Are you ready? The question is "Where can I take greater responsibility?" Before I analyse any situation, be it a transaction, business or property deal, I always ask myself this question and am brutally honest with myself.

I recently negotiated a very large property transaction on behalf of some close friends of mine. By asking myself "where can I take greater responsibility" it enabled me to close up and handle every single potential pitfall and loophole. I had everything covered, no loose ends, and no maybes. I was in complete control of the transaction, and as a result, was cause for the outcome, as opposed to being at effect. It could only have gone my way. Now, this approach requires you to have knowledge in the area you are dealing in, obviously, take an amazing amount of responsibility and be willing to control your actions. I found that this approach is far better than looking back and asking, "Where could I have taken greater responsibility?"

An interesting story happened to my wife and me many years ago when we were just learning about developing a winning mindset. We had come off a very up and down type of day, mostly down. One of those days where you wish you never got out of bed.

We were driving home from a personal development session where we were dealing with a lot of stuff that was coming up for us, emotionally. We were sitting in peak hour traffic on the freeway and all of a sudden … Bang! This car hits us from behind. Excellent, just what we needed to cap off the day. I knew that my wife and I were becoming more aware of having the right mindset and vibrating at the right frequency or energy level when, as soon as we got hit, we looked at each other and said, yep … we created that. Now, most people would say, Anthony, you were not moving, you were sitting still and got rear ended. It's the other guy's fault. Makes perfect sense, right? Here's the thing, there were hundreds of cars backed up in traffic at that moment, why were we the only ones that got hit?

The truth is this. We created and attracted that accident. My experience has taught me that as soon as one is able to take responsibility for everything in their life and confront the areas that they are avoiding, you start creating and attracting the things you do want and desire. That experience taught me that in life, things don't happen to you, they happen because of you.

Be Real, Be Great, Be Everywhere!

Chapter 15

Awakening the Vitality Within

By Caradi Miller

As a young girl growing up in a small farming community in North East Tasmania, my sisters and I were always out saving injured and abandoned animals. Our house was like a mini wildlife park with everything from goldfish, mice, guinea pigs, cows, sheep, possums, chickens, dogs, cats and birds. My parents had a massive vegetable garden in our back yard and I was always in there eating all the peas and carrots. The taste of fresh delicious goodness that ignites every cell in your body is something that once experienced is never forgotten. This was the beginning of my love for all things healthy.

It was my first year of high school and as part of our home economics class, we had to pay a visit to our local butcher shop to learn about where all the different cuts of meat came from and were prepared. Being a small community, our local butcher shop was the real deal. They still used the intestines for the sausage skins and did all things that are now called the "old fashioned way". I loved animals and had grown up caring for them. I nursed them back to health when they were sick or injured.

There was no way that I could continue to eat these beautiful creatures and to see them all cut up did not sit well with me. It was from that day onwards that I made the decision to become vegetarian with the exception of fish, which really made me a piscatorial. I went home from school that night and announced to my family that I was now a vegetarian and no longer ate meat or poultry. For weeks after my big announcement my mum tried everything to encourage me to eat meat before giving in and accepting my decision.

Over the years with my new way of eating I found myself gorging on pasta, bread and huge amounts of dairy especially cheese. I'm Tasmanian and we know how to make cheese. It was so tasty especially the soft cheeses such as Brie and Camembert. It didn't take long before I started putting on weight and growing outwards.

Despite my weight being on the rise my love and passion for personal health, sport and fitness were still there. Following in the footsteps of my father, I went and did a weekend basic massage course where I learnt about bones, muscles and where they were within the body. I even got myself a little job massaging elderly people's feet and their lower legs. Seeing the smiles on their faces when I rocked up to their houses with my little bag of oils and creams made me feel worthy. I loved knowing that I was helping others and giving them something to look forward too.

Shortly after I turned 18 I got myself a one-way ticket from Tasmania to Cairns in far North Queensland. I got a full-time job in one of the big backpacker's hostels as a cleaner. The owners of the hostels also owned some of the local nightclubs. All their staff were given VIP passes with free entry, cheap jugs of cocktails and pots of beer, what more could an 18-year-old want? My nightlife in Cairns just got wilder. I was out partying it up until all hours of the morning. I'd sleep in the cleaning locker at the hostel for a few hours before starting work at 6am. I was too drunk to ride my pushbike up the esplanade to the home I was sharing at the time. I was eating a lot of highly processed foods, toasted croissants with cheese and tomato had become my new favourite morning tea.

I would buy one from the old lady who owned the shop attached to the hotel every morning for "smoko", they tasted so good and were highly addictive. While living in Cairns, I became a member of the local gym and begun working out regularly. I got a trainer to do me up a program.

I would work through these boring tedious weight exercises, which I really didn't enjoy doing, about 3-4 times a week. Even with all this added exercise on top of a physical cleaning job my weight was still creeping up. The job at the hostel was awesome. I even got $20 bungee jumps and free trips out onto the Great Barrier Reef. I went bungee jumping a couple of times. Before you jump they need to take your weight and write it in your hand. That way the guys knew what tension to put on the bungee cord. 76 kilograms was written in my hand both times and I'm really short. At the time I shrugged it off, again telling myself stories about how it was okay to be big.

After 9 months of living the party girl life, I quit my job at the backpacker's hostel and begun travelling. I lived my life out of a backpack for almost 5 years. Following my instincts, exploring the world, eating, drinking and just going with the flow. It was a true sense of freedom. The only thing still hindering my overall freedom was the emotional attachment I had with food. Mostly highly processed, high carbohydrate, and high fat and sugar content foods. All this combined with beer and other sweet alcoholic beverages meant that my weight was still slowly creeping up and my overall health was declining. Not only was I getting fatter I also felt uncomfortable in my clothes, I had bags under my eyes, acne, joint pain and my energy levels had dropped.

In 2002 at the age of 24, I returned back home from being overseas and begun picking apples in an orchard in the South West of Western Australia. It was here that my life started to settle down. I bought a house, met a man who I later married and decided that it was time for me to begin living life as an adult. Living life with responsibilities meant that I no longer went out partying. I stayed home after work and on the weekends cooking and doing household duties. My husband and I both worked and we were both eating large amounts of high processed foods.

Now, not only was I still slowly getting bigger my husband was too. Looking back, I can see that I really was beginning to dislike my life, the life I had created. I began crying often in the shower at night and was wondering what on earth I was doing and asking questions such as "why am I not happy?" I would pull myself up and dust myself off so to speak. I'd make up stories and tell myself that it was okay to be slightly bigger and that it runs in the family.

To help with the depression that was slowly creeping in, I decided to take up Fit-ball classes at the local town hall. I had always exercised and was missing the social interaction of being with other women who were interested in health too. This class was a hoot! It was so much fun bouncing around on this huge round ball for an hour and the ladies in the class were so full of life and super friendly to be around. Fit-ball became my weekly outing.

After about six months of bouncing around on the Fit-ball. I regained some of my fitness back, feeling good about myself again and meeting new friends. I enrolled in an online gym instructor's course. Before I knew it I was a registered Fitness Professional and bouncing around teaching Fit-ball and Aqua Aerobics classes of my very own. There was still only one big thing that I was struggling with. My weight. Despite doing copious amounts of exercise regularly and teaching fitness classes galore. I still struggled to lose any weight. In 2007 I topped an all-time high on the scales, 97 kilograms to be exact.

I began working offshore in the oil and gas industry where your body weight needs to be taken before departing on the helicopter to and from work. Never ever before had my weight in figures been displayed in public for others to see. I felt ashamed and embarrassed as most of the men I worked with weighed less than me. I was just this fat, round unhealthy blob, however this did not stop me gorging myself on all the treats that were available. I was eating an assortment of chocolates, ice creams, indulging in the cheese platters, cooked breakfasts, pancakes and desserts galore. Some mornings I just sat on a box of water in the cool room indulging in 250g blocks of chocolates like it was normal.

On an emotional level, I was feeling very sad, lonely and angry with myself that I had let myself get that bad. This is not who I was, this is not how I was brought up. New Year's Eve 2007, I remember it as plain as day. I sat in my cabin on the ship and just stuffed my face with boxes of assorted chocolates until I felt sick and could no longer eat anymore. It was then that something or that little someone within me "clicked" and said, "Enough is enough".

My life as I knew it was in a bad way, both emotionally and physically, I just knew that something needed to change. I returned back home to my husband New Year's Day 2008 and I began to make a few changes. I wasn't happy with my whole life, I was not far from turning 30 and my marriage was going down the drain. I started exercising out in my home gym and begun to eat more fruit and vegetables again. It wasn't long before I begun to notice differences in my body and I began to feel better.

The more I moved my body the more I felt like exercising and the happier I started to become. I returned to work with a brand new iPod full of music for exercising. Every night after work I did some kind of exercise for an hour. After working offshore for 7 months, I lost a total of 13 kilograms. During this time I had also made up my mind and decided that I needed to leave my husband and begin living the life that I desired to live. Making the decision to leave was one thing but telling him that I could no longer live a lie and that I wanted a divorce was another. I stewed over this for the best part of 6 months. The stress of it all probably, actually most likely, helped with my weight loss.

The feeling of shame, failure and guilt are soul sinking and I struggled to come to terms with those feelings. I brushed them under the carpet, as I needed to be strong for my now ex-husband who was contemplating suicide. I stayed living in the farmhouse that the two of us had bought and continued to renovate it for a few months after our split. I slept on the floor in the spare room in my swag. My drinking had escalated and it became normal for me to drink every night to the point of passing out. While it's not a good thing, I also know that it's not really me and that it was going to be a short-term thing. I organised counselling for my ex-husband as he begun to spiral downhill fast and I felt responsible for his unhappiness. We had counselling together and then separately. Not much came out of it for me, apart from the fact that I was not happy and no longer felt I could stay married to my husband.

My best friend at the time asked me to join her and her parents in Sydney for a big four-day personal development conference in September. With only a month to get myself ready for the event and to help me feel good about the separation, I took myself off on a shopping spree for some new clothes. I shopped up a storm, buying dresses, bras, underwear, tops and jeans. When I was 97 kilograms there was no way that I would go shopping like this, I was so ashamed and embarrassed about my weight. I had been wearing clapped out old bras, jeans that were miles too long and undies that not even your grandma would wear. I felt like a million dollars that day with my sexy new lace matching underwear, jeans that fitted and dresses that looked amazing on.

I was all set to go to Sydney. I was with my best friend at the Sydney Exhibition Centre learning about property development, stocks, and shares and how to manage your mindset. Four days of complete mind blowing information which opened up all new pathways for my future. I signed up to do a property development course with a lady who was about my age and who inspired me to think outside the box. She gave me the tools to see past the negativity and to look at the positives in every situation. In the midst of all these amazing new learning's were my divorce and the sale of two properties.

My ex-husband had basically buried his head in the sand. This meant that I needed to take charge and see that the property was sold and to make sure that our divorce went as smoothly as possible. It was an exhausting few months. The day came when I could no longer stand to be in the house and I'll never forget that day. I packed everything up into boxes that I wanted to take with me. I had a lot of expensive kitchenware that I wanted to keep as it was given to me over the years as presents or I had bought it with birthday money. When it came time to pack up my car it didn't all fit in.

Emotionally I broke down, stumbled to my knees in the red dirt driveway and just howled my eyes out. Lockie my border collie came up to me and kindly licked away the tears. It was from that moment that I decided that all the expensive kitchen stuff in the world would not make me happy. The only thing that could make me happy was to find happiness within myself. I unpacked my car and repacked it. With only my basic personal belongings and Lockie we drove on out never to return.

For the following year after leaving the south-west of Western Australia Lockie and I lived out of my car staying at friends' houses on their couches and spare beds. Lockie stayed on a farm with a good friend of mine while I was at work and life became very nomadic. I was still drinking quite a bit of alcohol, eating lots of dairy and highly processed foods. My weight seemed to have plateaued out to about 82 kilograms. Mid 2009 I returned to Sydney to do a weekend property boot camp, which was apart of the development course I had enrolled in. I made a whole bunch of new friends and I was introduced to a man who worked on ensuring that you had the right mindset. This is critical for taking on such big high -risk property development opportunities. He had the million-dollar mindset club, which I joined. It is to this day that I thank this man for directing my mind away from the past and to focus on the future. His big saying is "Where your focus is today your future is tomorrow" and he is right in so many ways.

At the beginning of 2010, I decided that it was time to start renting out a bedroom in someone's house and get my life in order. I went from one friend's house to another and finally ended up living with a lady whom I had met at the local gym. She was vegetarian and loved animals too. After living with Julie for a few months, we sat outside soaking up some Sunday sunshine when she begun to ask questions about my financial situation. She used to work at the local bank and had been involved in situations involving debt and lenders mortgage insurance. Once I explained to her my divorce situation with the properties that were being sold she assisted me with all the legalities. Despite all the stress of my divorce, life really was great living with Julie. We ate an abundance of fresh salads, vegetables and fruit, exercised regularly and I had pretty much given up drinking.

By the end of the year, my divorce had come through, the farm in W.A. had sold and we were just waiting to sell the property in Queensland. Finally, there was light at the end of the tunnel and I felt like I could breathe again financially and emotionally. The Queensland property sold at a loss just before Christmas of 2010. Despite the loss, which meant that we still had some money owing to the bank. It was still a relief and such a huge weight off my shoulders, knowing that I could go into a New Year divorced and property free.

The following year brought about all new beginnings for this now single 32-year-old. Including a new house to live in along with a new housemate. I even taught myself how to roller-skate and before I knew it I was lining up as "fresh meat" in the beginners roller derby. Learning how to "booty block" and "whip" my way around the skating rink. I was still very much the novice at skating. I was heavily padded up even with bike pants, which were all padded around the bottom area. I had a tendency of falling over backwards.

I attended a huge six-day personal development event on the Gold Coast, which to this day I still say "it changed my life forever". I had never attended a course so powerful in my life and the outcomes for me personally were amazing. From here I went on to complete my master practitioner training in NLP and Hypnosis. As a result, I was able to expand my personal development knowledge and skills even more. Every course I attend allows me to grow and expand my mind, which in turn allows me to help others. I began feeling good about myself and naturally the weight was taking care of itself which made me feel happy and free again. October 2011, aged 33 I suffered a setback in my health and weight. I had a fall while at work trying to get down from the top bunk. As a result, I had to have minor shoulder surgery and eight months off work. Not being able to exercise properly due to my hip being badly bruised and with my shoulder needing rest. I began eating lots of dairy, especially cheese and chocolate. My weight was creeping back up around 85 kilograms and I was beginning to feel unhappy within myself and like a fat blob again. I remained as positive as I could by taking myself off to the swimming pool and walking my dog Lockie.

Not be able to do all the things that I really love to do was wearing me down both emotionally and physically. Along with a high alkaline-based diet, the rehabilitation work finally paid off and I returned back out to work on my birthday in May 2012. I was so delighted to be given the all clear from the surgeon and the company doctors it was the best birthday present. My life was back on track. So much so that I enrolled myself into doing the 5km Mother's Day Classic fun run along the river in Perth.

I began training by running a little bit and then walking a little bit and soon enough, I found myself running more than walking. I was never a runner and despised running with a passion so this running business was a whole new concept for me. I completed the fun run feeling proud and with a smile. From that day forward, I decided that I would keep running and over the years I have really grown to like it.

Towards the end of 2012, my love and passion for life, people, animals, personal growth and development, the environment and the planet we live in had grown. The more I researched and learnt about the effects of an over acidic body, the more it made sense about the reasons why I wasn't losing any weight. Despite the copious amounts of exercise, I was doing. Nothing until now seemed to make a difference, until I woke up one day and decided that I no longer liked or ate chocolate, or cheese, or milk, or eggs or fish. I was now vegan.

This just didn't happen overnight this happened over a period of a few months. It was a struggle at first, as I didn't want to tell my friends. I still ate food with animal products in them if I went to their places or out for dinner. Just to be polite and as always I am extremely grateful for their hospitality. However, the time came when my body could no longer tolerate animal products of any kind. I kindly told my friends one at a time that I was now a vegan. The more alkaline my body became the more weight I started to lose. I began feeling on top of the world with an abundance of energy, passion and drive for life. I didn't know many vegan people in Western Australia so I joined a vegan meet up group. From there I gained tips on how to make yummy vegan dishes and desserts, as all I really knew was salads. I also learnt about eating good quality unprocessed carbohydrates and how important they are for the body as it is where the body gets its energy.

Early 2013 I made the move to live back over the east coast of Australia. Choosing the Gold Coast in Queensland as my new home. It wasn't an easy choice to make. I was leaving all my close friends that I had relied on so much for everything over the past few years. I just knew that deep down, I needed to be living somewhere where it was warm. Somewhere I could get a variety of fresh fruit and vegetables and close to the beach. I liked the environment where it was lush, green and mountainous.

Life on the Gold Coast is perfect for me. I now eat more food than ever before. I weigh less than I did at 20 and have completed two Gold Coast half marathons and the 100km Oxfam walk. Today, I am 37 years old weighing about 67 kilograms. That's 30 kilograms lighter than my heaviest in 2007. I have an abundance of energy, my skin and mind are both clear. I eat an abundance of fresh fruit and vegetables, I don't feel bloated or constipated any more. I haven't been on any medication either prescribed or over the counter (with the exception of contraception) since my shoulder surgery in early 2012.

I donate blood regularly, I no longer suffer joint pain and I have a profound compassion for the world I call home. I enjoy pushing my body to limits that I once thought were impossible and my mindset is growing every single day. I'm living, breathing, dreaming and believing beyond doubt that simply everything that you put your mind to is achievable. Now I'm stepping into the space of helping other people to do the same. Life is here to be lived to the fullest.

Chapter 16

Walking the Path of Transformation: Stumbling One Step at a Time

By Tim Hammons

Awareness of a wisdom which flows through all things.

It was late on a cold winter night, a few days before Christmas. The house was filled with the quiet of a family asleep. Outside, stoic street lamps stand bravely in the frigid midnight stillness, their lamps reflecting the day's old snow and ice on the ground, and the street of our sleepy suburban neighbourhood. I put on my heavy coat and boots over my pyjamas, to go out into the cold. I have a box of matches.

I had just finished watching a particularly stirring version of the classic holiday movie "A Christmas Carol", with the famously bitter Scrooge. I watched his encounters with his mortality, his legacy, and his opportunity, the ghosts of Christmas Past, Present, and Future.

Alone on the couch and covered with a thick warm blanket, which belonged to my grandmother, I follow him on his journey through the bittersweet impressions of childhood and the struggles of his earlier and current adult life. I am moved by his pain, his confrontation, and follow him on his joyful change of heart.

As he is transformed, I feel something stirring in me as well. I want to follow the transformed Scrooge into the streets and shout "happy Christmas" while showering gifts and warm wishes to everyone. It's passed midnight, dark and cold, everyone's in bed, the streets are asleep. I'm alone on the couch. In the glow of the black and white movie credits, I reflect on my experience. The words "God", and "offering" appear in my mind. So, I determine, I would make an offering to God. I didn't fully understand 'WHY', I just wanted to do this. I wanted to take action.

As a 12-year-old middle school student, I had earned money in the winter by shovelling snow from the neighbourhood driveways. The going rate was $10 per driveway. I remembered one winter I had earned enough to reward myself with a coveted dual cassette radio-recorder, so I could record songs from the radio. I took $5 of my hard-earned money, out of my ceramic frog bank on my bedroom shelf, and a pack of matches from the kitchen. I was going to make an offering. The cold surrounds me like a frigid still box, as I step outside onto the front porch. "I don't want anyone to see me", I remembered feeling somewhat self-conscious as I considered the execution of my symbolic deed. I walked around to the side of our car parked in the driveway, off to the side where no one could see me. I was going to burn this money and send it up to God. I considered a montage of religious stories of offerings and selflessness.

I felt noble and humble as I considered myself among them. I struck my first match and suddenly the wind picked up, and it was quickly blown out. I held the dollar bill closer to my body, removed my gloves for better control, and lit another one. Out by the wind. I did this, again and again, each time with a growing determination to follow through on my offering. It was no use and I was running out of matches. I slumped down on the cold icy pavement, and considered "why"? The message I received that night was that this was not the way to do it. That it was something to do with giving to others. My "reward" for my action that dark and inspired night was this sense of "knowing" that there is a tangible presence running through our lives that is intimately woven into our intentions and actions. I recall this as one of my first and more graspable experiences with "Spirit".

Life offers opportunities for deeper connection

There have been many other connections with this presence before and after this event. Many of them had to do with my experiences of art or nature. I would feel a sense of the divine working through my childhood pet cat as he would come to sit on my lap in times of sadness. I am sure many a kid would recall similar connections with pets. As a young artist, I would sit and sketch a tree, and during one inspired sitting, I felt as if the tree was "speaking" to me. This was one of my first experiences around a lifelong interest in the intersection of art and spirituality. I now understand this experience to be one of focused mindfulness and full presence of awareness.

As a boy, I loved to climb trees. One day, while waiting for a friend parents to pick me up for a birthday bowling outing, I was climbing higher in our front yard tree than I had ever climbed before. I wanted to be able to see their car coming down the street from this vantage point of 2 stories off the ground. My older brother was out on the rooftop nearby doing some simple repair work. I remembered boldly declaring to him "if I make it to the top I will go down in history, and if I don't, I will just go down". Shortly after that, while suspending from an upper branch, go down I did. The branch snapped, and in slow motion, I felt my body falling, limbs tumbling, branch by branch, I was falling. When I came to rest, I noticed a large branch, which was "caught" in my right armpit. I looked around, and this was the last branch of the tree before I would have hit the ground. The tree had caught me in its strong arms. Coincidence or luck? I'll let you decide. Once again, I felt this clear presence, connection, and protection by nature. I went off to the birthday party with a few Band-Aids on my hands, a scratch on my face and a big bruise on my armpit. I was feeling reassured and reminded of something bigger. I knew somehow there is "more" to life than just what we see.

I continued searching. I am sure that many of these youthful experiences sparked my curiosity for life, for learning and for seeking. I wanted to know more about what we don't know. About that which is not apparent on the surface of our day-to-day experiences. As a young adult, after working in design firms in San Francisco and London, and now, in Singapore, I began to see a parallel between the creative journey, the journey to find inspired ideas and solutions, and to the spiritual or personal development journey.

I read books and attended seminars and meditations for personal growth. I was fuelled both by this sense of knowing and of "not knowing". Books such as "The Way of the Peaceful Warrior", "The Celestine Prophecy" "The Tao of Physics" were early works which resonated with my worldview and sparked a deeper interest. At the time, I was dating a woman who was running a personal development company and I was privileged to attend courses on Reiki, Rebirthing, and to host meditations and discourses by Lazarus, Osho and the like. Many of the practitioners of these courses stayed in our home, and so my interest turned to intimate and in-depth discussions and experiences on the many facets of this "other side" of life and knowing.

I can do it all! I can't do it all!

I had set up a small design company developing corporate identity programs, logotypes, and various print communications. I loved the work and the opportunity to engage in the process of finding and developing ideas and the parallels I was discovering. My interest in learning brought me to teaching and training, first at a local design college. I was also invited to facilitate youth motivation camps and eventually into corporate training. I soon found myself in front of rooms full of executives, teaching creative thinking tools, communication skills, presentations skills, team-building, emotional intelligence, and stress management. I embraced the challenges and I told myself that I could do anything and everything! I eventually came to the obvious realization that by taking on everything, I was only spreading myself too thin. In my quest to find the edges and my love of learning, combined with a tricky little voice which drove me to try to please everyone, I continued to say, "Yes" to just about every job that came my way. As we all know, when you're trying to do everything, you'll never be really good at anything. My tricky little voice wouldn't allow me to see that at the time, and so I kept on going, trying to redeem myself with each new challenge. Sometimes it went well, and sometimes it didn't. I remember one particularly challenging situation. I was a support trainer who would facilitate group learning activities in support of the main trainer.

On this particular day, I was tasked to replace a senior trainer who was sick for the day. This was 1.5 hours before the class was to begin with no time to prepare. The thought of saying "no" never really entered my mind at the time. I felt like I was being parachuted in only without a working parachute! I was in front of a group of very senior leaders, stumbling with my faulty parachute, through a workshop on customer service.

All too quickly it became apparent to everyone that I was obviously in over my head. I was good at what I did, but, without the natural industry experience, I was unable to flow through the nuances of their issues. I couldn't quite grasp their questions and make the vital connections between theory and practical application. It's that weird burning deadness in the pit of your stomach when you realise something just isn't right and you wished that you could be anywhere but here. I also realised that, if I were to continue in this way, that I am doing a disservice to the participants and to their learning. With this kind of "take it all" attitude, I began to notice a cycle appearing.

I was offered a project, it was low pay, and I felt I had to do it. I felt lousy for doing it afterwards for such low pay. I would beat myself up a bit, and vow to do something different next time. When next time rolled around and I would attempt to assert a greater sense of my value and my fee, the organizer would refuse and say there's no budget, take it or leave it, and so the process repeated. I felt lousy and stuck.

Step into the Darkness. Keep on moving

One time, this stickiness led me to confront "Spirit" once again. I recall that I felt particularly stuck with my work and my desperate money situation. I felt stuck in my relationship and didn't know how to move forward. I felt like I was going nowhere in my life. Frustrated, I didn't know what I could do or how I could change. I felt trapped. To move my emotions, I needed to move my body. I began walking around the room, stomping around the room, the words "what can I change" came in my mind and out of my mouth. "What can I change", I was soon shouting. I slumped on the couch exhausted from my fit. In that moment of respite from my rant, a quieter thought snuck in: "what am I holding onto", then, "what can I let go of?"

As a design practitioner and teacher, I had a particular image going on which I needed to uphold. For me, at the time, it was my long hair. This was my "brand" which said: "I'm different' (read: "I'm cool)", especially in what was at the time a very conservative culture in Singapore. My hair said that I'm a rebel! I secretly felt proud of this and had been for some time.

I realised that I was holding onto that image and that, at some level, it was running the show. My need to "be" a certain way was getting in the way of whom I really was. In my spirits' questioning of "what can I let go of", the picture that came to me was, my hair. I recognised by now that spirit rewards our actions. As a demonstration of trust in this voice, I went and cut it short. It was no big deal in the end. My little ego fought and imagined it to be so, as a biblical "Samson" losing his divine powers upon the slashing of his most powerful locks. A trip to the barber and it was gone. I was, gulp, "normal" again. A little slice of humble pie is good medicine for the soul. Within one week of this decision and action, three distinct things happened.

1. I developed a very high fever, which stayed for several days. As a context, I had been blessed with sickness-free health for over 10 years. A by-product of the mind-body connection journey I believed.

2. One day "out of the blue" my girlfriend of 4 years at the time declared that she would like to take a break from our relationship (which was very scary to me).

3. My father, who sold commercial real estate, called me up and announced that he had just landed a couple of big contracts and was buying me a ticket to fly home to the USA for Christmas. This was in October.

Earlier that year, I had set an intention that I would go home for the holidays, the first time home in 9 years. Having no idea how or if I would be able to afford it, I allowed the magic to happen. These 3 unrelated yet distinctly disruptive occurrences happened within one week. I have since come to recognise that, when unusual or significant things happen in a group of 3, that it is Spirits way of getting your attention. Yet, two out of 3 of these occurrences were unpleasant and seemingly unwanted.

I began to step back a bit, and learn to detach from the outcome, from what I had, as a preconceived notion of what was "good" or what was "bad". I began to allow a sense of the bigger picture of my life. I felt as if these experiences were guiding me to learn how to trust in a different, perhaps in a "bigger" way. I firmly believe now that there is more going on at any one time or place than we are privileged to understand at the moment. I also look back at this experience as a further acknowledgement of the power of clear intention and action. In response to my sincere seeking and asking, Spirit posed to me a challenge. With no idea as to what the heck it was about or why, I took it on and took action.

I had two very powerful realisations around how to deal with a challenging situation. First, I recognised the power of opening to and listening to both the questions and the responses from my intuition. Second, I recognised the unexpected power of making a clear demonstration of trust in my intuition through my actions when faced with a tough situation. Things worked out in the end. I enjoyed my time with my family that years end, fever passed with its blessings, and my girlfriend and I got back together. A few years later we eventually were married briefly and had a wonderful daughter together.

I could go on about my daughter, Aurora, and the many blessing she has brought us. From her early scans, we understood that she would be a "special needs" child, but this was no deterrent. She brought joy and happiness in abundance and opened the hearts of everyone who was able to connect with her. She continues to be a light of joy to those around her to this day.

Her mother Ming and I made a promise to each other of absolute honesty. If we ever felt the relationship no longer was serving us, that we had space, trust, and understanding to communicate this to each other. It was not an easy conversation to have, but it was honest and came from a space of love. After 7 years together, we decided to separate and eventually divorced. All the while, we remained close, and Aurora remained central in both of our lives.

Several years later, Ming became diagnosed with cancer. After months of various natural, alternative and allopathic forms of treatments, healing, therapies, she succumbed and passed on. Aurora was 5 years old at the time. We were all thrown into an abyss of numbness, loss, and disbelief. She was always such a strong and eternally optimistic woman, and now she was gone.

The days and years following were challenging on many levels, and I struggled to make things work as a single dad. Aurora shared her time between living with myself and with her grandmother. I prayed and meditated for guidance, seeking some answers from these devastating events. Catharsis made way for deeper self-reflection: who am I, what is my purpose here, why is all of this happening? I felt her mothers' presence often with me, somehow whispering to keep letting go, and keep opening up, to keep allowing the light to shine. I interpreted these messages to basically mean to step up, to be the guidance and strength for my daughter, to keep searching, finding, and drawing forth the light and strength in myself. It was time to reach more deeply inward, so that I could extend further outward, for myself, and for my daughter. While reassuring on one level, life continued to be challenging on other more practical levels.

Breakdowns and breakthroughs: Tools for transformation

Aurora was with living me. I was still caught in that familiar but painful pattern of financial struggle. Accepting work that really no longer supported who I was and we carried on. We had plenty of love and support around us from friends and extended family. At one point there was a concern over what was the best living arrangement for Aurora, given my unstable financial situation. Around the same time, I was faced with the painful reality of moving out of my home-office and apartment of 15 years, to somehow squeeze into a smaller and simpler place.

Aurora, now 9 years old, and I shared a single room for a while which was also my office. Faced with these two realities: losing my home, and, the possibility of "losing" my daughter, was, to say the least, one of the lowest points in my life. This challenge hit at the core of what it means to be a man, to provide the basic necessities for your family. Prayer and meditation provided little to appease my failing sense of self. The only way that I can best describe this is basically a wake -up call, a kick in the ass by the Universe.

I had remembered an analogy expressed in a powerful workshop many years earlier, "life gives you either a tap on the shoulder or a Mack truck". When you don't respond to the taps on the shoulder, the Mack truck will show up. I know that it's the way that we respond to our life challenges that define who we become. I felt like I was up against that wall, and I needed to transform my life and myself. I thought, "What are the actions I can take"? First, I had to honest with myself about what was working and what wasn't and do something about it. One thing that wasn't working was that bloody unproductive cycle or rather, that work cycle that was sucking my blood. I had to start saying "no" to those jobs that just didn't feel right. You know, we can all say, "I know it doesn't feel right, BUT... and that "but" is the most toxic but on the entire planet. It will kick your butt every time.

It was scary because it meant saying no to the money, which I needed. If I was to look Spirit directly in the eye and summon all of what I had learned and knew to be true, there really was no choice here. My spirit had brought me to this edge and it was time to test my wings. I began to say no. It still isn't easy to say, however, with practice, the momentum grows. There were many days and months of more questions than answers. The people I had usually worked with didn't understand this new more assertive version of me and they tried to bring me down through common sense justifications. "The market will only pay so much for this, it's very competitive, you can't charge so much", Yaddayada yadda. They were practical and well-intended voices but they rang toxic in my head as fingernails on a chalkboard. I needed to find a different conversation, or just step off this path altogether. Eventually, the voices of the energy drainers moved further into the background, as I began to create space to work with new and different voices.

Secondly, I became very conscious and protective of what I allowed into my head. I cannot completely control what happens to me but I can control and choose how I respond. The thoughts I choose to have and the words I choose to say are the keys to my experience. Much as a bouncer at a nightclub will assess, select, and allow only the "right" people through the doors, I became the gatekeeper of my thoughts, words, and actions.

Over the years, I had accumulated a small library of files, tools, resources from various personal growth workshops and learning events. The next thing I did was to go through some of these tools, which I had used and then abandoned, to pull them out, and work with them again. One particular tool was affirmations. Powerful, positive, present tense statements such as "This day, the wisdom and love of God shines through me, I create something of value this day" became part of my daily routine.

I began, 3 or so times a week, to go running or walking while singing, declaring, and creating my list of personal and professional affirmations. This list included areas of relationship with money, health, work and career, effective use of time and resources, professional relationships and opportunities, travel, family, and so on. I would modify or amplify as required based on what was showing up in my life.

Run for my life

Running, declaring, and energizing my goals and thoughts became an important part of moving stuck energy. I would run in my favourite park, MacRichie Reservoir. I ran on a raised wooden plank walkway with a semi-tropical forest on one side, beautiful clear lake on the other, singing and declaring my affirmations into the trees until my head was spinning. It felt as if the trees and the sky were silently cheering me on as I celebrate in their midst. Often, my daughter would accompany me to a small neighbourhood park, which is near our home. While I was running and declaring my affirmations, she would be sitting on the swing nearby, listening to me. She would create and shout out her own playful variations. When I declared, "I'm a genius and I apply my wisdom", she would declare back, "I'm a genius and I apply my makeup". We would both crack up laughing, and the power and energy of these affirmations became amplified.

I began every morning with a routine which included these declarations, stretching and visualising the details of my day unfolding in a "pink ball of light". I would visualise meetings, details of projects I was to work on being realised and cheques of a specific amount written to our company name. It was all manifesting tools, which had been learnt, let go of, relearnt, and more recently made more mainstream through the movie "The Secret". The key to all of this was, of course, to believe it, feel it, see it, and then let it go. You must do this, every day to see the desired results.

In my work, through the suggestions and sharing by friends and colleagues, I was beginning to become aware of different and new things happening in the field of facilitation and training. Mainly involving large scale visuals, drawing tools and processes. I had been using mind mapping, visual and creative tools in my teaching and consulting businesses for over 20 years. I began to explore further and soon identified professional opportunities where I could apply my visual tools and experience in these new ways. Through more research, I found a community of practitioners of this visual work, which was called the IFVP, "International Forum of Visual Practitioners". I noticed that they have an annual conference of skill sharing and networking. That year it was to be held in Honolulu Hawaii and it was coming up in a few months' time. Something told me "I have to be there".

Integration and growth

I worked out what it would cost to attend, and wrote down the amount. Then I worked out how many jobs I would need to create between now and the deadline for conference registration. I had a number. This number, amount, and the reality of my going now entered into my routines of affirmations visualising and believing. When the jobs and the subsequent amounts of payment that I was visualising showed up later, I wasn't really surprised. Grateful, of course, but not really that surprised, as I had already "known it to be true". I share this not in a boastful way, but in a sort of reassuring way, the way that you might speak of a trusted friend who you just know somehow will always be there for you in your times of need.

I attended that conference in 2010, together with my girlfriend and future wife Irene, and it proved to be a turning point in my career as a visual practitioner and facilitator. Together with Irene, we now have a thriving business doing this visual facilitation work we love, with amazing clients and collaborators. The opportunities to do inspiring and meaningful work in incredible places which I could only have dreamed of before is now my reality. I have participated in this conference every year since then. I now am blessed to call many of the practitioners in our community friends. This community and the annual conference have continued to be my greatest professional investment in this young and rapidly growing industry.

These tools and processes I've shared here are mainly personal, something I do on my own. Ultimately, the journey of growing is something that is a personal journey and will be unique for everyone. However, my journey couldn't have really happened if not for the support of some wonderful individuals. Around the same time that I was caught in the "take every job I can get" vortex, I attended an intensive training program in Phuket called "Making the Stage". This incredible 5-day program stretched participants on our abilities to connect more deeply with our emotional capacities, ourselves and of course with our audiences. It also confronted your relationship with selling and leading a group to a point of decision. Very powerful stuff. I love these kinds of programs as it provides many opportunities for participants to connect with our authentic selves, and to confront all that stands in the way of getting there. I also connected with many of the participants, and with two more specifically.

A lady from Hong Kong who's a coach and presentation skills trainer, and an Australian man with many passions for family, sport and business, who lives in Malaysia. They both invited me to join them as a small mastermind group. Not much at first, this informal connection grew into a powerful support structure for the three of us. Each week or two, we would share our challenges, issues, highs and lows.

We had given each other permission to kick each other's butts in various ways when required. I have never experienced a richer, more intimate and meaningful gift in the context of personal growth than I have with the connection to these two individuals and the network of love, support, and butt kicking we shared. We have all grown to be more than close friends, electing to call ourselves the "family that we choose".

A statement that rings true for me is "a true friend will push you harder than you will ever push yourself." To me, this sums up the essence of our mastermind group.

Perhaps the greatest resource I have, and the greatest support I have had through much of these challenges, is my wife and partner "Sunshine" Irene. She keeps me stable and steady and focused on making clear progress one step at a time in forward motion. She is always there to offer everything she is capable of and one way or another, to remind me of what I am capable of, to keep us on track whenever life gets too sticky.

I am so lucky and blessed. Each day we get to experience life unfolding together, through our love for each other and through our 4 wonderful children. This loving and supportive relationship is my greatest asset, and it is something that we have both consciously created together. My greatest lesson I take from my experience with Irene is to be there for each other and to be fully present with each other.

A few keys I have learned around transformation are:

1. Learn to trust and let go. Put yourself in environments where you don't have all the answers, and where you might experience life rising up in unexpected ways to guide and support you.

2. Develop a burning curiosity to understand the intangible world: energy, emotion, how things work and how we're all connected.

3. Create a fertile "inner garden" by using the tools for manifesting; affirmations, take the time to meditate and build a relationship with your inner spirit.

4. Take clear and decisive action in the face of uncertainty.

5. Allow yourself to be supported and create support structures around you.

Each new day I am presented with new opportunities to learn and grow. Some are sweet smelling roses, and some are rotten eggs. To me, it's all the same, and I do my best to embrace them both equally. I step out of bed and then start the day with affirmations, my positive expectations, and then I let them go. I focus on the moments of laughter and joy I can create with my children and my family, and the value I can create in all of my personal and professional relationships. I savour the joy of moving further every day along the journey of my life's work. Exploring and understanding the rich potential and exciting possibilities, which emerge, as we travel deeper along the parallel paths of creativity and spirituality. Life is an adventure to discover and co-create with the Universe day by day.

***

Various resources, which I have found helpful on the journey:

"Blessing Ball of Light" and other techniques for manifesting by Christie Marie Sheldon

"Ah Meditation" and select works by Wayne Dyer

"Date with Destiny" and the work of Tony Robbins

"Meditation on Twin Hearts" by Master Choa Kok Sui

"New Earth" and *"The Power of Now"* by Eckhart Tolle

"Master Your Mind" and other events by T Harv Eker and Success Resources

"The work of John Kehoe

Select Affirmations:

My circumstances and my situation are controlled by my thoughts and my beliefs. I can choose my thoughts, my words, and my actions, and consciously change my life.

Chapter 17

Thoughts That Change Your Life

By Kevin Southern

There I was, 28 years old, living in England in my own house (well mine and the Banks), had a great job that I loved to do, lived in the village near to all my family and friends opposite a park. I had a company van to travel to work and home. In my garage, I had a high-performance car and a very high-performance motorbike. I lived on my bike when the roads were dry and I wasn't at work. My life was fantastic, I was super fit after years in the gym and earned more money than I had time to spend. I had almost everything I wanted and the future looked so bright, then I met her, my wife.

Eleven years later she said the four words I had wanted to hear for some time and I knew they were coming; - I WANT A DIVORCE, she said to me one night after a somewhat heated argument. I can remember the morning after, as clear as today. I felt ten thousand tons had been lifted off my shoulders, I had a spring in my step I hadn't felt for years. I was excited about my future, and what I would do with it and also how this would affect my three amazing children. Within 5 days we had split up for the final time. All that I had been now gone, I had no home and a crappie car that was just about worth its money in scrap. Not to mention 16,000 pounds worth of debt. But more than anything I had my freedom and all the choices would be made totally by me from now on. My very kind parents offered me a home until I could get back on my feet. A very good friend gave me work, I know he didn't need to, but he created work for me to help me out. (Thanks Tom)

I needed a good paying job, the places I had worked before I went into the public -house business were in no need of my skills anymore. I'm a boilermaker by trade and I was clear on the opportunity that I wanted.

The company would need to be a decent size with lots of opportunity for overtime, to get me back on the road to financial recovery. I kept applying for jobs, but at the interviews, I was only to find out that there wasn't a great deal of money to be made there. Deep inside me, I knew I had to get a job where I could make big bucks and I wouldn't settle for anything less. Within a month or so, I had found a job that more than suited my talents in a place where overtime was a plenty. They weren't joking when they promised me lots of overtime. I was working twelve hours a day, seven days a week, yes eighty-four hours a week. That was what I had done most of my working life, you see I am a farmer's son and very proud of it. My Dad had always taught me, 'that when the sun shines you make 'hey' meaning that when there is the work there, you take it and make the most of it.

After a couple of months, they promoted me to charge hand, I then knew my job was secure, so it was time to find a fresh house for me to buy. Having come from running a Pub and making good money to now starting from scratch, the banks weren't too happy about giving me another mortgage yet, so I was looking at a high-interest mortgage because of the risk.

The fact that I had only had my job a couple of months was a concern for the bank. It didn't worry me, whatever I had to do was what I had to do. I started to look for a new home to purchase. Within a month I found a house for sale, it belonged to the parents of a friend of mine. The house was in a terrible state, but was structurally good, well apart from a glass house they had put up. I made a deal with the owners to buy the house on a handshake, I don't trust any estate agent. I put my faith in the seller to keep to his word and honour our agreement. They had to find a new house to buy, now that I was buying their home.

Normally you would expect this to take a month at most, but ten months later we were still in the same position and house prices were going up very fast. I was becoming worried about the situation, but on my frequent calls to see the seller he always assured me that the sale would go through. I put my faith in the man as he had given me his word and shook hands on it. You see he had old-school values, and that means you stand by what you say and agree upon on. Sure thing, another four months went by when the seller phoned me and said we were good to carry out and settle the sale of the house.

By this time the house was worth nearly thirty percent more than we had agreed on, but he said my word is my word and apologised for making me wait for so long. If only there were more people like that around today, I do think the world would be a much better place. Now because I had been working for sixteen months and had not only paid off my debts but saved up a good bit of money, I was able to get a great deal on a mortgage, which was fantastic. I received the keys to my home, I can't use the word new home because the house needed to be gutted from top to bottom. It needed new wallpaper, skirting boards, doors and frames, complete new bathroom, kitchen, fireplace, central heating, all new carpets and last but not least new gardens front and back. Basically, I had to take it back to a bare shell and start again, this was going to take some time and I already worked seven days a week.

I grew up on my parent's farm and loved every minute of it and would never swap one second of that time with anybody else. Growing up on a farm in the late sixties and early seventies provided plenty of health and safety challenges. I learnt early on in life what doesn't kill you, will make you stronger. I had some very close calls with the machinery on the farm and yet I always seem to walk away without too much of a fuss. My Dad used to say; 'Everything has a way of working out okay son'.

I carried that saying with me through my life. I remember being knocked down one Christmas Eve when I was 13 years old. I was in a very bad way with my skull fractured, and yet a week later I was partying with my friends. I have had motorbikes since I was eleven and still do, 9 broken bones and 68 stitches but everything has a way of working out okay and I still ride. I had never heard of the law of attraction at that time in my life, not even life coaches and I didn't have a computer.

I was just a country lad, who grew up on a farm. I knew everything would always work out okay, my dad always told me that and so it must be true. The reason I am expanding on this is because over the last few years I have studied human behaviour and the law of attraction in some depth. I can assure you that what you focus upon expands and not only that, your deep core beliefs hold your focus of that which the outcome will certainly come true for you. The tricky part is to control these beliefs, thoughts and emotions, but at that time in my life I always knew that everything would work out okay, we will come back to this later.

There I was working seven days a week, twelve hours a day. I needed the income, but also, I needed to find time to renovate my new home. Monday morning at work I got called into the director of the engineering's office. I wasn't worried at all as I am a confident man and stand by my convictions with pride. I wasn't there for the usual boring lecture on saving cost and time etc. My director wanted to enquire if I was prepared to go and work away on site for four months. I would be installing a very large amount of steel work we had been building for some time. I would run the project and I would need to work very long days. I would also receive an extra bonus for working away from home, but I could only work on the site.

The opportunity would be five days a week, so to translate that I would be earning the same money working away on five days a week as I was on seven days a week. This was absolutely perfect. I explained this point to show you a definition of what you focus on you attract. Now working away from home Monday to Friday and then working in my new home on the weekends I was making great progress with my house.

Leading up to this time I had been seeing my children at their mother's house which was some ninety miles away every couple of weeks or so. Boy did I miss them, which was the hardest part for me. It was even harder because my ex was in a relationship with another man. Sometimes I got on well with my ex and other times we didn't see eye to eye. Eventually there was a very heated and hostile environment between us and I knew this wasn't good for my kids.

I was hoping that I would get to have much more time with my children when I had the new home finished. Maybe even have them with me most of the time and let their mother visit them, a big turnaround of the tables. I often had thought of and dreamed of how great it would be to have my children back living with me full time when the house was finished. I was working on my house one evening and out the blue my ex-wife phoned me to say that she and her new partner were starting a new family together, and they really didn't have room now for our three children with a new baby. We agreed that when my house was finished that my children would come and live with me full time. Once again what I had focused upon with deep desire had come to me.

The big day had arrived and the inside of the house with the exception of the kitchen had been finished. All the bedrooms were finished and there was newly painted ceilings, new wallpaper, new carpets, new beds and new furniture throughout. The lounge room was new, the bathroom completely new and the hall and stairway all new. I was still working in the kitchen, but it was good enough to go and bring the three most important people in the world to me back home. Ready to start our journeys together under my care. My children loved being back home where they had all their friends and family, but most importantly to them they were back with me. It took me another three years to finish the house, as I wanted it to be. It had a full new kitchen, a big garage that I built myself and fully landscaped the gardens by myself, job done.

I think that in all this time I had never felt exhausted because I was a driven man and the only thing I was able to focus on was the house being finished, and getting my children back with me again. This is something to note, and the point is that you should make your goals a HAS TO BE, or HAS TO HAPPEN and be totally clear about the outcome. Put yourself in a place that you will not accept anything else, everything seems to just flow into place. You don't feel exhausted, you never get bored, or weary, you know you have to complete a task. When it is something as powerful as getting your children back, nothing will stop you. I am sure you have all heard of goal setting, well just in case this is a new concept to you, I will just lightly touch on the subject for you, as this is one of the most powerful tools you can be armed with to build the future you desire.

Most people, I believe, think or believe that life just happens and you have to ride what comes along like a loose boat riding the waves on the sea, ups and downs, highs and lows, calms and storms, and with no clear direction of where this journey will take them. I call this just drifting through life taking what comes to you, good and bad. Just drifting through life with no destination point other than the certainty that one day you will die. You must make the most of what you have or get before that day arrives. Every journey should have a designation point otherwise, how can you get to where you want to go if you don't know where you are going.

It's impossible, so step one you have to create your designation point, your goal. The next step is to get clear about why you want to go to that designation. If it's only a loose or lame idea of just somewhere to travel to, then there is no purpose in even trying to attempt to get there. You have to decide that the place you are going to is going to be amazing and because of that you will stop at nothing to get there.

You have to be clear that arriving at this designation will bring you so much joy that you won't let anything stand in the way of you reaching your destination. Your designation has to be like the HOLY GRAIL to MOSES, you will stop at nothing no matter how big a challenge you have to overcome to get there. You have to be clear that you will do whatever it takes to arrive at your destination. Clarity is power. Once you make a choice that this is what you desire and nothing will stand in your way there will be no wall high enough that you can't climb over it, no wall thick enough so as you can't break through it and no wall long enough that you can't walk around it. You become an almighty force that will not be stopped until you have reached your designation, you will not tire, you will not second guess, you will not take a rest, you are CERTAIN that this is your designation and nothing will stop you.

The second step is to get clear about where you are now with total honesty. You can't catch an aeroplane to England from Australia if you live in Japan. What do I mean, well if your life is at the bottom of a very deep shit hole that is where you have to start? You need to make tough choices and changes to yourself that you are not comfortable with. No matter what you do in life you will always be faced with challenges, some big and some little. It's how you deal with them that will set you apart from the rest of the crowd. These days in my own life I welcome challenges with excitement. I see a challenge as a message to tell me that there is a part of my life that is not the way I desire it to be. It's a warning signal to me to say that something needs to be looked at because it's going on a different journey than the one I have chosen. I need to change it or redirect something to the same path that I have chosen. You see if you embrace change or challenges, it will move you closer to where you desire to be in life.

***

There I was, my home finished, my children living with me again. I had motorbikes in the garage, one each for my sons and my very high-performance road bike. I stopped working on Sundays to have time with my children and take them out on their dirt bikes. My life consisted of getting up at 4.30am, having breakfast, packing lunch for my children and myself. Heading out to work at 5am, it usually took fifty minutes and I would start work at 6am. I would finish work at 6pm arrive home around 6.50pm, quick shower, make dinner for us, eat dinner, tidy up after the kids, get them showered and to bed by 9pm. I would have 30 minutes to myself before I went to bed for another 4.30am alarm.

Life was good, but there was something missing. I felt I was in a rut, was this it now, is this all that life had to offer me until my children had grown up. I was happy in one sense but very bored in another. One Monday morning I went to work at a site where I was in charge of erecting a very large building. One of the men came to me and gave me an envelope, it was a notice to say he was leaving the company. Have you got a new job I asked, no he said, don't give your notice until you have a new job I replied, with a sense of concern for his welfare? He just laughed and replied I am off to live in Australia. I felt like he had just got a big sword and cut through me. You see my friends and I had tried to move to Australia when we were around 22 years of age. They weren't interested in us then and it just brought it all back to me, the sadness of the rejection. Knowing now that I would never be able to go with my children, as the ex-wife wouldn't allow it. For weeks I was walking around like a Zombie with my jaw dragging on the floor, depressed.

A friend came around one night and we chatted, but he knew I wasn't myself, and said what's up with you. I told him about the man going to live in Australia with his family and that I had tried years ago and failed, that I was sure there would be no chance that my ex would allow me to take the children out of the country and I also felt England was heading for a bad time, as there was that many people going to work there from

Europe for little money and that it was ruining our future. How do you know that your ex-wife won't let you take the children to Australia? How do you know that you won't succeed in your application to live in Australia? Stop your sulking and at least try. My friend continued. Four years ago, you got divorced and were broke and had nothing and no job. Now you live in a beautiful house with your children and do a bloody great job of bringing them up on your own. You're also a site manager in a huge company running million pound projects, and you always told me you can do anything you want if you set your heart on it. You best get up and make it happen, because you have always been the man to inspire me. I'll kick your arse if I hear you talk like that again. In that moment my life changed again, I had worked so hard to reach where I was and achieved it.

The only thing was I had failed to set up another goal. I had nothing to look forward to, no driving force inside me to ignite my passion. It took four weeks to do the necessary research to decide on where I was going to live in Australia, and my chances to be allowed to move there with my children. I was on fire I had a vision again and my goal was to live with my children in Australia.

There was one big hurdle to jump over and I wasn't sure how high this hurdle was going to be. I prepared for a few weeks, for all the reasons that the children would be better off living in Australia with me rather than in England. I phoned my ex-wife and planned a time for us to have a long phone call about something. I had three days being nervous but I was certain that I could achieve the outcome I desired. After a three-hour phone call, the only thing I can say is, I have great respect for the mother of my children.

She sacrificed seeing her children grow up so that I could bring them up in Australia and give them the great life we both wanted for them. That was it, green flags and off we go, now it's not quite that simple to get into Australia. It took two years, thousands of pounds and a ton of paperwork. We did it, on the 17th of April 2007 we flew out to start our new journey in life and we had never even stepped foot in Australia before, it was an amazing feeling.

***

Coming back to the Law of Attraction or The Secret as some call it. I only heard of this a few years ago and I have made a somewhat detailed study of what people mean by the law of attraction. I have read books, bought coaching programs, even been to seminars on the subject. Let's face it if there is an easier way to get through life then I want to know about it. Why have I had to work so hard for everything in my life? I have often looked at me and seemed to see people with much more than me and yet I bet they didn't put 85 hours a week in for it. I must be doing something wrong I thought, let's change things around and see if we can make life a little or a lot easier. I have invested tens of thousands of dollars studying this subject. Not really being an academic person, I took my time to understand it the best as I could. The theory is we are all connected to a universal source and what we give our deep focus and emotions to we attract it to us through this universal power. How much more easily could it be, well I want that, I will focus on having it, and feel how happy it makes me, then, sure enough, it will come to me, job done, life is awesome.

Well, I am sorry to tell you it isn't quite as simple as that. In my opinion, if you research the Law of Attraction, most of the people promoting their products will make it sound as easy as this. The missing link, the three easy steps to living the life of your dreams and what they didn't tell you in the film, the Secret. What most of the good people are trying to sell you is their interpretation of the universal power of attraction and if you follow their guidelines then it should work. I don't doubt the power of this, the trouble is, I believe, that most people who are promoting this idea are addressing you as if you are a blank canvas.

If you were a blank canvas then what they promote I believe should work for you. Sadly we are not blank canvases. All our lives we have been listening to, watching and affected by social conditioning. This is where all the barriers to stop this great universal power from assisting us through life come into play. I know it does work, but the problem is you have a way to many other beliefs locked into your mind. All these beliefs will counteract any chance at all of you working with this universal power.

It has a darker side, you see the universal power of attraction is working all the time, always has been, and always will be. Think about it, it's working 24hrs a day 365 days a year, every moment of your existence this is working. The problem is it happens at a quantum physics level, to my best interpretation of the research I have done over the years. The way it would all sound on a glossy brochure is you can have anything. Just focus on what you desire and with some great magic you will receive it. Now here is the problem, the universal power of attraction can't distinguish the differences between good from bad. To put this in real terms what you focus on you attract both good and bad.

A short story of a lady I know who had to have her breast removed because of cancer, I went to visit her when she arrived home to show my support for her. We were talking about the cancer that she had. She went on to tell me that her mother, her grandmother, her auntie and two of her sister's had had this same cancer. Her belief was that it wasn't if she got cancer but more a question of when she got cancer. Now my belief is that she had brought this upon herself subconsciously by believing she would get it.

If you are in some financial crises and you are short of money and keep getting bills through your door and you really you can't afford them.

You then ignore them until the reminder comes and even then you ignore that until the final demand comes. You have to pay that one, then the next thing, next month's bill arrives. In this process, all you are ever giving your focus to is being short of money and getting bills you can't afford and guess what the universal power will send to you, no not a big fat cheque to help you out, but more of what you have focused on. Yes, that's right more lack of money and more bills.

This becomes a vicious cycle of events that just keep repeating itself over and over until you break the chain of events. I wrote earlier that I had lots of broken bones and stitches in my body through mainly motorbikes. What I didn't write was that this happened over a six-year cycle, because when I had hurt myself crashing motorbikes, I gave my focus to it and attracted more of the same. I broke my last bone when I was 23, I changed my job then and took on a much bigger role in my career. This changed my focus in life to my work and I have never crashed a motorbike since.

That was 30 years ago and I still ride them today. I could write lots of different ways in which your focus, emotion, social conditioning and core beliefs are controlling your life and you don't even know it. I believe this is why you need a fuller understanding of how you attract things to you that you don't want and block the things that you do. The universe seems to know how to make all the dots join up in the puzzle. Never judge what it brings you, just see if you can use it or not, you would be surprised at the outcome of strange events.

This leads me to another event in my life, I hired a coaching company that I pay to help me understand and work with the law of attraction. A few months ago, I was chatting with my coach and she asked what one of the things I desired was? Like most people I stated that I would like financial freedom, no surprise there, I am only human. Eighteen months after moving to Australia, I started to work for myself as a contract welder and fitter. For six years it has been providing me a great income.

Six times the amount I had ever earned in England, but a change of events this year has brought my income crashing down. I still make a good living but none to spare so to speak. My coach asked me how I was going to create financial freedom. I said well I couldn't split my body into parts and go to different customers. I also work in a very specialized field of work. I'm not really willing to train somebody else to do it and work for me. For fear that they would just then set up a company for themselves and undercut me. I said if I want to earn millions of dollars I needed to find millions of customers. How are you going to do that she said, just off the top of my head so to speak, I will write a book on everything I know and have learned in the law of attraction. It just came out of the blue, I had never thought about it even once before. Her reply was unexpected to me. Was I expecting a response like 'Well do you think you can do that? Or something else like 'Well that's a tall order for you?' No to my surprise, she replied, I wish you would. I said really, yes she said, I have rarely talked to anybody that has the understanding of the law of attraction that you have. I for one would certainly buy it.

That day I started to write; why do we make an easy life hard? I just opened it up and banged away on this keypad like it was second nature to me. And all was going well. I had written the introduction, and preface and then put thousands of words down and was excited about it. The coaching company tried to sell me something else and this alienated me towards them. I thought, just another company keeping me on a hook trying to get as much money out of me as they can and I allowed this to stop my writing for some time.

A couple of weeks ago, my sister had contacted me through Facebook. I'm not one for going on Facebook, months could pass by and I wouldn't even turn it on. I'm not a big fan, but there was a message in my emails that my sister had written a comment about me on Facebook. Knowing my sister, it would be some joke or something funny. I checked it out and I was right, it was something funny. While I was there I check all the interactions with other people who basically wasted their time trying to contact me that way. There was a message from my good friend John Spender.

The man who has put together this book, A Journey ofRiches and John was inviting me to write my short story for his anthology. It was with great joy that I accepted Johns offer, to write my short story. Now having written it. I feel deeply inspired to carry on writing my own book again. Thank you, John. I don't tell you this to advertise my book, but to put an emphasis on that you don't really know what the law of attraction will bring you. Or how it will bring you something you desire, but let's just assume that I will finish my book and it becomes a best seller. I make some good money out of it, then I am asked to write another book to follow it up and that book sells well. This may even bring me to the point where I get invited to do some public speaking and then get requests to have my own seminars. All this is something that I had given some thought to over the years and I'm sure it would be something I could enjoy. Travelling around the world doing public speaking and writing books. This would seem like a holiday to me after the working life I have had, making lots of money doing something I love to do. Now I am in the state of travelling around the world and getting very good money to do this instead of doing six, ten hours days a week. I think that would be classed as financial freedom, don't you. I received one hint to take action and then stopped. I now have an even bigger reason to complete the action. This is how the law of attraction can change your life and if you want a greater understanding of it then you may like to buy my own book when I get it finished. Why do we make an easy life hard?

Just to summarize, the things I need to happen in my life I gave focus to with a total belief that I would have them. I found a rundown house, I trusted the man's word, I found time to work on my house and I got my children living back with me. I brought my children to Australia and gave them a greater upbringing that I ever believed I could in England. Even now I may find financial freedom through all the years of studying the law of attraction by writing about it. Life is something you have more control over than you think. I believe that we have just been taught the wrong things in life, some say to keep us living like slaves, for the people with money and power. My strongest feeling on this is, you must design your own life or you will be a slave to somebody else's plan.

Chapter 18

Life's Challenges

By Kirrilie Oates

September 1975 it all started when I was born 2 months early and the doctors thought I would kill my mother in childbirth, as I was a breech birth. To make it worse I had a big forehead and a bump on my back of the head. All hereditary as my mother's family was to blame for the forehead and my fathers was to blame for the back. I went through tests after tests as they thought I could have had water on the brain, as it was not common in the 70's.

Starting school at Ashbury Public School was a challenge for a quiet 5 year old who had trouble making friends. It wasn't until 1985 that I changed schools to a catholic girls school in Strathfield in Sydney and that was where this story starts.

Starting year 4 at a new school had its ups and downs however the challenges that I faced having an older sister at the same school was nothing compared to coming home one day and announcing that I could not see the board. I wasn't learning properly and missing vital information the teacher was trying to impart on her students. I was too shy to put my hand up in class. I thought I would look like the dumb child and therefore be bullied which happened anyway. So off we went to the optometrist where I received the news I was dreading, I had what is know as wandering eyes or strabismusas it is known in the medical field. I would be looking straight ahead and seeing one person but my left eye would look like its looking at the side. The right eye was doing the same, but in the opposite side. Oh I could live with that but then the optometrist also advised I was short sighted. Taking after my mother and then I also switch my left side of my face off without knowing it so my right eye is way weaker than my left. Trying to get use to wearing glasses especially when you have the ones that look like your grandmothers in year 4. This left me wide open to the bullies and that's what happened. Even down to my sister and brother picking on me. Looking back on it, it builds character. School was a challenge and the following year it was agreed that I would be kept back to repeat year 5 for various reasons. Being held back had its challenges, as I was the oldest of my year group, however my sister had moved onto high school by then which did help. I concentrated on my studies made new friends and in 1988 left primary school. I lost most of the friends I had made, but I made new ones which some of them are still friends today.

One of the more challenging subjects that I did enjoy in primary school was learning Italian and I carried my love of the language right through high school undertaking 2 unit Italian as part of my HSC. The other thing I most enjoyed whilst I was in primary school was our annual trip overseas. I got to experience Asian cultures at an early age having extensively travelled through countries such as Indonesia, China, Japan, Hong Kong, Philippines, Korea, Malaysia and Singapore to name a few. It wasn't until later in life that I realised the benefit my parents gave me to understand and respect different cultures.

1989 was a new year and a new school. First day of year 7 as a very shy student wearing glasses (granny style) still. I had more appointments with the Optometistrist and the eye specialist my grandmother went to, where they insisted I do eye exercises to try and build strength in the muscles. The exercises didn't work but left me disappointed and exhausted. The preceding years saw more challenges come my way, as my family moved to Bali Indonesia. That meant boarding school and another new school. Making new friends has always been a challenge being shy, but to add to it when people looked at me they thought and assumed I was not looking at them. Of course there was bullying and jokes that had hit me hard sometimes being teenage girls.

Life in Boarding school being shy and still wearing glasses had it challenges, but I thoroughly enjoyed the experience first time living away from home. There were the ups and downs of life, but 3 out of 4 holidays I had to look forward to returning to Bali. We would have a shopping list to take various things my parents were missing from Australia. One of the things I remember about Bali was trying to learn Indonesian, as we had to live like the locals. Our house help was also trying to learn English, so there were certain times we talked in English other times was Indonesian only. I remember the first time I meant to ask for a banana but it came out as something completely different. In Bali I had to be known as my full name of Kirrilie and my sister had to be known as Amanda as if we were to use our nicknames of Mandy and Kirri – translated into Indonesian it was turn left at the bathroom.

School was still a struggle being an average C grade student but to make it worse my sister and brother were A grade students. I did have my select group of friends however I usually kept to myself and kept out of trouble unlike my sister who was the rebellious one. Living away from Mum and Dad and having to rely on my uncles to take me out for the weekends was interesting. I did get to know one of my cousins who are two years younger and we used to get up to mischief. At school I participated in sports, which I was involved in the Senior Girls Cricket team, volleyball and Hockey (my all time favourite as I was the winger). Wearing glasses I use to miss the ball in cricket and volleyball so I believe my coaches weren't too happy, but they tried not to say anything. Later in school being shy I was always picked last for teams. One occasion especially I was given the staring role in our year 10 big night out presentations for the year 12s. I was the girl in fishnets and short skirt saying "Thank you Mr Hooker". It didn't go over well with the school and all year 10 were sent to detention and not allowed to go out that weekend.

My last year was trying, struggling through the pressures of the Higher School Certificate. All sport had been stopped and by then my parents had returned to Australia. I was travelling each day from the Inner western suburbs of Sydney up to Hornsby NSW to attend the same school. I spent the train times reading and catching up on schoolwork. It wasn't until 6 months into that year, I was to attend an appointment to try and get Special Consideration as my writing skills and eyesight took a turn for the worst.

It was decided that I could use a computer, an optional scribe and given 30 minutes extra. Looking back on it I took the computer and extra time however believe I could have done it as a normal student. After getting my results that weren't good I thought my life had ended. As it destroyed all my dreams of going to University, my marks simply weren't good enough. Until my late grandmother came to visit and saw my tears, she wiped them away one at a time and took me aside and gave me some simple advice. " Whatever you do never give up". I didn't believe her at that moment, as it wasn't until later in my life I found it does ring true. What was I to do? I couldn't follow my dreams at the time but what I didn't realise, was there was a better road that I would be travelling down. If you are reading this and you or someone you know is in a similar position, there is a better road and some of us are meant to take the road less travelled. My Late grandmother took the time to write to me a special letter, to let me know that she believed in me and that I was loved, which I still have up to this day. This gave me the inspiration to go on and take a different route in life. If it wasn't for her I would of seriously given up and possibly landed on welfare for the rest of my life.

Choices, choices, choices – it was made clear to me that I undertake full time TAFE and then get a job or try and get a job and do part time study. On the 9th Feb 1995 I enrolled in full-time TAFE only to withdraw the next day. As I won a clerical traineeship with the NSW State Government for 12 months, which pleased my parents as both of them are former NSW State Government employees. Off to work, not knowing what to expect. I hadn't even held a part time job before. Wearing glasses I was asked whether I needed any extra support or a wider screen with large print. I said no as I wanted to fit in and enjoyed my 12 months learning all about the office. On the first day we were advised as there was 7 trainees that we had 12 months and then you had to walk through the door and never return.

Lucky for me there was an election that year and by the end of the year my section was looking for staff and so a submission went up for 3 trainees to be made semi permanent. When the paperwork came back the Director General had made us permanent. I stayed with that section going off to various secondments for another 17 years.

During that time especially around 1998 I was getting more and more headaches caused from my eyesight problems and looking at a computer all day. I was coming home to my parents with the worst headaches and I would spend hours and hours in blacked out rooms. They were as fierce as migraines or worse and I couldn't do anything until they passed. I got my first set of contact lenses and they were the ones you had to take out at night and keep in protein mixture. I had to clean them in another mixture once a week. If I forgot like I did and wore them too long they would end up hurting my eyes. Eventually I swapped to ones I could do anything in, especially swimming and sleeping, which meant I'd throw them away after a month. One of the funniest experiences with contacts has to be when I was in Vietnam and ran out. I went to the local optometrist and bought what I thought were the equivalent. They only lasted an hour as they gave my eyes major issues so I had to wear glasses ever since.

I learnt to drive and came across an uphill challenge, as wearing glasses and having wandering eyes didn't help me to learn to drive. After a number of lessons through driving instructors and 2 failed attempts. I ended up passing my licence and bought a car, which I had for 2 and half years, until I eventually sold it. I use the money as a deposit for the unit I'm currently living in.

My life changed for the better. I went for my regular check-up with the optometrist and I asked them if there was anything they could suggest. What a relief as I was referred to a very experienced specialist in Macquarie Street in the city, who advised I was a perfect candidate for surgery. I took some time off work and my wandering eyes were fixed. I was still short sighted and having to rely on glasses, but at least all the headaches had disappeared. It did leave me with no peripheral vision, so I choose not to drive, but still have my gold licence just in case I do decide to get behind the wheel. He also asked why I had not had the surgery earlier? I told him that my parents wanted to try the specialist my late grandmother used in Pennant Hills. And he only gave me eye exercises to do, which never worked. In a couple of years, it will be the 20-year anniversary, of making that life changing decision. My eyes have reasonably stabilised which reduces a lot of the issues I faced through school.

Life in the NSW public service, took turns with me working for various departments, such as Public Works and Services, Q-stores and Education. I grew as a person and realised that I was changing lives through working there. Especially in 2010 where I was lucky to win a 2-year secondment to the Priority Schools area. We looked after the lowest 20% of the state until 2012 where the Government disbanded the section and I took Voluntary Redundancy. I was able to pass on my experience to kids who were being bullied and who wore glasses in a constructive way so they could change their lives.

It was during that period, I joined an organisation called Toastmasters. It changed my life for the better, as up till 2003 I still found it hard to participate in discussions and would shy away from speaking up in meetings. I attended my first meeting in Nov 2003 and gave it 6 months. What I was to find was something completely different as I was accepted as myself. It took me 6 months to present my first speech and the ride I have been on and still on amazes me each day. I was given a mentor that never really helped me and it was members of my second club Canterbury Hurlstone Park RSL Toastmasters, which encouraged me the most. I successfully completed my Competent Communicator in the first 12 months and took on the opportunities that took me out of my comfort zone. This led me to setting up and managing a brand new Area of corporate clubs. When I take on leadership positions my motto is always lead by example and that's how my areas were so successful always meeting the goals of the members. Twelve and ½ years later I have completed the Toastmasters program 4 times and have met amazing people here in Australia and overseas. One of the best moments was when I was awarded the Area management Award from my district in 2009 for my achievements. Also receiving the first ever Competent Leader Award (6 months after it was introduced in 2006) was another highlight. I have managed to coach 2 struggling clubs back to health. This was achieved through listening to the members of the clubs and what they wanted rather than working the program. One of the most common points of feedback when I was presenting speeches was always eye contact. Had they known what I already had been through in regards to that challenge the feedback may have been different.

Also during that time I fulfilled a dream in completing a Bachelor of Commerce majoring in Management Accounting, Business Law and Marketing from University of New England Armidale graduating in 2007. This was completed online and by correspondence after successfully completing an advanced diploma of accounting through TAFE college. Attending evening classes 3 times a week after work was very tiring and my eyesight did play a part in the tiredness. Studying by correspondence did have its ups and downs, especially when I had to take time off work to attend compulsory residential schools in Armidale. This is when I met an 85-year-old student studying a Bachelor of English Literature. It made me realise that learning never stops and if she could do it so could I.

In 2009 I decided I needed a completely different challenge and so I got elected to my local Catholic Club Board as a Casual Director never having done anything like this before. I was the 2nd woman on the board and the youngest by far as most of the other directors were in their 60-80s. I met some amazing people and was welcomed with opened arms. However to get new technology ideas through was another challenge, as most of them had very little experience with computers, let alone the latest technology. My biggest win was the installation of free WIFI and that I was asked to MC the annual mass and luncheon one year which took me out of my comfort zone. In October 2010 I was fortunate enough to attend the Annual Conference for the NSW Club Directors on the Gold Coast, where I networked with other Directors from various clubs and went to specialised training sessions to enhance my role as a director.

In 2011 I decided to take up another challenge at University and I started on my second degree. A bachelor of Media and Communication, which is still being completed as I decided to swap Universities due to issues outside my control. I am halfway through this degree and it does have it challenges especially to fit it around my employment.

In March 2013 I landed a new job, something completely different, as I was bored working in an office. I spent 18 months face-to-face fundraising with a company called Fundamental World Wide. Raising money for the Australian Red Cross and Oxfam Australia. What an experience and I met some very lovely people along the way. Especially the CEO who asked me at the interview why he should hire me, as I didn't have any sales experience. I replied how could I get experience if no one is willing to give me a go? I had many challenges during that period, as it was a very small company and we had a different location each day. Sometimes going away on road trips for weeks at a time and often getting rejected, as people in Sydney don't always like street fundraisers. I made many friends and met a lot of travellers through the company and am still my friends today.

Eighteen months later I was ready to move on and I have taken the best experiences with me as I move into a new stage of my life. I am currently studying Media and Communication and Early Childhood as I was always told that I should be working with children. Currently I'm about to finish a Diploma of Early Childhood after putting University on hold and look forward to working in the industry. Maybe in the future I will go back to University and study my masters however money has to come first.

Maybe in the future I will look into having laser eye surgery to correct the short sightedness. As I grew up, it has become less and less of an issue and challenge, as I thought people were accepting it more until I went to teach English in Vietnam in 2014. To my shock and horror, I didn't get a contract after spending time, to be trained. One of the reasons they gave me, was I was not the image of a teacher, as I wore glasses and no other teacher did. I ended up staying in Vietnam for a month and a half, most of that time was volunteering with special kids in a centre in Ho Chi Minh City. These children were inspiring but have challenges ahead of them and their carers shared their stories. Often amazing and the reasons they were doing this type of work were spectacular. I wish I had a video camera with me to record them as they made my time in Vietnam memorable. Wearing glasses was a challenge with the kids, as most of them didn't realise, what they were and were fascinated with them. They had fun taking them off my face and throwing them on the floor. I was amazed they survived. If I do go back to Vietnam in the future, I will make the effort to go and spend more time with the kids at the centre. I do recommend if you want to do something different and you are in Vietnam, Toastmasters District 3 is worth a visit.

What about the future? Well I know I will always travel the road less travelled and hope there is room for me to grow as a person. I have started this journey with going from a size 16 to a 10/12 and my goal being an 8/10 before my 40th Birthday. I'm achieving this thanks to a wonderful mentor and the Herbalife program. I thought at the time the program would not do anything and judged it similar to the others, I had tried in the past but I was wrong. It is a lifestyle change, rather than a change in diet and is working so I will keep up with it. My 40th is going to be big and will be a celebration of what I have achieved. The challenges, I have overcome and most of my close friends will be invited to assist in the celebration. They say your eyes change after 40, I will just have to take the challenges as they come. Am also aiming to continue to study. Eventually the goal is to have my own business. My plan is I will not be working for anyone else by the age of 50. I would love to share and present my story and experiences with a larger audience. Especially those who believe they can't do anything or are being bullied, as that should not happen.

As for family of my own, I'm still on the hunt. I have had certain people in my life however they don't seem to stick around or maybe I'm just too picky! I would love to have children one day, even if I sponsor children from overseas or adopt. There is a lot more I would love to achieve and I set new goals each year, having overcome major issues in my life. I look on the positive side of life now. I don't look on wearing glasses, as an issue rather, as a benefit. I know friends and family, who have had to get use to glasses later in life. I hope I wont have to rely on them as much.

My advice to you as the reader, never give up on your dreams. Our challenges only make us stronger and are character building. If I can overcome things in life so can you. Believe in yourself as we were all created to be individuals, don't follow the crowd if it doesn't suit you. Make sure you are living life and having fun not the opposite. Life is too short to not do what you are passionate about in life.

Some of my favourite quotes I have lived my life by are:

'Don't wait for the rest of the world to recognise your greatness: live it and let the world catch up to you.'

~ Unknown

'Never get so busy making a living you forget to make a life.'

~ Dolly Parton

'It's not what you look at that matters, its what you see.'

~ Zig Ziglar

'Life is not about finding yourself, life is about creating yourself'

~ Lolly Daskal

'Strength lies in differences, not in similarities'

~ Stephen Covey

'Getting knocked down is a given, getting up and moving forward is a choice'

~ Zig Ziglar

Chapter 19

From Existing To Living

By Jaki Bent

Signs of Hope

It is only a few short years since I suffered so badly with panic attacks, lack of confidence, self-esteem and courage. I was often paralysed by fear and only left my home when it was absolutely necessary. If you had seen me on the street I would probably have been walking super-fast, not because I was confident - but because I was in a mad dash to get to the safety of my car. I was a single mother for a number of years, three children, three different fathers, all at a time when it was seriously frowned upon (and probably still is). I was a 'good catholic girl', who had a 'good catholic up bringing and I had 'let the side down'. In fact, one day the nuns at my school had told my mother "You have two such wonderful daughters" - well I was the third daughter who apparently, according to them, was either going to be a nun or end up in jail!

Some key life moments from my life:

- Just six weeks before my wedding my husband to be, my eldest son's father, gave me the ultimatum "Have an abortion and the wedding will go ahead - don't and it won't". I didn't and the wedding was called off.

- 5 years later, when I was expecting my daughter, my long-term partner went to work one morning only for me to discover, later that day, he had gone to Paris for the weekend with 'his girlfriend'.

- I did marry my youngest son's father, however, that turned out to be what could be described as emotionally abusive. It ended in divorce after 12 years. Leaving was traumatic and my husband was given a suspended prison sentence for breaking a court order, 18 times, to stay at least 100 yards away from me.

Fast forward to April 2007. I was at home recovering from a major operation, waiting to hear if I had breast cancer or not. I saw a program that changed my life. It made me realize that I existed instead of living. I had still been living as though I was trapped in my marriage. I was too afraid to do this or that, wore pyjamas as a layer of protection at night, kept the curtains or blinds shut for fear of being 'watched'. I was worried about buying the foods or things I liked for fear of repercussion. In that moment of realisation, I started to take back control and personal response-ability for MY life. The big question was where to start, after some careful thought I chose three questions to help me to start my journey:

- Does the way we think to create the way we feel?

- Do our thoughts and interpretations of our past 'dictate' the way we live our lives today?

- Can I change my past?

My answer, to all three, was a resounding YES!

It was time to set out on a journey of self-discovery and empowerment. Over the next few years, I literally spent thousands of hours and travelled thousands of miles in pursuit of my dream - to learn how to really live my own life. I:

- Studied

- Watched DVD's

- Attended courses

- Analysed body language

- Read hundreds of books

- Wrote and delivered workshops

- Spoke with as many people as possible

- Listened to hours and hours of audio programs

- Tried out a multitude of different tasks & exercises

- Had multiple 'Light Bulb' and 'Ah-Ha!' moments

And all of this started just after I was given the all clear - no breast cancer.

One of the great things about talking with other people, being honest and really listening is that you discover that you aren't the only one. For me, it soon became obvious that more and more people really are becoming increasingly frustrated with their lives and they were feeling the same as I was. As though they were existing, stuck in a rut and not living their own lives.

I realised that Emotional Baggage from the past was weighing down not only mine but many people's lives. It was distorting how they and I were seeing ourselves, how we were interpreting everyday situations. It is becoming like this unseen virus that was seeping into our lives, seeping into every single cell of our body and leaving us feeling frustrated and dissatisfied. I made up my mind, that if you can go on a physical diet – then surely it is possible to go on an 'Emotional Baggage Diet'. It would mean exercising my thoughts to lose the weight of those that were not good for me.

Removing the negativity from my daily diet and replacing it with positive and empowering thoughts and actions. It was time to exercise my emotional muscles. This was a turning point, a step towards healing internally. Maybe others may wish for wealth and riches based on money and possessions, but for me, riches and wealth meant finding a daily internal peace. The ability to claim my life back, to have a future that I was in control of, rather than one that was being 'dictated' by my old negative thoughts.

Changes didn't happen overnight. In fact, for me, they are still happening (I love the journey of discovery). When doing physical exercises to get a flat stomach, you can't see the difference after the first session. You need to persevere and after a few weeks, you start to notice the results. Gradually you notice that your body becomes healthy, you have more energy, you feel more confident and your self-esteem can soar. It is exactly the same with exercising your thoughts and to let go of Emotional Baggage.

Losing the weight of past and present negative thoughts and experiences can literally create a freedom that changes how you see and interact with the world. I had been like so many other people in life. I had 'learnt lessons' and accepted them as though they were fact, unchangeable, they just were, and that was the way it is ... Yet in reality, if something is not working for you, you can change it - or at least, change the way you think about it! The process of learning to be in control and actually live my life and not just exist wasn't all plain sailing, the universe seemed to want to severely test me at times. I was:

- Diagnosed with fast progressing Osteoporosis (2008) and told that I would probably be in a wheelchair within 5 years. However under 12 months later I walked a 1/2 marathon in Denver as part of a team that helped to raise $211,000USD for the Make a Wish foundation. Just for the record, I am still walking and standing tall & I have no intention of ending up in a wheelchair!

- Then in 2009, I was diagnosed with skin cancer and I told to prepare for facial disfiguration. That didn't happen and most people don't even notice the scar that runs down my nose.

Even though I faced those 'tests', giving up has not been an option. There have been quite a few times when it has been a persistent thought when things got tough or challenging! Occasionally those moments still crop up but I have found some 'tools' that make them manageable, that help me to have an inner strength I didn't know was possible before. They have given me an opportunity to learn, develop and to keep faith in myself. I no longer expect perfection from others or myself, we are all on a journey. E.g. we should be more forgiving of each other, it has made a big difference in my life. Around that time I found what is now my favourite quote:

"Insanity is doing the same thing over and over again and expecting different results".

~Albert Einstein

Doh! How obvious is that.? I had been doing the same things over and over again, day after day. Those little routines that had made my life feel safe were actually like a prison cell that I was locking myself in. I mean when you think about it: Would I wear the same clothes that I wore when I was 2yrs old or 16yrs old? Would I make a meal from last year's leftovers, a plate that has accidentally been left in a hidden corner, left to fester a bit and grow a 'personality of its own'? My answer was an emphatic no I wouldn't - and yet that was exactly what I was doing with routines and habits. I was letting them run my life.

Facts and Figures

I read something that really got me thinking. Research by Dr Daniel Amen[*1], a world-renowned brain imaging specialist, shows that every single day of our lives we have approx. 60,000 thoughts. That is one thought per second for every waking hour. Now of those 60,000 thoughts 95% of them are the same thoughts that we had yesterday, the day before and the day before that. Our minds are like a stuck record repeating the same song again and again - but what if you don't like that song. Dr Amen goes into those figures even more - of that 95 % of thoughts that are the same as yesterday and the day before a staggering 80% of them are said to be negative! So out of 60,000 thoughts - 45,000 of them are negative! Are you shocked by that figure? I know I was. He calls those thoughts 'Automatic Negative Thoughts' or ANTs for short. Now just the thought of having all of those ANTs running around in my head was enough to make me want to get rid of them.

Another Staggering Fact:

Did you know that in an average dictionary, approx. 30,000 words*2, there are only 1705 words that can be deemed to be positive, encouraging, uplifting, strong. That is just over 5% of the words available for us to use. Yet in that same dictionary there are just fewer than 6000 words that can be seen as negative, disempowering, belittling, sniping, griping or critical. No wonder then that it is easier for us to think negative thoughts or speak in a negative way to either others or ourselves.

And Another:

Author Darren Hardy - "Did you know that your brain is NOT designed to make you happy? This may be alarming to you, but your brain has only one primary responsibility - to keep you alive. Thus, your brain is constantly on the lookout for danger and attack warnings. Your brain is programmed to specifically to seek out the negative. Left unguided, your brain will stew in the negative all day, every day of your life. The conundrum is —what you think about comes about or where your attention goes, energy flows."

After learning those facts, figures and statistics, I admit that for a moment it seemed as though I could use them as an excuse. It wasn't my fault, what could I do about it, excuse, excuse, and excuse! I remembered that a part of me is actually really stubborn. I didn't want to be a statistic, to just accept that this is how it is. I also didn't want all of those ANTs running around in my head.

My next task was to find a way to break both my daily habits and the cycle of my negative thoughts as both were interlinked - because as you will see from the statistics above: 'Your past is your future unless you change it.'

Embracing the Past & Refusing To Give It Power

For me, and maybe you, it was a few things from the past that haunted me that were the original source of many of my negative thoughts. Finding a place to start unravelling my past was actually quite easy. I had a memory from childhood that had 'haunted' my self-esteem and 'stolen' my self-confidence. I had a memory that was so strong I didn't even need to close my eyes to be back in the moment.

I was about four or five year's old, standing in the front room of our family house. I was trying to tell my mummy my side of something that had happened. I was trying to be heard. My older sister had already said that I had done whatever the deed was and I hadn't, she had. I was being told off for doing something that I had not done. Yet I was innocent. I kept trying to say what had happened, but my mummy did not believe me. We had this wonderful chair in the lounge - it was huge and comfy. Suddenly I was picked up and bent over the back of the chair. My bottom was smacked! It was such a shock - I wasn't expecting it. It only took a second to happen but afterwards I shouted that it wasn't me.

I was told that continuing to lie would only get me another smack. I was told how wrong it was to lie and that nobody liked liars. I was sent to my room. I remember feeling total confusion. I had told the 'truth' and was then told off by telling a 'lie'. A few weeks later there was another incident, again I don't remember what it was. I was the guilty party this time and I lied about it. I didn't get into trouble. In fact, I got praised for telling the 'truth!' I was told how much better it was to tell the 'truth' and how people who told the 'truth' were liked.

So came about a tragic misunderstanding. I believed that a lie was the 'truth' and that the truth was a 'lie'. I honestly had the meanings mixed in my head. That was my young understanding of the definitions of those two words. It would be like a child being told that the grass was blue and the sky was green. A child trusts that what they are told is correct - they have not yet learned that mistakes and misunderstandings exist. Life is black and white to a child - they are not aware that there are shades of grey. A childhood of lies and exaggeration began. I could make up the most fantastical stories - my imagination would run riot and the stories were literally unbelievable. A reputation for being a fantasist and liar followed. I couldn't be trusted. I found it hard to keep friends and those I did make were pushed to the limit at times.

Another problem came when I realised the misunderstanding, it felt like it was too late to change, and I was already labelled. Life became a vicious circle of trying and giving up. I ended up feeling that no matter what I did, it was not worth the effort. It is very easy to get a reputation, but very hard to lose it. I found that I would often get blamed for things I hadn't done, so, in the end, I thought 'well I may as well do them'. I gave up. No one knew the agony that I experienced inside. It was years before I realised the 'mix-up' I had made in the meanings of those two little words. When I did I felt so 'stupid', so 'thick', so ... ... well, virtually every negative description that my brain could give me (and it gave me a lot!). I couldn't tell anyone. I had to keep on putting on a 'front' to the world & I became nervous about what people would think of me. It 'weighed' me down, held me captive and took away my freedom to be the real me. From the story above you may see how easy it is for negative thoughts to get hold of you, to become filtered into every aspect of your life.

Time to share the first - and I think the most empowering tool that I created on my journey.

A Mini Visualisation to Getting Rid Of Negative Thinking

The simple, but effective tool that I am about to share with you has helped me, and thousands of others from around the world, to let go of, or take control of negative thinking. It is genuinely powerful and empowering, takes only 15-30 seconds, can be used anywhere, anytime and forms the basis of breaking habitual negative thinking, providing remarkable and lasting results.

And even better, it will become even quicker to do, as it becomes second nature. Earlier, through Dr Daniel Amen, I introduced you to ANTs. I don't know about you but I didn't like the thought of all of those ANTs (Automatic Negative Thoughts) running around in my head. So I set out to find a means of removing them in an organic and healthy way. During my research, I also came across CATs - Capability Affirming Thoughts, in other words 'positive thoughts', a way of thinking that supports you in your every day life. The ANTs&CATs led to the creation of this visualization and it really can be used again and again, anywhere at anytime. This one simple staple 'ingredient' quite literally has changed not only my life but also the lives of countless clients.

The Visualisation

Imagine a kitten (yep - that's the CAT), small, fluffy and full of playfulness. It sees an ANT crawling along the floor. (I'm not into animal/insect cruelty, I promise). What will the kitten do? It will play with the ANT until the ANT is gone.

When to use the Visualization - Each time you catch yourself having one of those sneaky little ANTs, congratulate yourself, pat yourself on the back, for being aware, then think of the fluffy Kitten playing with the ANT until it is gone. Just like magic you are smiling, the ANT has gone and you are breaking the chain of those repetitive negative thoughts :)))

The ANTs & CATs tool is a key step in releasing and letting go of The Emotional Baggage that can weigh down your life - it is a core ingredient, a staple food for your mind and thoughts.

Next Tool: Finding a Positive, Time Lines and Reframing

Going back to that situation where I misunderstood the meanings of a lie and the truth. Well, to start with finding a positive from it was difficult. Surely there must be a positive hidden in there somewhere. It was hiding from me. In the end, I chose to take a 'global positive' from the situation. My thought process was ~ 'If the initial situations and all those experiences that followed had not happened, then I would not be the person that I am today. I am actually very happy with who I am (Now).

One knock on effect that has come from this life experience is the fact that I am as honest as possible. I can't stand the thought that anyone may think I am not being truthful. I have often given unnecessary explanations when I felt that I might not have made myself totally clear. And if I felt that someone might have misunderstood what I was saying or my intention. Surely that cannot be a bad thing. Another positive was that I had a very sharp learning curve. I learnt that we are all human and mistakes can be made.

They are not necessarily intentional - It is a fact of life that people can jump to the wrong conclusions. I now try to make sure that I understand what other people are saying to me. When my children were growing up I tried to really listen, I know that I didn't get it right every time. I know that when I realised I had made a mistake, I would apologise. There were times though when people around me would use this honesty against me and I 'felt' that they manipulated me. However if I had learnt from this - then I could learn from those experiences as well.

This revelation may seem small, actually, it wasn't, and it was massive. Can you imagine a jigsaw puzzle falling into place, pieces suddenly fitting together, where before they hadn't? It was as though just by 'reframing' that one incident literally hundreds more 'misunderstandings and moments of confusion' slipped into a new 'memory category'. Suddenly I was able to look at other incidents with a different type of understanding. I was able to see them in a different light, one where they were no longer disempowering, and one where they changed from heavy to light. One of my clients, now a friend, once said to me that it is like taking the thorns off a rose! I was excited if I could do that with one memory then what could I do with more? I set out on a conscious journey to visit my past. I set about creating a timeline of my life to date, making notes of things that I could remember, both good and not so good. I started collecting photos and pictures that helped me to represent memories. This wasn't about just looking at the not so good memories. It was about the whole picture. I created a sheet and marked down my age and corresponding year along the centre. Then I added notes and picture representations. I put down happy and sad.

I really thought about the wording that I used in referencing the sad memories. Awareness was 'key' - was it fact? Or was it just the way I had seen and felt it? Was there another side to the equation? Next I created lines in my mind that linked the not so good to good or great memories. I was a bit of a computer lover so I found a program that I could use to create a 'banner' that showed my life in pictures. Be creative - have fun, remember the ANTs and CATs, the number of Positive and Negative words in the dictionary and set yourself the challenge to frame everything in a way that lifts you. Yet so many of us live our lives based on out dated ideas, thoughts and interpretations from things that may have happened to us years ago. I have shared a few small strategies and tools that can be incredibly freeing. They are just the tip of the iceberg, but each of these tools can be mixed and matched together, just like when you make a meal you can chose what goes in it. Pick and choose the things that work for you that give your life the flavour that tickles your taste buds the most. Remember that for every negative thought there is, at least,one equal and opposite positive point of view. The decision always rests in our own hands as to which option we want to give value and energy. Our deepest tragedies can become a springboard for the next phase of our life. Life is a Tapestry full of colours, textures and shapes. Without the dark there is no light, without the dark we would not notice how brightly the sun is shining!

1. Statistics from Dr Daniel Amen, world-renowned psychiatrist and brain imaging specialist (Via - Marci Schimoff ~ 'Happy for No Reason

2. Source - The A-Z of Positive Thinking by Neil James

3. Source - Darren Hardy - The Compound Effect

Let the Waves Wash Away Your Fear

As I walk along the water's edge

I leave my footprints in the sand

The waves lap gently at my feet

The breeze stirs my senses.

A split second of peace before my fears return.

A moment of freedom from the thoughts that have been tumbling round and round in my mind.

The terror of 'what if', of made up scenarios,

Of failure, ridicule and obvious public humiliation.

My dream had seemed so real, so possible …

And yet now in the cold light of day,

At the point where it is about to become reality,

Myself-doubt, my past, my lack of belief in me

Comes back with a determined vengeance.

Laughing in my face, taunting me, haunting me,

Overwhelming me - leaving me feeling as though

I am being tossed & turned in the stormy seas within my head.

Yet my worries, my concerns are all tricks of my mind.

My conscious brain tells me there is no truth to them.

They are pure fantasy created partially by a fear of success.

Life prepared me for failure,

With words of caution from the moment I could walk:

Be careful, watch out, and don't be so ridiculous, that won't work,

Get real, who do you think you are!

Those who loved and cared for me

Believed they were keeping me safe.

Yet in reality, they were programming me to

Stay within a small box of 'safety',

Not to step out and take chances.

Failures were seen as something bad,

Something negative, something to avoid at all cost.

Many years later I now know

That failure is not something negative,

It can be positive and powerful.

It means that I took a chance,

I was prepared to learn a lesson.

It means I stepped out of my comfort zone

And tried something new.

It means I get to have an opportunity to try again

With more knowledge than I had before -

Or I could choose to let it go and know it wasn't for me.

The choice is mine - it is always mine.

So often we are programmed to believe the voices in our head,

To think that they are real, that they are truthful

And to be treated as fact.

Yet they are not!

The only truths for the future are that

The sun and moon will rise and set,

Even if it is behind a dark and stormy cloud it is still there.

Everything else is pure fiction, story-telling,

Whether it is something that someone else is telling me

Or that I am telling myself.

As I leave the water's edge I have

A new confidence and determination in my stride.

No matter what - I always have a choice

And today, in this moment, I choose to take a chance,

To step up and step out,

To use my voice and actions

To make a difference.

I choose to follow my passion and purpose,

I choose to admit when I need help

And accept it when it is offered.

I choose to stop living in fear

Or letting fear run my life.

I choose to see the sun - even if it is behind a cloud.

I choose to accept me and to be me.

AUTHOR BIOGRAPHIES

John Spender

John started his first business at the age of 6 selling Plaster Of Paris statues of Mickey Mouse and Donald Duck with his older brother. He later delivered pamphlets, papers, collecting trolleys, delivering milk and many other ventures all before he was 16. At 22, he had his own landscaping company completing council and government contracts.

After giving up on that business, due to an emotional breakdown, John learnt the value of balance in life, of investing in systems and the power of developing people to do the work for you, while they and the business grow together. He sold his last business for a healthy profit and began learning and studying about personal development and coaching with his journey taking him all around the world and learning many different modalities. That led John to transition into Coaching and Mentoring where he has now helped thousands of people all around the world to live a life of freedom, fun and passion.

www.ajourneyofriches.com

Angi Kim

Angi Kim is a freelance visual artist and Sydney-based wanderer, dedicated to using her creative skills for good. With a BA in marketing communication and diplomas in graphic design and photo imaging, Angi has a deep understanding of how to effectively reach different audiences using visual tools and has enjoyed helping her clients meet their communication goals for over ten years.

Born in Taiwan and adopted by an Australian family, travelling is in Angi's blood and she uses photography to document her global adventures. She wants to encourage people to try something new or see things from another perspective; and strive to create images that inspire others to sit up and notice the beauty of the human spirit and this amazing world we live in. An avid hiker, climber and diver, much of her inspiration is drawn from exploring the great outdoors and by connecting with people and nature.

Please call for coffee, prints or project enquiries.

Phone (+61) (0) 409 050 701

Email: angikimcreative@gmail.com | www.angikimcreative.com

Ais Sarah

Blogger, Peak Performance Life Trainer and Entrepreneur, Ais Sarah (pronounced as "Ice" Sarah) is an enthusiastic advocator for "Following Your Heart and Instinct". Her purpose in life is to use her positivity and motivation to inspire and motivate others to follow their dreams and achieve all they want in life. Ais is currently conducting training around the world in the area of Entrepreneurship, Image Consulting, Financial & Information Literacy, Tax Sale Wealth, Alternative Cancer Healing and has designed several programs including her specialty program called "Designing Your Life". As a successful real estate entrepreneur and investor, Ais invests and assists others to achieve their financial abundance in the area of real estate. As a blogger, image consultant and model, Ais imparts the importance of taking pictures and looking at one's best.

Find out more about her at www.aissarah.com

John W. Newman

John W. Newman is the founder of My Road to Financial Freedom.com and creator of The Stepping Stones of Wealth System. He is a lifestyle entrepreneur, avid investor, and proud husband and father! The aim of his business is to empower, inspire and equip people with money management, mindset and strategies for success and financial freedom. His aim is to help people to create both time and financial freedom, escape their comfort zones, and to live a balanced life with their health, wealth and relationships. He believes this can best be achieved by building a successful online business that will create both the cash flow and the lifestyle, so people can FINALLY live the life of their dreams, WITHOUT the money worries! Join him on your OWN road to financial freedom!

Email: john@myroadtofinancialfreedom.com

Website: www.myroadtofinancialfreedom.com

Jane Thorpe

Having been through many challenges externally in 2010 Jane Thorpe decided to commit to the challenge of the internal quest to know her true self. Having studied Self Awareness since then, Jane has spoken internationally about what it means to simply be and to create a life you love rather than one of reaction. Jane is currently writing a book on awakening and continues to integrate a conscious lifestyle. Mother of 2 daughters, Jane currently lives in Sydney Australia.

Cecilia Yeung

Cecilia Yeung is a firm believer of realizing self-potential and lifelong learning & development. She is a Human Resources Specialist with over twenty years of work experience in Asia Pacific, currently based in Hong Kong. In her day job, Cecilia works with senior executives from multi-national companies across a wide range of industries in leadership development to support and facilitate their enhanced effectiveness and productivity. Her secret mission to save the world is through serving others in discovering personal power, exploring self-awareness and enabling contribution. Cecilia has committed to studying and trained under the world's top experts in the areas of personal growth, mindfulness and self-development since 1995 and brings her unique blend of organizational and personal development experience to her presentations, writing and workshops.

Helen Ingrid Appleton

Helen Ingrid Appleton resides in Sydney, Australia and has had 25 years' experience as a business owner/entrepreneur and professional speaker.

Her life has been dedicated to studying principles that relate to the universe and the application of them. Helen's challenging childhood was the turning point for her intense desire to learn and master the ability to overcome extreme obstacles. Since the age of 13 Helen has been working in a sub-editorial capacity on publications such as the Australian Encyclopaedia and other academic work. Helen excelled in writing at school and speaking on stage and has done so since then. Her desire to help others through both her writing and speaking is what fuels her and her own life experiences aid in her desire to help others overcome their personal challenges with proven techniques and strategies.

John Ifergan

John Ifergan from All Total Coaching is a specialist in overcoming one of the biggest phenomena of our generation Depression and Fear. We can assist you with overcoming mental and emotional issues.

We can also help you empower you emotionally and mentally to get over the past with simple meditation onto the road of success happiness and prosperity. We also tailor programs that are specifically for you, we provide the 1st free session with no obligation what so ever. We pride ourselves, by being different, by providing Testimonials and evidence with Real names and phone numbers of people we worked with so you know before you even start.

John Ifergan

All total Coaching

E john@sosdating.com

www.alltotalcoaching.com

Vanessa Tran

I am Vanessa Tran. I was born in Vietnam. My grandparents were from China. I am very fortunate and proud to call Australia home. I am a wife and mother of 2 wonderful teenage children. I am a co-founder of Shine Real Estate.

My passion is creating wealth and financial independence through investing in real estate. I started investing in real estate since 2000. I love learning and watching everything to do with self-development and real estate. Hence, I have carried this passion into my business, assisting people to invest in the right property to build their wealth.

Elaine Mc Guinness

Elaine Mc Guinness is an expert in the field of personal and spiritual development, as well as self-empowerment. As a clinical hypnotherapist, Hypno-psychotherapist, co-active life coach, master NLP practitioner, reiki master and nurse, she is passionately dedicated to inspiring and empowering you to live a life on purpose with freedom and fulfilment in the journey to the actualization of your Authentic Self. Elaine is a certified trainer for Oneness University, India. She also has a BA degree in the Humanities.

Adam Todd

I have been a personal trainer for 9 years. I love my job of helping people get healthier and feeling better about themselves. My website and Facebook page are Action Time Fitness (actiontimefitness.com). I love keeping fit myself with different types of exercises in and out of the gym including playing basketball. I have just started coaching district basketball, which is great for educating some of the youth of today through my love for the game and life. I am still working on my hobby of making electronic music. I have two releases available on discovery records called "Peaceful Dreams" and "Mr Hypnotizer". You can listen to other tracks I've produced on my Soundcloud page "attt" and my YouTube channel "amtodd3", I hope you enjoy reading my story.

Caradi Miller

Caradi Miller is a passionate, life loving, consciously aware, world globetrotter. She has dedicated her whole life to studying and learning as much as she possibly can about the human body and human psychology to awaken in others a more purposeful and meaningful life. Caradi's strong mindset and drive to perform and push herself to achieve many personal goals such as Tough Mudder, The Gold Coast Half Marathon, 10km fun runs and the 100km Oxfam Walk has helped her to understand that if you want something bad enough then you can achieve greatness in all areas of your life. Caradi has been in the Health and Fitness industry for over ten years now. As a qualified Massage Therapist, Personal Trainer and Sports Trainer, Caradi has had to overcome some of her own personal demons to find true happiness within herself before she could help others. Today she is the founder of her own business inspiring and helping others all around Australia to find true happiness within themselves.

Timothy Hamons

Graphic Facilitator and Visual Thinking Consultant.

Timothy Hamons is a dynamic and creative trainer, facilitator, and speaker with over 20 years' experience in leading teams and individuals towards success, through his programs on personal and organizational creativity.

As a speaker, he uses live sketching and drawing in his presentations to frame the key messages and boost engagement with his audiences. He also teaches the skills of visual thinking to business professionals, educators, trainers and facilitators, to transform learning environments and meetings into places of inspiration and engagement.

He has worked with many organizations, throughout Asia and around the world, using these tools to design and deliver programs on innovation, change management, brand and leadership strategy, and team development. He is a highly experienced facilitator and trainer with expertise gained in corporate, non-profit and government sectors. He has facilitated programs in China, Indonesia, Hong Kong, Thailand, Philippines, Malaysia, India, Brunei, Vietnam, and Australia.

Kevin Southern

Kevin Southern was born in Lancashire England on his parent's farm with 3 siblings. His love of machinery took him to a construction plant in which he became a fully qualified fitter/welder, working on bulldozers, excavators etc. At 39 yrs. he got divorced and was bankrupt, 18 months later he brought his children home to live with him and brought them up as a single parent ever since. If you know Kevin you would know that his children are his no 1 passion in his life. Feeling somewhat stuck in life he started his personal development journey in 2005 and in 2007 he and his children moved to Western Australia where they still all live. He is now a small business owner and works for himself. Kevin had started to write his own book when he gave time to this project. To contact Kevin Southern, Facebook, or wmes@live.com.au

Kirrilie Oates

In 1995, she joined the Property Services Group (State Government) on a clerical traineeship and has never looked back. She successfully gained permanent employment with Department of Public Works and Services at the time in their accounts area and went on to complete an Advanced Diploma of Accounting in 2001. Her love for study was not complete as after completion of the Diploma she was accepted into a Bachelor of

Commerce majoring in Management Accounting, Business Law and Marketing, which was completed in 2007. Her love for Toastmasters and assisting others to change their lives still burns brightly today, as she has been awarded four Distinguished Toastmaster Awards in this space of time, the last one in 2014/15.

Jaki Bent

Jaki has a personal mission statement that she lives by which is:

"Jaki is 100% Committed to using her Knowledge, Experience, Energy and Passion in helping others to stop 'Existing' and 'Start Living' their lives in an Uplifting, Personal, Powerful, and fulfilling way"

She spent years in an emotionally abusive marriage, followed by a few years where she was still living as though she was still trapped in it. When she realised how 'stuck' she was she made a promise to learn how to truly live and to help others in the process.

Jaki does this through 'The Emotional Baggage Diet' - a series of tools and strategies that she uses and shares to help people to Let Go - Live Free and Love Life.

She is also the founder of If Everyone Cares™ - a UK Social Enterprise that is working on creating 'Ododow™ - The Interactive Community Map which will pin-point the Charities, Non-Profits and Community Projects that provide support to people in crisis.